The State of Black America® 2007

AN OFFICIAL PUBLICATION OF THE  National Urban League   www.nul.org

120 Wall Street New York, NY 10005

Published in the United States by
Beckham Publications Group, Inc.
P.O. Box 4066, Silver Spring, MD 20914

Library of Congress Control Number: 2007923099

ISBN: *0-931761-85-9*
EAN: *9780931761850*

1098765432

The State of Black America® is a registered trademark of the National Urban League

The State of Black America® 2007

Portrait of the Black Male

Foreword by Senator Barack Obama

AN OFFICIAL PUBLICATION OF THE ⊜ National Urban League

THE Beckham
PUBLICATIONS GROUP, INC.

CONTENTS

REPORT FROM THE JOINT CENTER FOR POLITICAL AND ECONOMIC STUDIES HEALTH POLICY INSTITUTE

REPORT FROM THE NATIONAL URBAN LEAGUE POLICY INSTITUTE

THE OP-ED SECTION

Afterword

APPENDICES

APPENDIX I

APPENDIX II

APPENDIX III

APPENDIX IV

THE STATE OF BLACK AMERICA® 2007

AN OFFICIAL PUBLICATION OF THE NATIONAL URBAN LEAGUE

EDITOR-IN-CHIEF

Stephanie J. Jones

EDITORIAL DIRECTOR

Lisa Bland Malone

MANAGING EDITOR

Rose Jefferson-Frazier

ASSOCIATE EDITORS

Valerie Rawlston Wilson

Rhonda Vonshay Sharpe

Mark McArdle

BOOK DESIGN

Pooja Bakri, Principal

Bakri Design

CHARTS

Cari Colclough

FOREWORD

by Senator Barack Obama

T here are at least two stories to tell about the state of Black America in 2007. One story celebrates the extraordinary fact that some of this country's top financial institutions have black chief executives, that a black woman is president of an Ivy League university, that the current and previous secretaries of state are black Americans, that a black coach led his team to victory in the Super Bowl, that the college graduation rate of black women has never been higher, that homeownership by blacks is as high as it has ever been, and that blacks have penetrated nearly every barrier in law, business, medicine, sports, education, politics and public service. Black influence on art and culture is as strong as it has ever been, and black voters should feel empowered by a reauthorized Voting Rights Act.

These accomplishments are the fulfillment of the hopes and dreams of black Americans who marched, bled, sat-in, voted and toiled against all odds and obstacles. Some of these achievements were perhaps beyond even the imagination of the millions of black Americans who labored without reward or compensation to help build this country despite being denied its rights, privileges, and opportunities.

Thanks to the success so many black Americans have realized so far, the dreams of my daughters can be bolder and brighter than the dreams of their parents, their grandparents, or any forebears. This story of continued progress toward our highest ideals of freedom and equality affords us pride and hope.

But another story must also be told about the state of Black America. A quarter of all black Americans live below the federal poverty level, a poverty rate about twice the national rate. More than a third of all black children live in poverty and almost two-thirds grow up in a home without both parents. In some cities, more than half of all black boys do not finish high school, and, by the time they are in their 30s, almost six in ten black high school dropouts will have spent time in prison. Half of all black men in their 20s are jobless, and one study a few years ago found more black men in prison than enrolled in college. The typical black household earns only about 60% of the earnings of white households and has a net worth only about 10% that of whites. The HIV/AIDS rate is highest for black Americans, and blacks are more often the victims of inadequate healthcare and preventable health maladies.

This sad story is a stark reminder that the long march toward true and meaningful equality in America isn't over. We have a long way to go.

These hard facts also remind us that politics is not a game. The decisions we make and the challenges we ignore have real consequences for the American people. And over the last six years, those consequences have led us to a crossroad. This is a unique moment in our history and the decisions we make in the next few years—on the war in Iraq, on education, on economic opportunity, on health care, on retirement security—will set the course of the next century. So we cannot afford more of the same divisive politics that keeps us from the real work we have to do together.

The world is changing at lightning speed. Globalization is transforming the game for all Americans, creating more opportunity but also greater vulnerability. At the same time, the black family, as a structure of relationships, love, support and sustenance, is endangered. And government institutions that support working families and ensure economic mobility have been damaged by irresponsible fiscal policies, cynical incompetence, and neglect. Young black males in particular have been left so far behind that their well-being is too often measured not by the richness and meaning of their lives—or their contributions to our economy and common lives—but rather by the costs they impose on others.

The public and private institutions that were so critical to African American progress over the past several decades are weaker and more vulnerable now. Even the large private organizations that have done so much to sustain the struggle and codify our progress, like the National Urban League and NAACP, are in the process of transitioning to new generations of leadership and new expectations of membership.

That's why this annual status report, *The State of Black America*, is so important. It is a moment to consider the opportunities that confront America.

Will we be able to use the greater financial, educational, political, and cultural assets that we have acquired in order to finish the fight for equality that others have started? Will we be able to coalesce around a commitment to strengthening the black family and reinventing community-based and national programs to support those who have been left behind or need assistance to get ahead? The crisis of the black male is our crisis whether we are black or white, male or female. The failure of our policies to recognize black men as husbands, fathers, sons and role models is being acknowledged, and we need a new ethic of compassion to break the cycle of educational failure, unemployment, absentee fatherhood, incarceration, and recidivism.

We all have a responsibility to instill in children the values of self-determination and self-sacrifice, dignity and discipline, honesty, accountability, and hard work. But it is too easy and sometimes too fashionable to demonize black men, especially young fathers, who have strayed. It's too easy to stereotype people even within our own community and to use them as an excuse for our problems. But in so doing, we degrade ourselves, we weaken the bonds of shared interests that are necessary to sustain us. We fail to give people the first chance they deserve, and the second chance that we all sometimes require.

Wherever we live, the wounds of Katrina that are still unhealed are our wounds; the failure of the federal government to respond with care and rebuild with commitment is our failure. It is the failure of those of us who don't get off the couch and register to vote. It is the failure of those of us who get so focused on making money that we suffer from a poverty of ambition and forget the golden rule. It is a failure of those of us who have allowed fate or circumstance to determine the lot of our children.

None of this will come easy. Every one of us will need to work more, think more, care more. We will have to slough off bad habits and take responsibility for our families, our politics, each other. Our kids will have to turn off the TV sets and start hitting the books. We will have to insist upon reforms in our schools that are failing too many. We have to recognize our collective responsibilities and do more than defend old programs.

History teaches us that equality must be fought for each and every day. We must redouble our efforts to close the health care gap that leaves minority communities with higher rates of disease and lower rates of quality care. We must close the achievement gap by committing to early education and ensuring that we teach all of our kids to take pride in educational achievement. We must close the empathy gap that lets us give up on people who may have lost their way and all Americans must embrace our common fate and shared destiny.

In this edition of *The State of Black America* report, there are many different approaches to solving our common problems. Some will work and others might not. But it is in our shared interests and in the interest of every American to stop ignoring these challenges and start finding the solutions that will work. For in the end, we want the story for Black America to be one universal story where success is the norm and struggles are overcome.

This is the journey we are on together.

Barack Obama / Chicago, IL / March 2007

Empowering Black Males To Reach Their Full Potential

by Marc H. Morial
President and Chief Executive Officer
National Urban League

I n the past year, several black men grabbed the national spotlight because of their singular achievements. Rep. Charles Rangel became the first African American to head the House Ways and Means Committee, one of the most powerful and prestigious committees in Congress. Two African-American coaches—Chicago Bears Coach Lovie Smith and Indianapolis Colts' Tony Dungy—led their teams to the Super Bowl, professional football's pinnacle contest. And Illinois Sen. Barack Obama, who wrote the Foreword to this edition, entered the presidential ring. Countless other black men of all ages, out of the spotlight, worked hard, found success, supported their families and improved their communities.

These men are all sterling examples of outstanding black men breaking through racial barriers to achieve the American Dream.

But while there are Barack Obamas and Lovie Smiths out there to prove just how far black men can go, there are many whose futures are far from bright. The National Urban League 2007 *Equality Index* shows us that black men continue to lag behind their white counterparts in every major category; a disproportionate number of black men are underperforming in our society in a variety of areas for a variety of reasons.

This state of underachievement, with its devastating and far-reaching ramifications, is the most serious economic and civil rights challenge we face today. It's a problem with a major rippling effect. Not only does it impact individual black men. It also hurts their families and communities. It's not just a problem for the African-American community. It's a problem for everyone in this nation.

In 2004, the National Urban League began the Black Male Initiative to address the obstacles impeding the success of black men and boys—especially the poor and young who've fallen off the nation's radar screen. This year's report, *The State of Black America: Portrait of the Black Male*, is part of our ongoing effort to bring attention to and develop solutions for this national challenge.

Young black men in this nation—especially those who live in poverty— face a daunting future. A 2006 *Washington Post* series on the black man suggested that young black boys faced three possible paths in their lives—incarceration, underachievement or success.

"Imagine three African-American boys, kindergartners who are largely alike in intelligence, talent and character, whose potential seems limitless. According to a wealth of statistics and academic studies, in just over a decade one of the boys is likely to be locked up or headed to prison. The second boy —if he hasn't already dropped out—will seriously weigh leaving high school and be pointed toward an uncertain future. The third boy will be speeding toward success by most measures," reporter Michael A. Fletcher observed.

According to this year's *Equality Index*, black men are more than 6 times as likely than white men to be incarcerated. At the end of 2001, 16.5 percent of the black male population had been to prison, compared to 7.7 percent of Hispanic and 2.7 percent of white men, according to the Bureau of Justice Statistics. And of single-parent black households in 2005, only 12 percent were led by men, according to the U.S. Census.

The scourge of diminished expectations and underperformance also underscores that need for the African-American community to focus on raising our children in two-parent households, which tend to be more affluent than their single-parent counterparts. According to the U.S. Census, more than two-thirds of black children live in one-parent households in 2005, the majority headed by women. And over 42 percent of female-headed black households with children were poor, compared to slightly more than 9 percent of married black households.

I am by no means advocating a mass movement to the altar. What I am suggesting is that we raise our children with two parents in the picture. Young black men, faced with discriminatory hurdles as well as a brand of self-doubt fueled by negative images in society, need hope in the form of role models to help them achieve their dreams. They require a modicum of financial and personal security to assure that they get the tools they need to excel later in life. It's difficult enough for two parents with two incomes to support their children financially in this day and age. There's no doubt that children raised in one-parent households are more likely to live in poverty, which is much more likely to perpetuate the cycle of underachievement and drastically diminished expectations. The absence of the black man in the black family will only lead to greater poverty for our community as a whole. It helps exacerbate the disparities already existing between minorities and whites in the United States.

The State of Black America 2007 report takes up this challenge with a fresh and in-depth look at the current conditions affecting the black male. We urge our public officials, policy makers, scholars and others committed to addressing the problems of race, poverty and justice to carefully study *The State of Black America 2007* report and use it as a blueprint to bridge the racial divide in this nation. Empowering black males to reach their full potential is the most serious economic and civil rights challenge we face today. Ensuring the future of the black male is critical, not just for African Americans, but for the prosperity, health and well-being of the entire American family.

THE NATIONAL URBAN LEAGUE EQUALITY INDEX™

by Rondel Thompson and Sophia Parker of
Global Insight, Inc.

everal occurrences in the past year have led some to suggest that African Americans have finally achieved equality with whites in today's society: we have seen African Americans win Academy Awards, coach in—and win—the Super Bowl, and even run for President of the United States with a considerable amount of support and anticipation.

But anecdotes and isolated examples such as these do not accurately assess the status of blacks in America. For this reason, the National Urban League developed the *Equality Index*™, which compares the conditions between whites and blacks in America using multiple variables. In this index, whites have been used as the control. So an index number of less than one means that blacks are doing relatively worse than whites in that category. An index value of greater than one means that blacks are doing better than whites in that category.

According to the 2007 *Equality Index*, Black America's index value stands at 0.733, fractionally up from 0.730 in 2006.

The *Equality Index* is a compilation of five sub-indices: Economics, Health, Education, Social Justice, and Civic Engagement. Each of these sub-components has an index value of its own. The sections below summarize how each of the individual sub-indices was constructed, the data available, and the weights used. Global Insight, Inc. attempted to use the most recent data available across these five indices to create the most current index value. Additionally, Global Insight attempted to ensure its methodology and data are as consistent and accurate as possible by, among other things, employing weighting schemes to manage any shortcoming in the data.[1] These weights are referenced both in the text and listed for each variable in the full index.

The weights are unchanged from last year:

Economics	30%
Health	25%
Education	25%
Social Justice	10%
Civic Engagement	10%

ECONOMICS—30% OF THE EQUALITY INDEX

The Economics sub-index is divided into six separate categories: Mean Income, Employment Issues, Poverty, Housing and Wealth Formation, Transportation, and Digital Divide. The weight of each category is based on relative importance and the quality of the data that was available. Of the six,

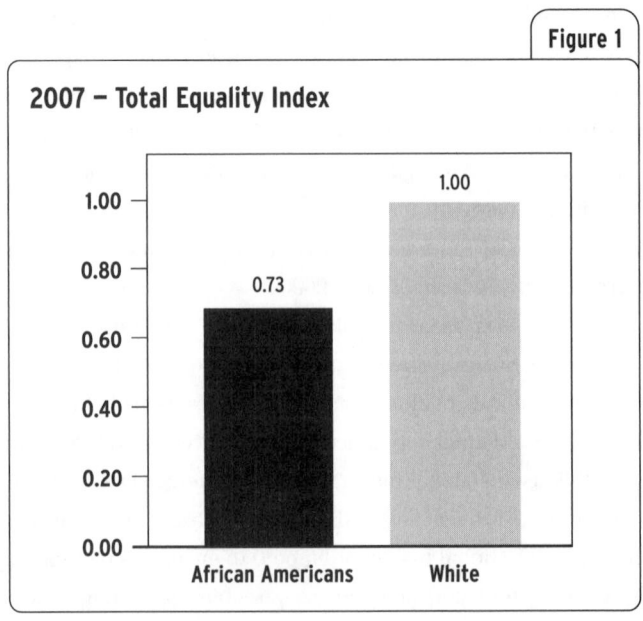

Figure 1

2007 – Total Equality Index

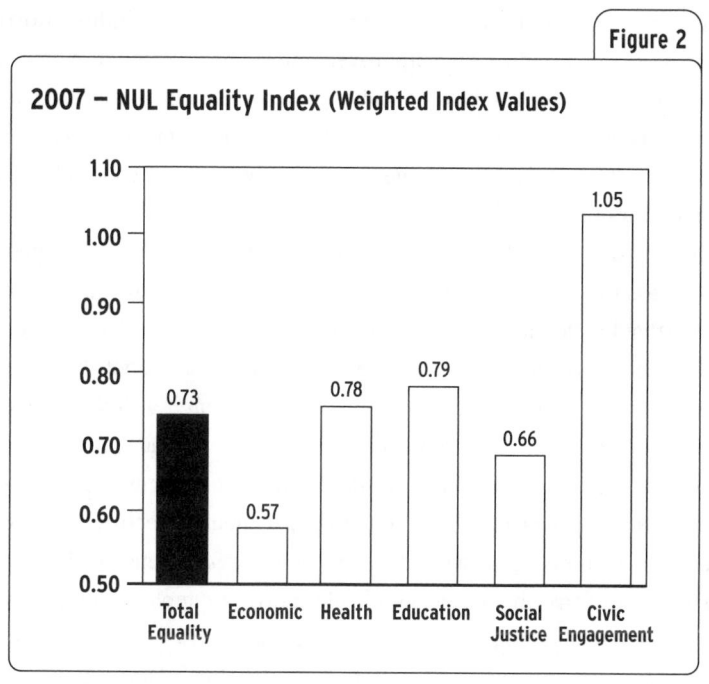

Figure 2

2007 – NUL Equality Index (Weighted Index Values)

Housing and Wealth Formation was given the strongest weight (34%), as it is the best measure of both a person's current assets and their economic potential. For example, it is easier to secure a business loan if one owns a home and can use it as collateral, thus housing can directly contribute to wealth formation. Median Income, which is assigned the second highest weight (25%), represents the current economic performance of the white and black employed populations. Employment Issues was given a slightly lower weight (20%), followed closely by Poverty (15%). The Digital Divide (5%) was given the second lowest weight. Finally, Transportation (1%) was given the lowest weight. The *Equality Index* number for Economics in 2007 was calculated at 0.57, a nominal increase over the 0.56 figure from 2006. This index number, the lowest of the five sub-indices, means blacks are performing disproportionately worse than whites in the economic area. A closer look at the sub-indices that make up the Economics index will reveal some of the reasons for the disparity.

Housing and Wealth Formation—34% of Economics

The Housing and Wealth Formation category includes Mortgage Application Denial and Home Improvement Loans (weighted at 8% each), Home Ownership (1%) and Home Values (1%). Home Values was given a lesser weight because the index for this is not based upon a current snapshot, but rather on historical material. Home Ownership was weighted less because it is somewhat correlated to Mortgage Application Denials.

Home ownership, calculated at 0.63, shows yet another separation between races. Less than 50 percent of black families in America own homes, a percentage that has actually gone down over the last two years. Conversely, nearly 76 percent of white families in America own homes. A contributing factor lies in the next series: mortgage denial was computed at 0.53. Blacks are rejected for home mortgage loans nearly twice as often as their white counterparts. A more detailed look at the data reveals some interesting characteristics. As a percentage of applications filed per their respective races, whites (40.9%) have more than twice as many joint applications filed as blacks (17.9%). When African Americans do file mortgage applications jointly, the application denial rate falls to 20.8% from 24.5%. Even when blacks do obtain credit, it is often at a higher rate. Data from the Home Mortgage Disclosure Act reveal the pricing inequity faced by black borrowers. The data shows that 54.7% of blacks purchasing a home received a high-priced loan (more than 3% above the Treasury rate) as opposed to 17.2% of whites.[2] The home improvement mortgage loans category was slightly better than mortgage denials, at 0.63. Still, blacks obtained home improvement financing at a rate that is well below whites. Consequently, if money is not made available to fix a home in disrepair, the value of the home and the surrounding neighborhood can suffer. Lower median incomes and often segregated neighborhoods also help to account for median home value, which was calculated at 0.65, translating into a $42,800 gap in black versus white home values.

There is also a large disparity between the numbers of black and white owned businesses. The U.S. Firms by Race index, which was calculated at 0.54, illustrates the sizeable gap. The current index number of 0.54 remains unchanged from last year's number. One possible reason is that black firms are not getting the seed money needed to create private wealth. The index does show that blacks are being rejected for home loans at a much higher rate than whites, and just as important, blacks have less collateral since they are less likely to own their home and the average black home is worth less than the average white home. All of these statistics point to the difficulty for blacks to obtain the financing necessary to start a business.

The remaining components comprise the Housing and Wealth Formation section of the Economics Index: Median Net Worth[3] (8%), Equity in Home (8%), Percent of People Investing in 401k (1%) and Percent Investing in IRA[4] (1%) further complete the wealth formation aspect of Housing and Wealth Formation. The heavier weights were given to Median Net Worth and Equity in Home as they are the strongest immediate indicators of wealth formation.

Median Income—25% of Economics

The index for Median Income is broken out into three components: Median Male Earnings by Highest Degree Earned (8%), Median Female Earnings by Highest Degree Earned (8%), and Median Income (8%). Median Male Earnings produced an index value of 0.74. Not only are black males beings paid less than whites, but black males would have to see their mean income increase by $12,374 annually for the index to equal 1. The indicator for Mean Female Earnings of 0.87 reveals that black females are closer in earnings to their white counterparts. However, a black female would still have to earn $4,602 more each year for the index to reach 1.

Employment Issues—20% of Economics

Employment Issues is broken out into three main categories. The Unemployment Rate portion of the index was weighted at 10%, Labor Force Participation (LFP) at ages 16-64 was weighted at 9%, and for the employment to population ratio weighted at 1%. The Unemployment category itself is comprised of the overall unemployment rate, the unemployment rate per race by gender and the unemployment rate of persons age 16-19. The unemployment rate for blacks is more than twice their white counterparts, as is depicted in Figure 3. The number of unemployed blacks would have to decrease by 867,580 people for the unemployment index to equal 1. When looking at gender, black females (0.48 index value) fare better than black males (0.42 index value) in terms of the unemployment rate. Figure 3 graphically depicts the higher unemployment rates that black males are subject to relative to their white counterparts.

The Labor Force Participation (LFP) rate, on the other hand, showed a nominal racial difference. LFP is the number of people in a population that are either working or looking for work. The 0.96 index figure illustrates a slightly higher labor force participation rate for whites. The LFP index number does not fully bring into perspective the difference in labor force participation, however. When this index is disaggregated by age and education level, the differences are interesting as higher education levels produce relatively higher LFPs for blacks. The LFP index for ages 16 to 19 was 0.73, but the LFP index for ages 20 to 24 showed improvement, at 0.90. The LFPs for higher age groups, simply stated as "over 25," are in addition broken out by education level. The LFP index number for Over 25 with Less than a High School Degree is 0.85. However, the remaining LFP index values (which were all weighted at .001) all registered higher than one: High School Graduate/No College (1.07), Some College/No Degree (1.06), Associates Degree (1.03), Less than Bachelor's Degree (1.05) and College Graduate (1.06). The numbers stress the importance of education. In particular, graduating from high school is a huge hurdle that can help to insure higher labor force participation for blacks. Higher education would not only increase LFP numbers but higher incomes as well. However, the literature indicates that there is a white/black wage gap among educated individuals that is not explained by differences in degree, major or age.[5]

Poverty—15% of Economics

The Poverty category is broken out into three subcomponents: Percent of the Population Below the Poverty Line (9%), Percent Living 50 Percent Below the Poverty Line (1%) and a newly-added category, Percent Living 125% Below the Poverty Threshold (5%). Figure 4 presents a visual representation of two of the variables in the Poverty category. As a percentage of their population, three times as many blacks live below the poverty line as whites. The index number of 0.33 is a marginal decline from the 0.35 index number in the previous *Equality Index*. Moreover, the Percent Living Below 125% Poverty Level data also shows that nearly three times as many blacks are living below 125% poverty than whites, when adjusted for their relative populations.

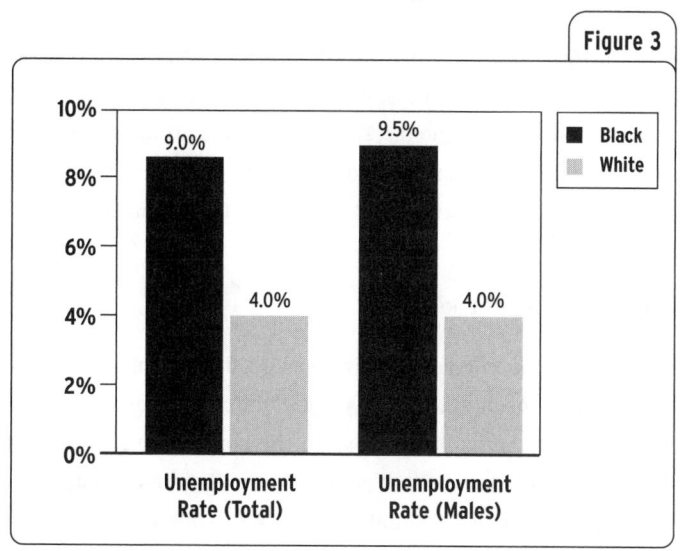

Figure 3

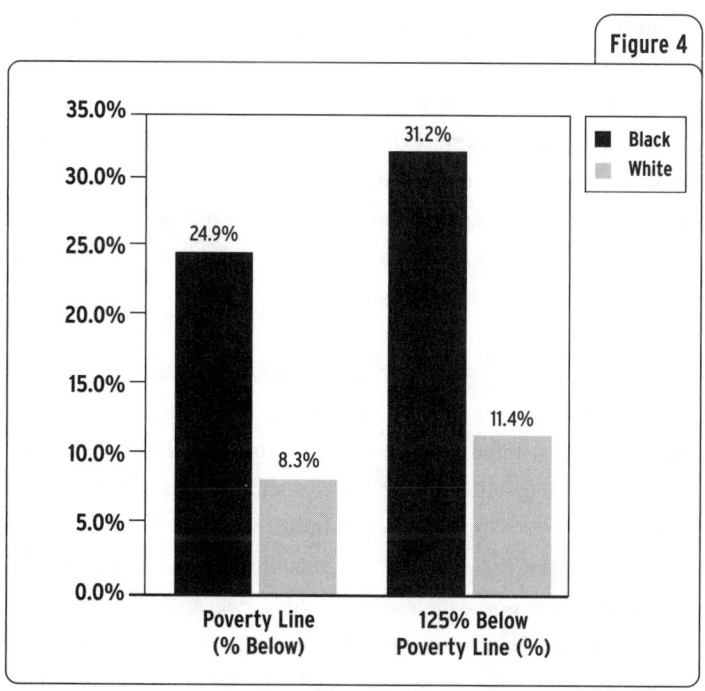

Figure 4

Digital Divide—5% of Economics

Each of the three items within the Digital Divide category (Households with Computer at Home, Households with the Internet, and Households with Broadband) is equally weighted. While there is a pronounced disparity in Households with Broadband, the index number is improved over last year. The 2007 index number of 0.61 rose from 0.54 in the previous year.

Transportation—1% of Economics

The Transportation category is divided into three items: Car Ownership, Driving to Work Alone, and Reliance Upon Public Transportation. These variables are important in that they speak to the ability of blacks to be mobile enough to have access to jobs that are not within their immediate vicinity. All three items produced index numbers that were below 1: Car Ownership (0.79), Driving Alone (0.89) and Reliance upon Public Transportation (0.23). The low index number for Reliance upon Public Transportation means that nearly four times as many blacks rely upon public transportation systems than whites. According to a Brookings Institution policy brief many new jobs are located in suburban areas. However, public transit rarely takes urban residents to within a close proximity of those employers. The document also goes on to say that poorer families often pay more for cars due to higher finance charges.[6] The consequences of this lack of transportation options include longer commutes to new jobs and a relatively higher cost of purchasing a car for many lower-income African Americans.

HEALTH—25% OF THE EQUALITY INDEX

The Health sub-index is divided into three major categories: Death Rates and Life Expectancy, Lifetime Health Issues, and Neonatal Care and Related Issues. Of the three categories, Death Rates and Life Expectancy is weighted the most at 45 percent within the Health Index. Lifetime Health Issues, which attempts to measure the struggles of individuals with failing or impaired health who are still to some degree functioning, was given a weight of 30 percent. Lastly, Neonatal Care and early childhood issues were given a weight of 25 percent, since this stage of development sets the table for one's entire life but is not always directly correlated to the health problems experienced later.

The overall index number for Health was calculated at 0.78, an improvement over last year's value of 0.76.

Death Rates and Life Expectancy—45% of Health

The white population in the U.S. lives over five years longer than our nation's black population, and this disparity is reflected in the Health Index. Life Expectancy at Birth is weighted at 15 percent of the Health index, and the Age-Adjusted Death Rate (per 100,000) for all causes is weighted at 30 percent. In the index we use the Death Rate for all causes to avoid skewing the measurement based on a particular cause of death. The black population remains significantly behind the white population in the Age-Adjusted Death Rate at 77%. Diabetes, homicide, and HIV prevalence in the black community are several times greater than in the white population. Diabetes is almost twice as likely to occur among blacks as whites. Blacks are ten times more

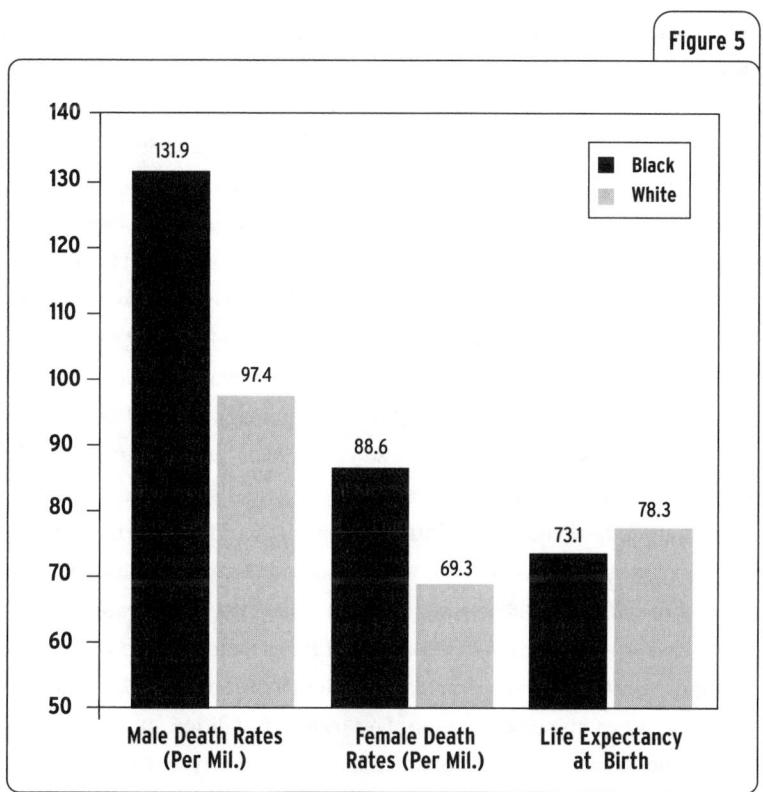

Figure 5

likely to die as a victim of a homicide. The disparity in HIV deaths is also strik-ing—blacks are over 8 times as likely to die from HIV compared to whites. A positive note is that blacks are less likely to be stricken with chronic liver dis-ease. In addition, the suicide rate of the nation's white population is more than twice that of blacks.

Figure 5 shows the differential between white and black death rates by gen-der. Though males have a higher death rate compared to females, black males have the highest death rate of any group. The 131.9 death rate for African-American males is substantially higher than their white counterparts. African-American females also have a higher death rate than white females, but that difference is less and produces a higher (more favorable) index value (0.78 for women versus 0.74 for men). The higher death rates lead to lower life expectancy at birth.

Lifetime Health—30% of Health

This subcategory is disaggregated into five sub-components. The sub-com-ponents are: Physical Condition, 10% (includes the former categories Weight Issues and AIDS); Substance Abuse, 10%; Access to Care, 5% (formerly Health Insurance); Elderly Health Care, 3%; and Mental Health, 2%. Substance Abuse and Physical Condition issues are given the most weight in the Lifetime Health sub-index as they affect the largest percentages of the population. Under physical condition, blacks are more likely to be overweight and have a much greater incidence of obesity than whites. Obesity is weighted twice as heavi-ly as merely overweight, since the health ramifications for being obese are far more significant. When looking at the data broken down by gender, it becomes apparent that black women are faring worse than black men in terms of being overweight or obese. Black men over 20 years old actually are better off than their white counterparts in terms of being overweight (producing an index of 1.06) and are only slightly worse off for obesity (.98). However, black women are doing considerably worse than white women in terms of being overweight (an index of 0.72) and for obesity (index of .60). Figure 6 shows the gender breakdown for the Overweight variable and for diabetes, which is correlated with being overweight and which blacks suffer disproportionately. Among the largest disparities in index values in the Physical Condition sub-index pertain to AIDS. The African-American population of this country is disproportionate-

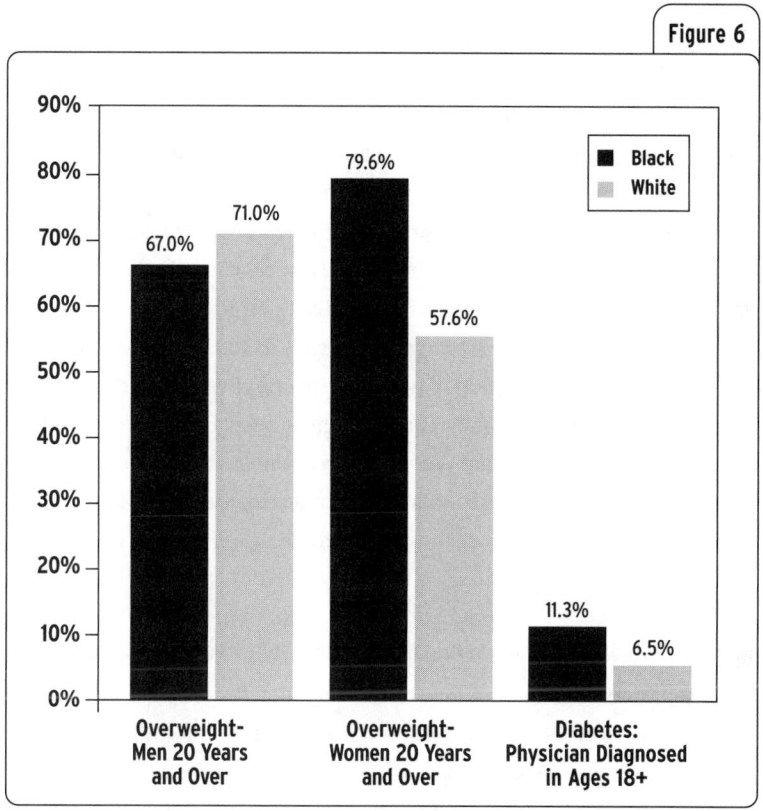

Figure 6

Black
White

79.6%

71.0%

67.0%

57.6%

11.3%

6.5%

Overweight-
Men 20 Years
and Over

Overweight-
Women 20 Years
and Over

Diabetes:
Physician Diagnosed
in Ages 18+

ly stricken with this illness compared to white Americans. African American males 13 and older have nearly 8 times as many AIDS cases per 100,000 people than white males. The statistics for African-American women show an even larger gap, with black females over the age of 13 having over 20 times the number of AIDS cases per 100,000 that white females have.

The Substance Abuse category reveals that blacks are significantly better off than whites in terms of binge drinking. In fact, whites 18 years and older are nearly twice as likely to binge drink as blacks. In addition, blacks 18 and over are marginally less likely to use tobacco products. The Mental Health sub-component reveals data with mixed results. Substantially less black male and female high school students consider suicide compared to whites. However, of those black female students who consider suicide, a higher percentage of them act upon that feeling compared to white female students.

The Access to Care category includes usage of prescription drugs, which is correlated with preventative health care. Additionally, data points measuring health care coverage highlight the low likelihood for African Americans to have health insurance coverage. Lower rates of health insurance are highly correlated with lower care, impacting health throughout a person's entire life. The All People Without Health Insurance variable remained unchanged at 0.58 compared to the 2006 index value, indicating that nearly twice as many blacks were without insurance compared to whites. The impact of this disparity affects not only the health of African Americans, but the health of our nation as a whole. When a person does not have insurance, routine medical visits tend to not be an option. Medical conditions are left untreated and become worse to the point where that person often ends up in an emergency room where costs are far higher. The cost of the operation or medical procedure is eventually passed onto the larger society and help push up the cost of health care for everyone.

Neonatal & Pediatric Care, and Other Early Childhood—25% of Health

Four separate components have been developed for this category: Delivery Issues, 10%; Children's Health, 10%; Pregnancy Issues, 4%; and Reproduction Issues, 1%. Delivery Issues focuses on conditions affecting black women during birth. There are more than twice as many total infant deaths per 100,000 births for black women, and that number is the same when looking at the prenatal and postnatal components. The Maternal Mortality index value of 0.24 indicates that four times the number of black women die in childbirth as white women per 100,000 births. Under Pregnancy Issues, nearly as many black women start prenatal care in the first trimester as whites (an index of 0.89); but the data also shows that far too many African-American women wait until the third trimester to begin prenatal care (an index of 0.39). Also, as a percent of live births, black infants are over 2.5 times more likely to be born with extremely low birth weight (a newly-added variable this year). The Children's Health sub-component yielded some promising results. All of the variables that comprise this sub-component produced higher index values compared to the 2006 *Equality Index*. The largest increases came from No Child Health Care Visit in Last 12 months, which rose to 1.16 this year from 0.92 in 2006. This is important since increased frequency in child doctor visits will help to detect many illnesses that could go undetected and worsen over time. Reproduction Issues revealed some relative decline in family planning. According to the index, less black women use contraception in this year's index (0.89 index value) relative to white women than in last year's index (0.94 index value).

EDUCATION—25% OF THE EQUALITY INDEX

The Education sub-index is divided into five major categories: Quality, Attainment, Scores, Enrollment, and Student Status and Risk Factors. Of the five, Quality is weighted the most at 45 percent. Attainment, the level of education a person achieves, is weighted at 20%. Test scores, an important indication of performance, are weighted at 15 percent within this sub-index. Enrollment, which does not take into account effectiveness or quality, was given a weight of 10 percent. Lastly, Student Status and Risk Factors were considered important measures of behavior, student confidence, and future accomplishment in life; but since these are closely related to attainment, a weighting of 10 percent was assigned. The overall index number for Education was calculated at 0.79 for the 2007 index, an improvement of .01 points over the 2006 index.

Quality—45% of Education

The quality of the product being received within the black community and the white community is not equal. This fact dominates how each population fares in high schools, colleges, and their jobs across America. Two broad themes emerge from these criteria: the quality, skills, and experience of the teacher, and the course curriculum of the student. The first is referred to as Teacher Quality (30%). This measure was consistently linked to student performance, and so was given the greatest weight. Four data series, each equally weighted, plus a fifth weighted less, comprise this key determination. The first two measure the percentage of out-of-field teachers—teachers lacking even a college minor in the subject being taught or in a related field. The first series measures this at the middle school level and the second at the high school level. It does not measure what percentage of teachers achieved qualification certificates, only their prior college training in the subjects they now instruct. Middle school showed the greater black-white discrepancy—49 percent of teachers of black students were out-of-field, compared to 40 percent for white students.

Two additional measures were used: Teachers with less than three years experience teaching in minority schools and public school funding on education per student. Funding was measured per student in high and low poverty

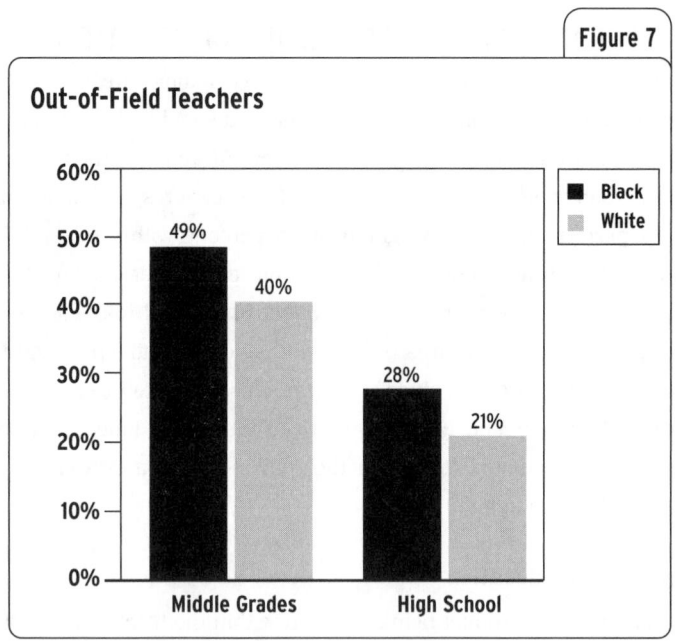

Figure 7

Out-of-Field Teachers

districts based on the total amount of state and local revenues each district received for the school year .[7] Even after applying a 40% adjustment for low-income students which takes into account the fact that these students need more support to reach the same level as higher-income students, there still remains a funding gap. Lastly, and given less weight than the prior four, is a California survey that asked what percentage of teachers in minority schools are underprepared—that is, had not completed the California preparation program and obtained a full credential before beginning to teach. There was a sizable improvement (0.18) for this index number, which shows that California made progress towards closing the gap of its under-prepared teachers between the 2005-06 school year and 2003-04 in high and low minority schools.

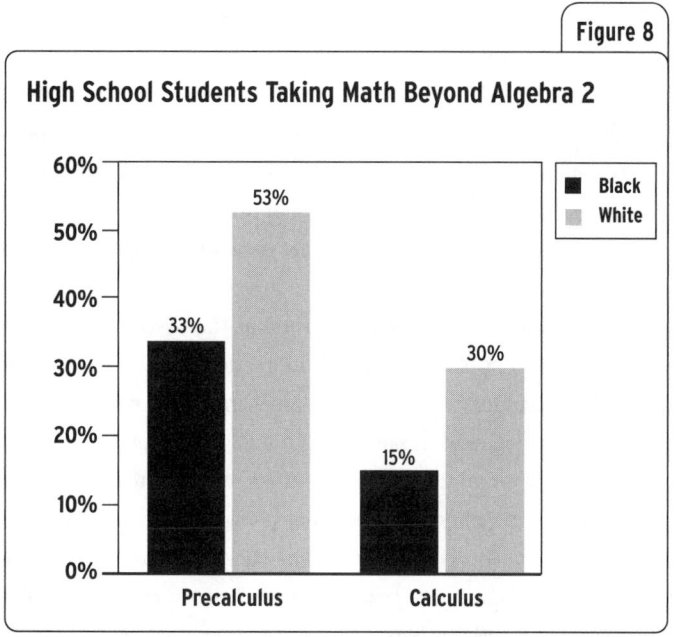

Figure 8

High School Students Taking Math Beyond Algebra 2

The second broad theme of this category is Course Quality (15%). There is some evidence that the intensity of courses taken in high school provides the most momentum for continuing education and completing college. Eight data series were included to measure the course curriculum of the student. Two series measured high school students who enter college and the general strength of their high school curriculum, while six others measured enrollment in algebra 2, precalculus, calculus, chemistry, English composition, and grammar. Studies have shown that taking math one step beyond Algebra 2 doubles the odds that you will earn a bachelor's degree.[8] Based on those students who took the SAT, the discrepancy between blacks and whites taking courses beyond algebra 2 is still large. Figure 8 illustrates the gap between blacks and whites taking math beyond algebra 2. Only 33% of black students took precalculus, compared with 53% of whites, and the index number *declined* from last year's index for this indicator. Calculus showed a slightly lower percentage point difference (15%) and no change from last year's index.

Attainment—20% of Education

Eight different gauges were used to measure educational attainment. Each of these gauges was given an equal weight. Two of them measure graduation rates of two- and four- year schools; these data sets track students over time. Additionally, NCAA Division I schools track how many of their college freshmen graduate within six years. For students who graduated in the 2001 cohort year, 27% of blacks graduated from two-year degree-granting schools versus 34% for whites. The discrepancy is higher for graduation rates at 4-year degree-granting schools: for the 1998 cohort year, 40% of blacks graduate compared to 58% for whites.

Three data sets measured degrees earned at the associate, bachelor, and masters level. High school and college attainment for those over 25 were both also included in the index. All levels of degrees improved over the 2006 index, with the most improvement in narrowing the gap between the percentage of blacks and whites who attain master's degrees. A separate data set was used to report the types of college degrees that persons over 18 hold. New data revealed that a greater percentage of blacks chose computer/information sciences, mathematics/statistics, social science/history and pre-professional than whites; while in others like medicine, engineering, agriculture/forestry, and philosophy/religion, white concentration is greater.

Scores—15% of Education

The same measures created in 2006 to measure Total Scores—Preschool, weighted at 10% of scores; Elementary, 40%; and High School, 50%—were used again for the 2007 index. The wide variety of tests used creates a range of different measures. For preschool children, a test score that evaluates skill sets (recognizes all letters, counting to 20 or higher, writing their name, and reading or pretending to read storybooks) was used. At the elementary school level, NAEP proficiency tests had the most data available, and included reading, writing, math, history, geography and science scores for 4th and 8th grade students. At the high school level, both the ACT and the SAT were included, since they roughly cover different parts of the country, and their results did not significantly differ. GPAs for those taking the SAT were also included, as was writing proficiency. Newly updated data for the 2007 index showed that the gap narrowed at the preschool level between 2001 and 2005. There was no change in this year's index for GPAs, NAEP, SAT or ACT scores compared to last year's index.

Enrollment—10% of Education

The Enrollment category is divided into school enrollment by age and college enrollment by age. Being enrolled in college during the more traditional age range of 18-24 was a higher weight than enrolling in college later in life because having a college degree at 20 rather than at 30 allows for the individual to earn higher wages for an additional 10 years. There was an improvement in the enrollment of young black children relative to white children, but the gap widened for the age groups between 18 and 24. For students enrolling in college, the greatest improvement in enrollment of blacks relative to whites was for 15 to 17 year olds, and the only declines came from the 20 to 21 and 30 to 34 age groups.

Student Status and Risk Factors—10% of Education

Eighteen series comprise this category, all evenly weighted. They reflect both school and home practices that affect performance in school. Of the

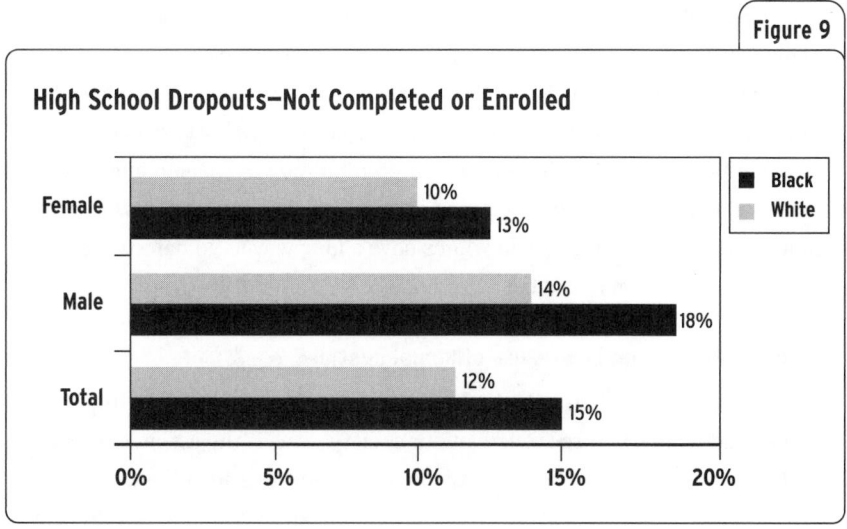

Figure 9

High School Dropouts—Not Completed or Enrolled

school factors, dropping out of school is an important and widely followed statistic. Not only does it indicate students who have left the school system and the benefits an education provides, it also may be an indicator that the schools themselves are failing. Results of School Age Children (5-15) with a

Disability, Elementary and Secondary Students Suspended a Grade and Repeating a Grade illustrate the preponderance of black children to be quickly taken out of mainline classrooms. Children in Poverty and Children with No Parent in the Labor Force were included since school performance is linked to conditions at home. In addition, home environments that foster Home Literacy Activities (measures include Read to 3 or more times a week, Told a story at least once a month, Taught Words or Numbers three or more times a week, and Visited a Library at Least Once in Last Month) do influence children's cognitive development.[9] Improvements in closing the gap came in all categories of Home Literacy Activities except Read to 3 or More Times a Week (which declined slightly since 2001). Unfortunately the number of black high school dropouts relative to whites increased from last year's index (Figure 9), as well as two attendance variables; black males had the highest rate of High School Dropouts at 18%.

SOCIAL JUSTICE—10% OF EQUALITY

The Social Justice index, computed at 0.66 is 8 points lower than last year's value of 0.74. The change in the index is largely due to the elimination of the Government Equality section, which consisted mostly of older data that could not be updated. The Social Justice index now contains two categories: Equality Before the Law (80%) and Victimization (20%). The sub-index number of 0.66 for social justice, the second lowest (after economics) in the entire index, indicates that blacks and whites have a long way to go before equality, or justice, have been achieved.

Equality Before the Law—80% of Social Justice

The first category in the Social Justice sub-index is the equal treatment of blacks and whites before the law in our society. This is the essence of a fair and colorblind nation. Four data series captured this idea best: Stopped While Driving, Average Jail Sentence, Probation, and Prisoners as a Percent of Arrests.

Stopped While Driving (0.10) measures the percentage of drivers being pulled over for a variety of reasons. The most recent index has determined that some gains have been made in terms of blacks being stopped while driving. While a higher percentage of blacks get pulled over compared to whites,

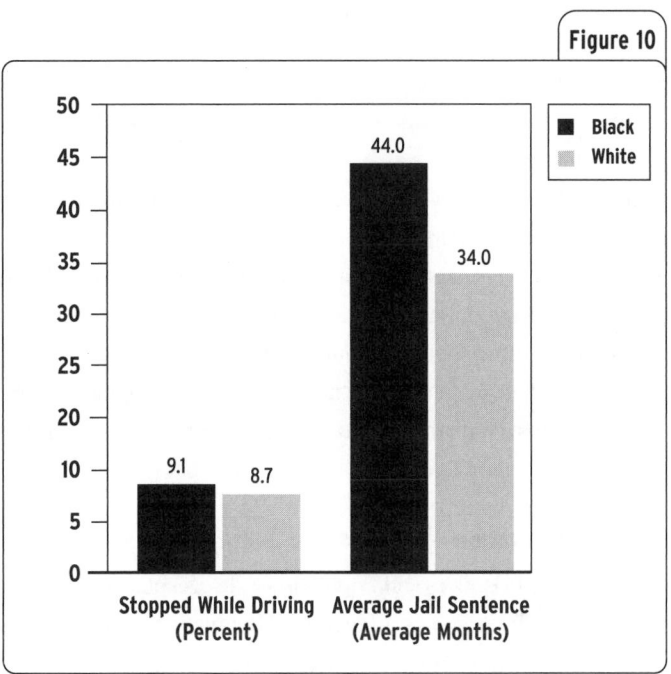

Figure 10

the 0.96 index value for 2007 is a sizeable gain over the 0.85 index value from 2006. It must be noted that though the index has increased, there was no available data that describes what transpired after an individual is stopped while driving. In Figure 10, the relatively close percentage of blacks and whites that are stopped while driving is contrasted by the noticeable difference in the average sentence in jail for a felony offense.

The index figure for Average Jail Sentence (0.20) shows that blacks are receiving, on average, a significantly longer felony sentence relative to whites. A black person's average sentence is ten months longer than a white's. This index has an overall value of 0.77, but varied significantly by type of crime and gender. The Average Jail Sentence sub-categories, which show sentences for particular crimes, have been recently broken out by gender. Of the sentences issued in 12 crime categories in the State Courts, sentences for black males were longer than white males in all of them. Black females found the justice system to be slightly more lenient than for black males. Of the sentences issued in 12 crime categories in State Courts, sentences for black females were longer than their white counterparts in all but four sub-categories. This brings up the question: is the justice system not only biased against blacks, but heavily biased against black males? While the data could not fully address this question, there is the indication that African-American males face bias in sentencing in our justice system.

According to Probation (0.10) figures, white male felons are more likely to get probation than black male felons. This result produced a Probation Granted index of 0.79. Again, this data series was adjusted for what kind of crime placed the person in jail, so a non-violent criminal offender was granted probation more often then a violent offender. Black females, once again, faired better than their male counterparts. The Probation Granted index was 1.14, which indicates a higher percentage of black females being granted probation compared to white females.

Prisoners and Population—20% of Social Justice

The weight of the Prisoners and Population index is split evenly between its two sub-categories: In Prison as a Percent of Population (10%) and Prisoners as a Percent of Arrests (10%). The Prisoners as a Percent of Arrests index measures the transition from arrests to prison and the discrepancy therein. The index value of 0.34 speaks to a disproportionate amount of black arrests that result in the person becoming a prisoner. In fact, as a percentage of arrests, there are three times as many blacks that become prisoners. This supports the operating theory that blacks are more likely to be imprisoned once arrested and indicates there may be racial bias in how the law is enforced. The In Prison as a Percent of the Population index made a nominal improvement but still indicates that there are seven times as many African Americans in prison, as a percentage of the population, compared to whites. The newly-added gender designations for this statistic illustrate the disparity not only between white males and black males, but between black males and black females. The index produced a low index number for black females (0.29), but an even lower index for black males (at 0.15). In fact, per 100,000 people, black men have an incarceration rate that is over 20 times that of black women.

Victimization and Mental Anguish—20% of Social Justice

The Victimization and Mental Anguish index (0.20) has most of its weight devoted to the male and female homicide sub-indices. The Homicide indices for males and females collectively comprise 50 percent of the index under this category, and the remainder is calculated with Adolescent Mortality (ages 13-19), Murder Victims (% of Population), Hate Crimes Against (% of Population), Victims of Violent Crimes (Per 1000 people), Delinquency Cases (Crimes committed by a juvenile for which they could be tried as an adult), Prisoners Under Death Sentence, Percent of Students Carrying a Weapon in School and Percent of Students who Carry a Weapon Anywhere.

Homicides Adjusted for Population, both male and female, paint a grim picture. The Homicide Index number for males (.16) shows a murder rate for black males that is over six times that of white males. Under Male Homicides, black male deaths due to firearms and stabbings are near the overall index value of 0.15. The Homicide index number for females was better than for males, at 0.35. However, the homicide rate for black females is nearly three times higher than white females.

There are other components of the Victimization and Mental Anguish sub-component that continue to show disparities between African Americans and whites. As a percentage of their population, blacks (index value of 0.20) are five times more likely to be the victim of a murder than whites. Blacks are also more likely to be the victim of a violent crime (index value of 0.74). The troubling thing about these figures is that the bulk of these crimes committed upon blacks are by other blacks. Finally, African Americans are nearly 17 times more likely to be the victim of a hate crime (index of 0.06) than their white counterparts.

CIVIC ENGAGEMENT—10% OF EQUALITY INDEX

The Civic Engagement sub-index is divided into four categories: The Democratic Progress (40%), Community Participation (30%), Collective Bargaining (20%), and Government Employment (10%). The Civic Engagement index number was computed at 1.05, indicating that, as far as Civic Engagement goes, blacks in America are slightly more involved than whites. The 2007 Civic Engagement value is slightly higher than the 2006 value (1.04).

The Democratic Process—40% of Civic Engagement

This category attempts to measure the degree to which the two populations exercise their right to vote. Registering to vote and the act of voting itself are excellent proxies for how invested people are in the fabric of their nation and to what extent they feel engaged in their society. Registered Voters (20 percent) and Actually Voted (20 percent) are weighted evenly within this group. The Registered Voters index figure of 0.95 speaks to a slightly higher percentage of whites who registered to vote than blacks. Actually Voted—which measures the percentage of people who voted in relation to those who are registered to vote—has an index value of 0.93. This shows a nominal difference between blacks and whites. Interestingly, despite the tremendous effort it took to gain the right to vote, blacks still participate somewhat less than whites. Yet there are also many blacks who are left out of the democratic process due to criminal disenfranchisement. The Voting Rights Act of 1965 confronted the issue of state disenfranchisement, but criminal disenfranchisement, which denies the vote to citizens convicted of crimes in varying degrees in most states, eliminates the potential votes of millions of Americans—a disproportionate share of which are nonwhite.[10]

Community Participation—30% of Civic Engagement

Participation has six components: Volunteerism, Percent of Population Volunteering for Military Reserves, Unpaid Volunteering of Young Adults, Attends Church, Church Attendance Among Youth, and Youth Group Participation.

The 2007 Volunteerism figure of 0.73 is higher than the 2006 index figure of 0.68, indicating an improvement in the percentage of blacks who volunteer relative to whites. Percent of Population Volunteering for Military Reserves was .99, the first year for which the index figure was below 1. This may reflect a larger trend of fewer blacks enlisting in the regular armed services, where members of the reserves usually have served, that has been observed since 2000.[11]

Collective Bargaining—20% of Civic Engagement

The two components in this category, Unionism (% in union) and Union Represented (% in occupations that are represented by Unions), are equally weighted. The Unionism index number of 1.24—unchanged from last year—reveals a significantly higher percentage of blacks in unions than whites, suggesting that unions remain an important vehicle for blacks' voice in the labor force. In addition, the Union Representation index value of 1.23 means that blacks also are more concentrated in jobs that are represented by unions. Union Representation barely changed from last year's index.

Governmental Employment—10% of Civic Engagement

State and Local Government Employment and Federal Executive Branch Employment comprise this category. Federal Executive Branch Employment is a newly added series, defined as total employment for Executive branch agencies participating in OPMs Central Personnel Data File (which excludes postal employees). The employment index tallies at 1.46, demonstrating a greater propensity for African Americans to be employed in the federal government. The State and Local Government index was even higher, at 1.67. The large index numbers may reflect the perceived job security and good benefits that are associated with government jobs and make them an attractive employment option for African Americans.

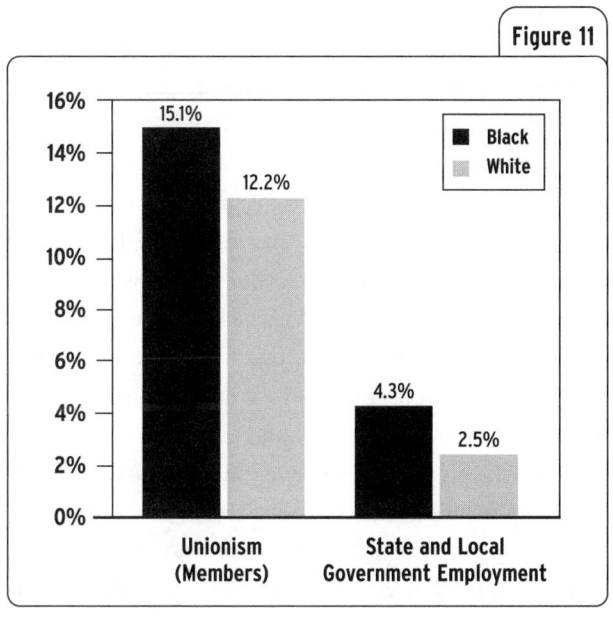

Figure 11

CONCLUSION

Overall, the Total Equality Index is virtually unchanged, registering 0.73 in both 2007 and 2006. This is not surprising, since wholesale national changes move at a glacial pace. However, changes in the sub-indexes did occur; thus the comparison between the two years' index values is not straightforward. As the *Equality Index* project progresses, Global Insight is improving the index both by updating the data as newer values become available and adding new concepts to further illustrate and better capture the totality of the Black/White experience in America. In the 2006 *Equality Index*, a total of 352 data series (2006-352 in Figure 12) were utilized to measure the gap between Black and White America; in the 2007 *Equality Index*, the number of series totaled 330.

Global Insight kept the 2007 weights exactly as last time around for all the five major sub-indexes and for the great majority of micro categories and even some individual series, adjusting instead the relative weights of new micro categories. For example Education scores represent 15% of the total Education sub-index. In 2004 seven different nationwide scores were used, each with 1/7 the weight of the 15%. In 2005 a total of 14 scores were utilized each with a 1/14 weight of the 15%.

For purposes of comparison, Global Insight has created charts showing the 2006 index value (2005-352) and the 2007 new index value (2007-330) below. GII also created a true apples—to—apples index comparison for the total index and the major sub-indexes (2007-330). This last index is what the 2006 value would have been had we just used the old 352 data series reflecting all the updated data available this year.

In the table and accompanying chart (Figures 12, 13), the Social Justice sub-index recorded the largest change of any index on a percent change basis. The decline is due largely to the eradication of the Governmental Equality section of Social Justice, which had variables that produced relatively high index numbers. Governmental Equality was not used due to a lack of recently updated data. The weights from the Governmental Equality section were shifted to other sections which had lower index values. The Health index recorded the next largest change compared to the 2006 *Equality Index*. The Health index was aided by large increases in the diabetes index number (though the number is still lower for blacks than whites). In addition, updated data

Figure 12

National Urban League Equality Index

	2007-330	2006-352	2007-352	Percent Change From 2007 2007-330	2007-352
Total Equality	0.733	0.730	0.667	0.35%	-8.68%
Economic	0.568	0.561	0.498	1.12%	-11.28%
Health	0.777	0.759	0.652	2.43%	-14.13%
Education	0.788	0.776	0.784	1.56%	1.00%
Social Justice	0.659	0.742	0.589	-11.12%	-20.61%
Civic Engagement	1.050	1.037	0.995	1.25%	-4.03%

KEY
• 2006-352 is the index value calculated in the 2006 Equality Index.
• 2007-330 is the Equality Index calculated with additional factors in it.
• 2007-352 offers the direct comparison with the 2006 Equality Index.

Figure 13

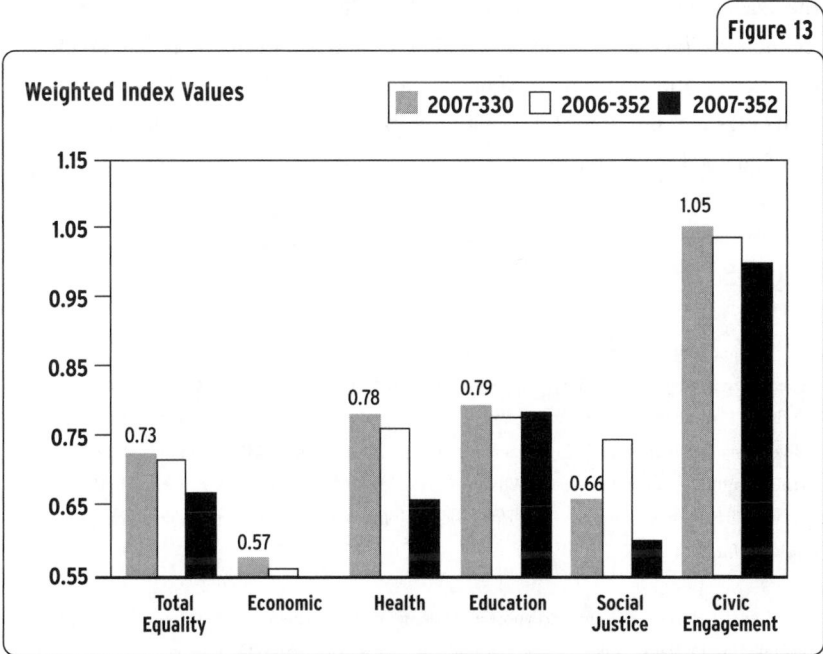

Weighted Index Values — 2007-330 ☐ 2006-352 ■ 2007-352

KEY
• 2006-352 is the index value calculated in the 2006 Equality Index.
• 2007-330 is the Equality Index calculated with additional factors in it.
• 2007-352 offers the direct comparison with the 2006 Equality Index.

showed that blacks are abusing alcohol less than whites, and have lower sui-
cide rates. The percentage of babies that were breastfed saw an increase in
this year's index and also helped to increase in the Health index. The
Education logged a moderate increase compared to the previous year.
Children's School Readiness Skills (Ages 3-5) increased from 0.81 in the 2006
Index to 0.94 in this year's edition. This variable has lasting importance, as
early readiness can lead to sustained academic success. The index value for
Preprimary School Enrollment also rose relative to last year. The Education
index was also boosted by a surge in the variable for College Enrollment of
Persons 35 years and older. This index figure rose from 1.43 in 2006 to 1.80 in
2007. Civic Engagement, which has the least amount of explanatory variables,
produced the second smallest change relative to last year, rising 1.25% on a
percent change basis. Most variables in this sub-index stayed relatively constant, although there was an increase in volunteerism—which rose from 0.68
in the 2006 index to 0.73 in this year's index. The Economic sub-index showed
the least variation, increasing only 1.12% since 2006. The increase in the
Economics sub-index came largely due to increase in the mortgage application denial and home improvement loan denial variables, which recorded
gains versus 2006. Households with Computers also recorded a sizeable gain
which helped the increase in Economics.

NOTES

[1] Index weights are represented within the text as a percentage of the sub-index: "Life
expectancy is weighted at 15 percent," or a shorthand percentage follows the description of
the data: "Live births per 1000 women was given the greatest value (5%) in the micro-index of
delivery issues." In all cases, the percentage refers to the percent of the sub-index—Health
in this example—being discussed. When referring to the entire *Equality Index* itself, the
text will directly mention this. "The Education sub-index comprises 25 percent of the
Equality Index."

[2] Avery, Robert, Kenneth Brevoort and Glenn Canner. "Higher-Priced Home Lending and
the 2005 HMDA Data". Federal Reserve Bulletin. September 25, 2006, p. A160.

[3] Net Worth is defined as the total value of held assets minus the total value of debts.
Included in net worth were interest-earning assets, checking accounts, stocks and mutual
funds, real estate and motor vehicles.

[4] The literature makes a correlation between black savings behavior, intergenerational wealth transfers and the black/white wealth gap. Altonji, Joseph G. and Doraszelski, Ulrich. "The Role of Permanent Income and Demographics in Black/White Differences in Wealth." *The Journal of Human Resources*, Winter 2005.

[5] Black, Dan, Haviland, Amelia, Sanders, Seth, and Taylor, Lowell. "Why Do Minority Men Earn Less? A Study Of Wage Differentials Among The Highly Educated." *The Review of Economics and Statistics*, February 2006.

[6] "High Cost or High Opportunity Cost? Transportation and Family Economic Success," the Brookings Institution, December 2005

[7] Eli Pristoop and Ross Weiner, "The Funding Gap 2006," accessed online at www2.edtrust.org.

[8] Adelman, C. *The Toolbox Revisited: Paths to Degree Completion From High School Through College*. Washington D.C.: U.S. Department of Education, 2006. An odds ratio indicates that every unit of change in an independent variable (in this case, each step up the math ladder) increases the odds of X happening versus the odds of X *not* happening by Y (the odds ratio).

[9] Christopher Jencks and Meredith Phillips. *The Black-White Test Score Gap*. Washington, D.C.: Brookings Institution Press, 1998. Their research showed that the effects of variables which account for a home learning environment are hardly reduced once children's cognitive genes are controlled for.

[10] Andrew L. Shapiro. "Challenging Criminal Disenfranchisement," *The Yale Law Journal*, Vol. 103, No. 2. (Nov., 1993), pp. 537-566.

[11] David R. Segal and Mady Wechsler Segal, "Army Recruitment Goals Endangered as Percent of African American Enlistees Declines," accessed online at www.pbr.org.

The Equality Index of Black America

Updated Series ▮ New Series (Index = 0.73)

	Source	Year	Black	White	Index	DIFF ('07-'06)
ECONOMICS (30%)						
Median Income (0.25)						
Median Household Income (Real)	Census	2005	30,858	50,784	61%	(0.01)
Median Male Earnings	ACS	2005	34,433	46,807	74%	0.04
Median Female Earnings	ACS	2005	29,588	34,190	87%	0.04
Poverty (0.15)						
Poverty Line (% Below)	Census	2005	24.9	8.3	33%	(0.02)
Poverty Line (% Below 50% of Poverty Line)	Census	2005	11.7	3.5	30%	(0.00)
Population Living Below Poverty Line 125% of Poverty Line	Census	2005	31.2	11.4	37%	
Population Living Below Poverty Line (Under 18)	Census	2005	33.5	10	30%	0.00
Population Living Below Poverty Line (18-64)	Census	2005	20.3	7.8	38%	0.00
Population Living Below Poverty Line (65 and Older)	Census	2005	23.2	7.9	34%	(0.01)
Employment Issues (0.20)						
Unemployment Rate	BLS	2006	9.0	4.0	44%	0.00
Unemployment Rate-Male	BLS	2006	9.5	4.0	42%	
Unemployment Rate-Female	BLS	2006	8.5	4.1	48%	
Persons 16-19 Who are Unemployed	BLS	2005	29.00	13.20	46%	(0.03)
Not in Workforce-Ages 16 to 19	BLS	2006	0.7	0.5	81%	
Not in Workforce-Ages 16 and Older	BLS	2006	0.4	0.3	93%	(0.00)
Labor Force Participants	BLS	2006	64.1	66.5	96%	(0.01)
LFPR 16 to 19	BLS	2006	34.0	46.7	73%	0.04
LFPR 20 to 24	BLS	2006	68.8	76.5	90%	(0.00)
LFPR over 25-Less than High School Grad	BLS	2006	40.1	47.4	85%	(0.01)
LFPR over 25-High School Graduate, No College	BLS	2006	66.9	62.5	107%	(0.02)
LFPR over 25-Some College, No Degree	BLS	2006	74.0	69.5	106%	(0.00)
LFPR over 25-Associate's Degree	BLS	2006	77.9	75.9	103%	(0.01)

The Equality Index of Black America

	Source	Year	Black	White	Index	DIFF ('07-'06)
LFPR Over 25-Less than Bachelor's	BLS	2006	75.2	71.7	105%	(0.00)
LFPR Over 25-College Graduate	BLS	2006	82.1	77.5	106%	0.00
Employment to Pop. Ratio	BLS	2006	58.5	63.8	92%	0.01
Housing & Wealth (0.34)						
Home Ownership	Census	2006	47.9	75.8	63%	(0.01)
Mortgage Application Denial	HMDA	2005	24.49	12.98	53%	0.05
Mortgage Application Denial (Male)	HMDA	2005	25.76	15.27	59%	
Mortgage Application Denial (Female)	HMDA	2005	24.78	14.66	59%	
Mortgage Application Denial (Joint)	HMDA	2005	20.81	9.99	48%	
Home Improvement Loans Denials	HMDA	2005	47.74	30.01	63%	0.10
Home Improvement Loans Denials (Male)	HMDA	2005	49.43	34.95	71%	
Home Improvement Loans Denials (Female)	HMDA	2005	49.91	34.77	70%	
Home Improvement Loans Denials (Joint)	HMDA	2005	41.74	24.72	59%	
Percent of High-Priced Loans (More than 3% above Treasury)	HMDA	2005	54.7	17.2	31%	
Home Values (Median)	Census	2000	80,600	123,400	65%	
Median Net Worth	SWA	2004	12	118	10%	0.01
Equity in Home	Census	2000	35000	64,200	55%	
Percent Investing in 401k	Census	2000	19.6	32.9	60%	
Percent Investing in IRA	Census	2000	6.5	27.5	24%	
U.S. Firms by Race (% Compared to Employment Share)	Census	2002	0.509	0.951	54%	
Digital Divide (0.05)						
Households with Computer at Home	Census	2003	44.6	66.6	67%	0.08
Households Using the Internet	Census	2003	36.0	59.9	60%	(0.09)
Households with Broadband Access	Stat. Ab.	2005	23	38	61%	0.06
Transportation (0.01)						
Car Ownership	Census	2000	70.2	89.2	79%	0.00

The Equality Index of Black America

	Source	Year	Black	White	Index	DIFF ('07-'06)
					▨ Updated Series ■ New Series	(Index = 0.73)
Drive Alone	Census	2004	72.3	81.1	89%	0.06
Reliance on Public Transportation	Census	2004	11.3	2.6	23%	(0.02)
Economic Weighted Index					**57%**	
HEALTH INDEX (25%)						
Death Rebates & Life Expectancy (0.45)						
Life Expectancy at Birth	CDC-H	2004	73.1	78.3	93%	0.00
Male	CDC-H	2004	69.5	75.7	92%	0.00
Female	CDC-H	2004	76.3	80.8	94%	0.00
Life Expectancy at 65 (Additional Expected Years)	CDC-H	2004	17.1	18.7	91%	0.00
Male at 65	CDC-H	2004	14.6	16.6	88%	0.00
Female at 65	CDC-H	2004	18	19.5	92%	0.00
Age-Adjusted Death Rates (per 100,000)–all causes	CDC-D	2003	1,065.9	817.0	77%	(0.01)
Age-Adjusted Death Rates (per 100,000)–Male	CDC-D	2003	1,319.1	973.9	74%	
Age-Adjusted Death Rates (per 100,000)–Female	CDC-D	2003	885.6	693.1	78%	
Age-Adjusted Death Rates (per 100,000)–Heart Disease	CDC-D	2003	300.2	228.2	76%	(0.02)
Ischemic Heart Disease	CDC-D	2003	195.0	161.7	83%	(0.01)
Age-Adjusted Death Rates (per 100,000)–Stroke (Cerebrovascular)	CDC-D	2003	74.3	51.4	69%	(0.02)
Age-Adjusted Death Rates (per 100,000)–Cancer	CDC-D	2003	233.3	188.5	81%	(0.01)
Trachea, Bronchus, and Lung	CDC-D	2003	60.8	54.5	90%	(0.03)
Colon, Rectum, and Anus	CDC-D	2003	26.4	18.6	70%	(0.02)
Prostate (Male)	CDC-D	2003	57.4	24.4	43%	0.01
Breast	CDC-D	2003	20.1	13.8	69%	(0.07)
Age-Adjusted Death Rates (per 100,000)–Chronic Lower Respiratory	CDC-D	2002	31.2	46.9	150%	0.00
Influenza and Pneumonia	CDC-D	2003	23.3	21.9	94%	(0.00)
Chronic Liver Disease and Cirrhosis	CDC-D	2003	8.4	9.5	113%	0.07
Age-Adjusted Death Rates (per 100,000)–Diabetes	CDC-D	2003	49.2	23.0	47%	0.02

The Equality Index of Black America

			Updated Series		New Series	(Index = 0.73)
	Source	Year	Black	White	Index	DIFF ('07-'06)
Age-Adjusted Death Rates (per 100,000)—HIV	CDC-D	2003	21.3	2.5	12%	0.02
Unintentional Injuries	CDC-D	2003	36.1	38.2	106%	0.03
Motor Vehicle-Related Injuries	CDC-D	2003	15.8	16.8	106%	(0.00)
Age-Adjusted Death Rates (per 100,000)-Suicide	CDC-D	2003	5.2	11.8	227%	(0.16)
Age-Adjusted Death Rates (per 100,000)-Suicide Males	CDC-D	2003	9.2	19.6	213%	(0.05)
Age-Adjusted Death Rates (per 100,000)-Suicide Males Ages 15-24	CDC-D	2002	11.3	19.3	171%	0.00
Age-Adjusted Death Rates (per 100,000)-Suicide Females	CDC-D	2003	1.9	4.6	242%	(0.77)
Age-Adjusted Death Rates (per 100,000)-Suicide Females Ages 15-24	CDC-D	2002	1.7	3.4	200%	0.00
Age-Adjusted Death Rates (per 100,000)-Homicide	CDC-D	2003	21.0	2.2	10%	(0.03)
Age-Adjusted Death Rates (per 100,000)-Homicide Male	CDC-D	2003	36.7	5.3	14%	0.04
Age-Adjusted Death Rates (per 100,000)-Homicide Males Ages 15-24	CDC-D	2002	83.1	5.5	7%	0.00
Age-Adjusted Death Rates (per 100,000)-Homicide Female	CDC-D	2003	3.2	0.9	28%	0.01
Age-Adjusted Death Rates (per 100,000)-Homicide Females Ages 15-24	CDC-D	2002	10.3	2.2	21%	0.00
Age-Adjusted Death Rates (per 100,000) by Age Cohort: >1 Male	CDC-D	2003	1,427.7	647.2	45%	(0.02)
Age-Adjusted Death Rates (per 100,000) by Age Cohort: 1-4 Male	CDC-D	2003	55.1	30.2	55%	(0.01)
Age-Adjusted Death Rates (per 100,000) by Age Cohort: 5-14 Male	CDC-D	2003	27.9	18.1	65%	0.02
Age-Adjusted Death Rates (per 100,000) by Age Cohort: 15-24 Male	CDC-D	2003	176.5	105.9	60%	(0.02)
Age-Adjusted Death Rates (per 100,000) by Age Cohort: 25-34 Male	CDC-D	2003	266.6	129.9	49%	(0.01)
Age-Adjusted Death Rates (per 100,000) by Age Cohort: 35-44 Male	CDC-D	2003	440.0	243.8	55%	(0.01)
Age-Adjusted Death Rates (per 100,000) by Age Cohort: 45-54 Male	CDC-D	2003	1,012.8	513.2	51%	(0.01)
Age-Adjusted Death Rates (per 100,000) by Age Cohort: 55-64 Male	CDC-D	2003	2,047.7	1,110.5	54%	(0.01)
Age-Adjusted Death Rates (per 100,000) by Age Cohort: 65-74 Male	CDC-D	2003	4,041.1	2,738.5	68%	(0.02)
Age-Adjusted Death Rates (per 100,000) by Age Cohort: 75-84 Male	CDC-D	2003	8,165.7	6,692.2	82%	(0.01)
Age-Adjusted Death Rates (per 100,000) by Age Cohort: 85+ Male	CDC-D	2003	15,082.2	16,234.4	108%	0.01
Age-Adjusted Death Rates (per 100,000) by Age Cohort: >1 Female	CDC-D	2003	1,146.9	502.5	44%	0.01
Age-Adjusted Death Rates (per 100,000) by Age Cohort: 1-4 Female	CDC-D	2003	40.7	24.9	61%	0.01

The Equality Index of Black America

	Updated Series	New Series			
	Source	Year	Black	White	Index	DIFF ('07-'06)
Age-Adjusted Death Rates (per 100,000) by Age Cohort: 5-14 Female	CDC-D	2003	19.6	12.9	66%	(0.03)
Age-Adjusted Death Rates (per 100,000) by Age Cohort: 15-24 Female	CDC-D	2003	56.0	44.3	79%	(0.01)
Age-Adjusted Death Rates (per 100,000) by Age Cohort: 25-34 Female	CDC-D	2003	118.0	61.2	52%	0.00
Age-Adjusted Death Rates (per 100,000) by Age Cohort: 35-44 Female	CDC-D	2003	278.4	138.0	50%	(0.01)
Age-Adjusted Death Rates (per 100,000) by Age Cohort: 45-54 Female	CDC-D	2003	595.7	293.1	49%	(0.01)
Age-Adjusted Death Rates (per 100,000) by Age Cohort: 55-64 Female	CDC-D	2003	1,201.6	705.0	59%	(0.01)
Age-Adjusted Death Rates (per 100,000) by Age Cohort: 65-74 Female	CDC-D	2003	2,531.2	1,807.9	71%	(0.01)
Age-Adjusted Death Rates (per 100,000) by Age Cohort: 75-84 Female	CDC-D	2003	5,454.6	4,720.5	87%	0.01
Age-Adjusted Death Rates (per 100,000) by Age Cohort: 85+ Female	CDC-D	2003	13,730.3	14,107.7	103%	(0.03)
Lifetime Health (0.30)						
Physical Condition (0.10)						
Overweight and Obese: 18+ years (% of Population)	CDC	2002	68.9	57.5	83%	0.00
Overweight-Men 20 Years and Over (% of Population)	CDC-H	2004	67.0	71.0	106%	(0.05)
Overweight-Women 20 Years and Over (% of Population)	CDC-H	2004	79.6	57.6	72%	(0.02)
Obese (% of population)	CDC-H	2002	34.8	22.2	64%	0.00
Obese-Men 20 Years and Over (% of Population)	CDC-H	2004	30.8	30.2	98%	(0.03)
Obese-Women 20 Years and Over (% of Population)	CDC-H	2004	51.1	30.7	60%	(0.03)
Diabetes: Physician Diagnosed in Ages 18+ (% of Population)	CDC-H	2005	11.3	6.5	58%	0.16
AIDS Cases per 100,000 Males Ages 13+	CDC-H	2005	103.6	13.1	13%	0.00
AIDS Cases per 100,000 Females Ages 13+	CDC-H	2005	49.9	2.1	4%	(0.00)
Substance Abuse (0.10)						
Binge Alcohol (5 drinks in 1 day, 1x a year) Ages 18+ (% of Population)	CDC-ER	2005	12.1	22.6	187%	0.63
Tobacco: Both Cigarette & Cigar Ages 18+ (% of Population)	CDC-ER	2005	21.4	22.5	105%	(0.00)
Mental Health (0.02)						
Students Who Consider Suicide: Male	CDC-H	2005	7.0	12.4	177%	0.61
Students Who Carry Out Intent and Require Medical Attention: Male		2002	5.2	1.1	21%	0.00

(Index = 0.73)

The Equality Index of Black America

Updated Series   ■ New Series

	Source	Year	Black	White	Index	DIFF ('07-'06) (Index = 0.73)
Percent of Students that Act on Suicidal Feeling: Male	CDC-H	2005	5.2	5.2	100%	0.82
Students Who Consider Suicide: Female	CDC-H	2005	17.1	21.5	126%	0.56
Students Who Carry Out Intent and Require Medical Attention: Female		2002	2.4	2.2	92%	0.00
Percent of Students that Act on Suicidal Feeling: Female	CDC-H	2005	9.8	9.3	95%	(0.37)
Access to Care (0.05)						
Private Insurance Payment for Health Care: Under 65 Years Old (% of Population)	CDC-H	2004	51	65.8	78%	0.04
All People Without Health Insurance	Census	2005	0.196	0.113	58%	0.00
People 18 to 64 Without A Usual Source of Health Insurance	CDC-H	2004	18.8	17.5	96%	0.00
People in Poverty Without a Usual Source of Health Insurance	CDC-H	2004	24	22.7	95%	
Population Under 65 Covered by Medicaid	CDC-H	2004	24.9	10.4	42%	0.05
Elderly Health Care (0.03)						
Population Over 65 Covered by Medicaid	CDC-H	2003	30	6	20%	(0.06)
Medicare Expenditures per Beneficiary	CDC-H	2002	15260	13010	85%	0.00
Reproduction and Pediatric Care (Mother's Health, Births & Early Childhood) (0.25)						
Pregnancy Issues (0.04)						
Prenatal Care Begins in 1st Trimester	CDC-B	2004	76.5	88.9	86%	0.01
Prenatal Care Begins in 3rd Trimester	CDC-B	2004	5.7	2.2	39%	0.03
Percent of Births to Mothers 18 and Under	CDC-H	2004	6.5	2	31%	(0.13)
Percent of Live Births to Unmarried Mothers	CDC-B	2004	67.2	29.4	44%	0.10
Mothers With Less than 12 Years of Education (% of Live Births)	CDC-H	2004	23.4	11	47%	(0.01)
Mothers Who Smoked Cigarettes During Pregnancy (%)	CDC-B	2004	8.4	13.8	164%	(0.06)
Low Birth Weight (% of Live Births)	CDC-B	2004	13.7	7.2	53%	0.01
Very Low Birth Weight (% of Live Births)	CDC-B	2004	3.1	1.2	39%	
Reproduction Issues (0.01)						
Abortions (Per 100 Live Births)	CDC-H	2003	49.1	16.5	34%	0.00
Women Using Contraception (Percent in Population)	CDC-H	2002	57.6	64.6	89%	(0.05)

The Equality Index of Black America

		Source	Year	Black	White	Updated Series / New Series — Index	DIFF ('07-'06)
Delivery Issues (0.10)							
All Infant Deaths: Neonatal and Post (per 1000 Live Births)		CDC-D	2003	14.01	5.72	41%	(0.01)
Neonatal Deaths (per 1000 Live Births)		CDC-D	2003	9.4	3.87	41%	(0.01)
PostNeonatal Deaths (per 1000 Live Births)		CDC-D	2003	4.6	1.84	40%	(0.01)
Maternal Mortality (per 100,000 Live Births)		CDC-H	2002	32.3	7.8	24%	0.05
Children's Health (0.1)							
Babies Breastfed (%)		CDC-H	2001	45.3	68.7	66%	0.21
No Child Health Care Visit in Past 12 Months (% of Children Up to 6 Years Old)		CDC-H	2004	5.5	6.4	116%	0.24
Vaccinations of Children Below Poverty: Combined Vacc. Series 4:3:1:3 (% of Children 19-35 Months)		CDC-H	2005	77	78	99%	0.10
Uninsured Children		CDC-H	2004	10.3	7	68%	0.09
Overweight Boys 6-11 Years Old (% of Population)		CDC-H	2004	17.2	16.9	98%	0.16
Overweight Girls 6-11 Years Old (% of Population)		CDC-H	2004	24.8	15.6	63%	0.05
AIDS Cases per 100,000 All Children Under 13		CDC	2005	59.0	6.3	11%	0.04
Health Weighted Index						**78%**	
EDUCATION (25%)							
Quality (0.45)							
Teacher Quality (0.30)							
Middle Grades–Teacher Lacking at Least a College Minor in Subject Taught		ET	2000	49%	40%	85%	0.00
HS–Teacher Lacking at Least a College Minor in Subject Taught		ET	2000	28%	21%	91%	0.00
Per Student Funding in Low and High Poverty Districts (Dollars)		ET	2004	5937	7244	82%	(0.01)
Teachers with <3 Years Experience (Hi vs. Low Minority Schools)		ET	2000	0.21	0.1	48%	0.00
Distribution of Underprepared Teachers (California Only) Small vs. High Minority		SRI	2005-06	0.08	0.03	38%	0.18
*had not completed a preparation program and obtained a full credential before beginning to teach							
Course Quality (0.15)							
All College Entrants		ET	1999	0.45	0.73	62%	0.00
Of All College Entrants What Percent Had a Strong HS Curriculum (Algebra 2 Plus Other Courses)		ET	1999	0.75	0.86	87%	0.00

(Index = 0.73)

The Equality Index of Black America

Updated Series | New Series | (Index = 0.73)

	Source	Year	Black	White	Index	DIFF ('07-'06)
HS Students: Enrolled in Chemistry	NCES	2000	0.6	0.63	95%	0.00
HS Students: Enrolled in Algebra 2	NCES	2000	0.65	0.69	94%	0.00
Students Taking: Precalculus	CB	2006	0.33	0.53	62%	(0.02)
Students Taking: Calculus	CB	2006	0.15	0.3	50%	0.00
Students Taking: English Composition	CB	2006	0.43	0.53	81%	0.07
Students Taking: Grammar	CB	2006	0.51	0.56	91%	0.07
Attainment (0.20)						
Graduation by Enrolled Students for 2-year Institutions	NCES	2001	27%	34%	79%	(0.03)
Graduation by Enrolled Students for 4-year Institutions	NCES	1998	40%	58%	68%	0.01
NCAA Div. I College Freshmen Graduating within 6 Years	NCAA	99-00	44%	63%	70%	0.02
Degrees Earned (Assoc)	NCES	2004	1.9%	2.5%	75%	0.02
Degrees Earned (Bach)	NCES	2004	1.9%	3.5%	54%	0.01
Degrees Earned (Master)	NCES	2004	0.5%	0.9%	59%	0.03
HS Educational Attainment (25 and Over)	Census	2005	81%	86%	95%	0.00
College Educational Attainment (25 and Over)	Census	2005	18%	28%	63%	(0.01)
Degree Holders (% of Persons Over 18)						
Agriculture/Forestry	NCES	2001	0.7	1.2	56%	(0.02)
Art/Architecture	NCES	2001	3.3	2.9	114%	0.78
Business/Management	NCES	2001	19.5	18.1	108%	(0.09)
Communications	NCES	2001	3.2	2.4	135%	0.44
Computer and Information Sciences	NCES	2001	3.9	2.2	177%	0.15
Education	NCES	2001	15.3	15.3	100%	(0.23)
Engineering	NCES	2001	3.6	7.7	47%	0.08
English/Literature	NCES	2001	2.6	3.3	80%	0.19
Foreign Languages	NCES	2001	0.8	0.9	96%	0.38
Health Sciences	NCES	2001	5.4	4.5	120%	0.13

The Equality Index of Black America

Legend: Updated Series | New Series | (Index = 0.73)

	Source	Year	Black	White	Index	DIFF ('07–'06)
Law	NCES	1996	1.8	3.0	60%	0.00
Liberal Arts/Humanities	NCES	2001	4.6	6.1	75%	(0.33)
Mathematics/Statistics	NCES	2001	2.4	1.4	169%	0.03
Medicine	NCES	1996	0.3	2.3	13%	0.00
Natural Sciences	NCES	2001	6.0	5.6	106%	0.40
Nursing & Public Health	NCES	1996	0.9	1.1	82%	0.00
Philosophy/Religion/Theology	NCES	2001	0.9	1.3	70%	0.01
Pre-professional	NCES	2001	1.6	1.1	146%	(1.21)
Psychology	NCES	2001	4.9	3.9	126%	(0.01)
Social Sciences/History	NCES	2001	8.1	4.9	165%	0.15
Other Fields	NCES	2001	13.1	17.2	76%	(0.24)
Scores (0.15)						
Preschool 10% of Total Scores (0.015)						
Children's School Readiness Skills: Ages 3-5 (% with 3 or 4 skills*)	NCES	2005	44	47	94%	0.12
*Skills: Recognizes all Letters, Counts to 20 or higher, Writes Name, Reads or Pretends to Read						
Elementary 40% of Total Scores (0.06)						
Proficiency Test Scores for Selected Subjects (NAEP) Elementary Ages	NCES					
Geography Scores for 8th Graders (Public & Private)	NCES	2001	234	273	86%	0.00
History Scores for 8th Graders (Public & Private)	NCES	2001	243	271	90%	0.00
Math 13 Yr Old (8th Grade)	NCES	2004	262	288	91%	0.00
Math 9 Yr Old (4th Grade)	NCES	2004	224	247	91%	0.00
Reading 13 Yr Old (8th Grade)	NCES	2004	244	266	92%	0.00
Reading 9 Yr Old (4th Grade)	NCES	2004	200	226	88%	0.00
Science 9 Yr Old	NCES	1999	199	240	83%	0.00
Science Scores for 8th Graders (Public Schools)	NCES	2000	121	160	76%	0.00
Writing Proficiency at or Above Basic 4th Grade	NCES	2002	79	91	87%	0.00

The Equality Index of Black America

Updated Series | New Series | (Index = 0.73)

	Source	Year	Black	White	Index	DIFF ('07-'06)
Writing Proficiency At or Above Basic 8th Grade	NCES	2002	75	91	82%	0.00
High School 50% of Total Scores (0.075)						
High School Scores						
Writing Proficiency At or Above Basic 12th Grade	NCES	2002	59	80	74%	0.00
Science 17 Yr Old	NCES	1999	254	306	83%	0.00
High School GPAs for Those Taking the SAT	CB	2006	3.01	3.40	89%	(0.00)
SAT	CB	2006	863	1063	81%	0.00
ACT	ACT	2006	17.1	22	78%	0.00
Enrollment (0.10)						
School Enrollment: Ages 3-34 (% of Population)	Census	2004	59	55.5	106%	(0.01)
Preprimary School Enrollment	Census	2004	67.0	63.8	105%	0.10
3 and 4 Years Old	Census	2004	59.6%	52.8%	113%	0.12
5 and 6 Years Old	Census	2004	94.1%	95.5%	99%	(0.01)
7 to 13 Years Old	Census	2004	98.6%	98.2%	100%	0.00
14 and 15 Years Old	Census	2004	99.0%	98.5%	101%	(0.00)
16 and 17 Years Old	Census	2004	95.7%	94.2%	102%	0.02
18 and 19 Years Old	Census	2004	59.2%	64.9%	91%	(0.05)
20 and 21 Years Old	Census	2004	40.0%	49.3%	81%	(0.05)
22 to 24 Years Old	Census	2004	25.1%	25.3%	99%	(0.03)
25 to 29 Years Old	Census	2004	14.3%	12.2%	117%	0.06
30 to 34 Years Old	Census	2004	7.2%	6.4%	113%	(0.26)
35 and Over	Census	2004	3.3%	1.9%	174%	0.18
College Enrollment by Age Cohort (15 and Over)	Census	2004	8.2%	7.1%	115%	0.04
15 to 17 Years Old	Census	2004	2.1%	1.4%	144%	0.17
18 to 19 Years Old	Census	2004	35.4%	49.8%	71%	0.08
20 to 21 Years Old	Census	2004	32.7%	51.2%	64%	(0.08)

The Equality Index of Black America

	Source	Year	Black	White	Index	DIFF ('07-'06)
					Updated Series / New Series	(Index = 0.73)
22 to 24 Years Old	Census	2004	21.6%	26.1%	83%	0.01
25 to 29 Years Old	Census	2004	13.1%	13.0%	100%	0.08
30 to 34 Years Old	Census	2004	6.2%	6.5%	96%	(0.25)
35 years Old and Over	Census	2004	3.1%	1.7%	180%	0.37
College Enrollment of Recent High School Graduates	NCES	2004	62.50	68.80	91%	0.04
Adult Education Participation	NCES	2001	46.00	46.00	100%	0.09
Student Status & Risk Factors (0.10)						
High School Dropouts: Status Dropouts–Not Completed HS and Not Enrolled, Regardless of When Dropped	Census	2004	15%	12%	79%	(0.03)
Children in Poverty	USDC	1999	0.331	0.093	28%	0.00
Children with No Parent in the Labor Force	USDC	2000	0.203	0.055	27%	0.00
School Age Children (5-15) with a Disability	USDC	2000	0.07	0.057	81%	0.00
Elementary & Secondary Students: Suspended	NCES	1999	0.15	0.35	43%	0.00
Elementary & Secondary Students: Repeated Grade	NCES	1999	0.09	0.18	50%	0.00
Center Based, Child Care of Preschool Children	NCES	2001	63.1	59.1	94%	0.00
Parental Only, Child Care of Preschool Children	NCES	2001	15.1	25.3	60%	0.00
Teacher Stability: Remained in Public School	NCES	2001	84.3	85.0	99%	0.00
Teacher Stability: Remained in Private School	NCES	2001	83.2	79.0	105%	0.00
Zero Days Missed in School Year (%)	NCES	2002	16.5	13.0	127%	0.01
3+ Days Late to School (% of students Reporting)	NCES	2002	46.1	31.5	68%	(0.05)
Never Cut Classes (% of students)	NCES	2002	64.6	72.9	89%	(0.08)
Home Literacy Activities (Age 3 to 5)						0.00
Read to 3 or More Times a Week	NCES	2005	78	92	85%	(0.02)
Told a Story at Least Once a Month	NCES	2005	54	53	102%	0.14
Taught Words or Numbers Three or More Times a Week	NCES	2005	81	76	107%	0.03
Visited a Library at Least Once in Last Month	NCES	2005	44	45	98%	0.18
Education Weighted Index					**79%**	

The Equality Index of Black America

| | | Updated Series | New Series | (Index = 0.73) |

	Source	Year	Black	White	Index	DIFF ('07-'06)
SOCIAL JUSTICE (10%)						
Equality Before the Law (0.80)						
Stopped While Driving	BJS	2002	9.14	8.75	96%	.11
Speeding	Census	1999	43.4	53.7	124%	0.00
Vehicle Defect	Census	1999	13.4	10.4	78%	0.00
Roadside Check for Drinking Drivers	Census	1999	1.4	2.5	179%	0.00
Record Check	Census	1999	11	9.1	83%	0.00
Driver Suspected of Something	Census	1999	2.4	2.3	96%	0.00
Other	Census	1999	28.4	22	77%	0.00
Average Jail Sentence (In Average Months)	BJS	2002	44.0	34.0	77%	0.00
Average Sentence for Murder-Male	BJS	2002	240.0	213.0	89%	0.00
Average Sentence for Sexual Assault-Male	BJS	2002	95.0	85.0	89%	0.00
Average Sentence for Robbery-Male	BJS	2002	92.0	78.0	85%	0.00
Average Sentence for Aggravated Assault-Male	BJS	2002	48.0	36.0	75%	0.00
Average Sentence for Other Violent-Male	BJS	2002	40.0	36.0	90%	0.00
Average Sentence for Burglary-Male	BJS	2002	44.0	37.0	84%	0.00
Average Sentence for Larceny-Male	BJS	2002	23.0	22.0	96%	0.00
Average Sentence for Fraud-Male	BJS	2002	30.0	25.0	83%	0.00
Average Sentence for Drug Possession-Male	BJS	2002	23.0	20.0	87%	0.00
Average Sentence for Drug Trafficking-Male	BJS	2002	45.0	38.0	84%	0.00
Average Sentence for Weapon Offenses-Male	BJS	2002	30.0	27.0	90%	0.00
Average Sentence for Other Offenses-Male	BJS	2002	23.0	22.0	96%	0.00
Average Sentence for Murder-Female	BJS	2002	247.0	121.0	49%	0.00
Average Sentence for Sexual Assault-Female	BJS	2002	34.0	43.0	126%	0.00
Average Sentence for Robbery-Female	BJS	2002	57.0	54.0	95%	0.00
Average Sentence for Aggravated Assault-Female	BJS	2002	29.0	25.0	86%	0.00

The Equality Index of Black America

	Source	Year	Black	White	Index	DIFF ('07-'06)
Average Sentence for Other Violent–Female	BJS	2002	25.0	39.0	156%	0.00
Average Sentence for Burglary–Female	BJS	2002	20.0	20.0	100%	0.00
Average Sentence for Larceny–Female	BJS	2002	16.0	16.0	100%	0.00
Average Sentence for Fraud–Female	BJS	2002	23.0	20.0	87%	0.00
Average Sentence for Drug Possession–Female	BJS	2002	15.0	14.0	93%	0.00
Average Sentence for Drug Trafficking–Female	BJS	2002	33.0	30.0	91%	0.00
Average Sentence for Weapon Offenses–Female	BJS	2002	23.0	17.0	74%	0.00
Average Sentence for Other Offenses–Female	BJS	2002	19.0	14.0	74%	0.00
Probation Granted for Felons (% granted)–Male	BJS	2002	27.0	34.0	79%	0.00
Probation Granted for Murder	BJS	2002	4.0	6.0	67%	0.00
Probation Granted for Robbery	BJS	2002	11.0	14.0	79%	0.00
Probation Granted for Burglary	BJS	2002	23.0	27.0	85%	0.00
Probation Granted for Fraud	BJS	2002	37.0	42.0	88%	0.00
Probation Granted for Drug Offenses	BJS	2002	31.0	42.0	74%	0.00
Probation Granted for Felons (% Granted)–Female	BJS	2002	47.0	45.0	104%	0.00
Probation Granted for Murder	BJS	2002	5.0	17.0	29%	0.00
Probation Granted for Robbery	BJS	2002	24.0	31.0	77%	0.00
Probation Granted for Burglary	BJS	2002	24.0	32.0	75%	0.00
Probation Granted for Fraud	BJS	2002	57.0	50.0	114%	0.00
Probation Granted for Drug Offenses	BJS	2002	45.0	49.0	92%	0.00
In Prison as a % of Population	BJS	2005	2.17	0.32	15%	0.01
Prisoners per 100,000 People–Male	BJS	2005	3145.0	471.0	15%	
Prisoners per 100,000 People–Female	BJS	2005	156.0	45.0	29%	
Prisoners as a % of Arrests	FBI, BJS	2005	24.4	8.3	34%	0.03
Victimization & Mental Anguish (0.20)						
Homicides (Adj. for Population)–Male	BJS	2003	0.4	0.1	16%	(0.00)

Updated Series ▪ New Series   (Index = 0.73)

The Equality Index of Black America

Updated Series   New Series   (Index = 0.73)

	Source	Year	Black	White	Index	DIFF ('07-'06)
Homicide Rate per 100,000: Firearm (aged 15-34)	BJS	2001	785.4	86.0	11%	0.00
Homicide Rate per 100,000: Stabbings (aged 15-34)	BJS	2001	50.8	14.3	28%	0.00
Homicide Rate per 100,000: Vehicular (aged 15-34)	BJS	2001	10.7	21.7	202%	0.00
Homicide (Adj. for Population)-Female	BJS	2003	0.1	0.0	35%	0.02
Murder Victims (% of Pop.)	USDJ	2004	0.0	0.0	20%	0.01
Hate Crimes Against (Incidents % of Pop.)	USDJ	2004	0.0	0.0	6%	(0.00)
Victims of Violent Crimes	BJS	2005	27.0	20.1	74%	0.01
Delinquency Cases (Cases Com. By Juvie that Adult Could Be Pros.)	NCJJ	2003	92.5	46.0	50%	0.00
Prisoners Under Death Sentence	BJS	2005	0.0	0.0	22%	0.01
% Students Carrying Weapons in School (9-12 Grade)	CDC	2003	7.0	6.0	86%	0.00
% Students Carrying Weapons Anywhere (9-12 Grade)	CDC	2003	17.0	17.0	100%	0.00
Firearm-Related Death (All Ages, Males)	CDC	2004	36.4	15.6	43%	(0.00)
Ages 1-14	CDC	2004	2.0	0.7	35%	(0.04)
Ages 15-24	CDC	2004	80.7	14.3	18%	(0.00)
Ages 25-44	CDC	2004	59.2	17.4	29%	(0.01)
Ages 25-34	CDC	2004	83.6	16.9	20%	(0.00)
Ages 35-44	CDC	2004	35.1	17.8	51%	(0.02)
Ages 45-64	CDC	2004	18.3	19.2	105%	0.01
Age 65 and Older	CDC	2004	14.6	27.6	189%	(0.21)
Firearm-Related Death (All Ages, Females)	CDC	2004	3.7	2.9	78%	0.12
Ages 15-24	CDC	2004	6.9	2.5	36%	0.05
Ages 25-44	CDC	2004	5.7	3.9	68%	0.07
Ages 45-64	CDC	2004	3.0	4.1	137%	0.10
Age 65 and Older	CDC	2003	1.8	2.2	122%	(0.69)
Social Justice Weighted Index					**66%**	

The Equality Index of Black America

Updated Series   New Series   (Index = 0.73)

	Source	Year	Black	White	Index	DIFF ('07-'06)
CIVIC ENGAGEMENT (10%)						
Democratic Process (0.4)						
Registered Voters	Census	2004	64.4	67.9	95%	(0.02)
Actually Voted	Census	2004	56.3	60.3	93%	(0.01)
Community Participation (0.3)						
Percent of Population Volunteering for Military Reserves	USDD	2005	0.9%	0.9%	99%	(0.05)
Volunteerism	BLS	2005	22.1	30.4	73%	0.05
Unpaid Volunteering of Young Adults	NCES	2000	40.9	32.2	127%	0.00
Attends Church (% Considering Self Religious)	BLS	2005	45.5	33.8	135%	0.02
Church Attendance Among Youth (Weekly %)1996	MTF	41	38		108%	0.00
Youth Group Participation (2 Years or More)	MTF	1996	59	57	104%	0.00
Collective Bargaining (0.2)						
Unionism (Members)	BLS	2005	15.1	12.2	124%	0.00
Union Rep.	BLS	2005	16.5	13.4	123%	(0.01)
Governmental Employment (0.1)						
Federal Executive Branch (Nonpostal) Employment	OPM	2005	1.2%	0.8%	146%	
State and Local Government Employment	EEOC	2003	4.3%	2.5%	167%	0.00
Civic Engagement Weighted Index					**105%**	

Re-imagining Black Masculine Identity: An Investigation of the "Problem" Surrounding the Construction of Black Masculinity in America

by David J. Johns

> Black masculinity is not merely a social identity crisis. It is also a key site of ideology and ideological representations where a major contrast of competing forces is played out.
>
> Maurice Wallace, *Constructing the Black Masculine*

The social categorization of black maleness, black masculinity, black male identity or any term by which we seek to understand the implications of being both black and male, in the United States, is an imagined social construct with real consequences.[1] The concept of black masculine identity was fashioned during and codified after the formal collapse of the American institution of slavery. Thus, black masculine identity is a product of American history. It has been socially constructed from narrowly defined understandings of white maleness.[2] Black masculine identity is heavily imbued with pernicious stereotypes introduced to strip enslaved Africans of humanity. These stereotypes are still prevalent in contemporary U.S. society and this prevalence is at least one factor contributing to the cycle of black male disengagement, alienation and misrepresentation.[3] The collusion of multiple factors, including being fashioned from restricted definitions of white maleness and the pressures of other socially imagined but life-shaping constructs like race, gender, and class, has resulted in archetypal categorization of black men and boys as easily understood, readily identifiable and operating in standardized and often counterproductive ways.

Black males continue to occupy the lowest rungs of most, if not all, quality of life indicators. The negative implications of how black men are identified and tracked by society deserve critical attention. This essay highlights the ways in which the concept of black maleness is a product of American history and examines the ways black males perceive themselves as well as the ways black males are perceived by others. This tripartite investigation makes re-imagining varied, complicated, and nuanced versions of black masculine identity possible and serves to disrupt and supplant negative and harmful understandings of black males.

Deconstructing Black Masculine Identity

> To put the matter yet another way, it is by an abiding bankruptcy of vision that black male bodies in the public sphere go phantasmically misrecognized. It is precisely the ineradicable image of the black male body in the white mind or what Freud called the "permanent traces" of perception [...] that forestalls the achievement of "real authority" black men, under patriarchy, might otherwise freely gain.
>
> Maurice Wallace, *Constructing the Black Masculine*

Peculiar to the creation of the Americas, the institution of slavery served as the mechanism through which chattel slaves, particularly African male bodies, became men.[4] African male bodies were denied any semblance of humanity, including gender distinctions or access to socially constructed identities. The equivalent of property, enslaved Africans were denied participation in or associations with humanity altogether. As such, social identities were not bestowed upon or accessible to enslaved Africans. Once enslaved Africans became free, the social matrix governing the slave/owner relationship shifted.

As enslaved Africans transitioned beyond the circumscribable boundaries of commodity, the establishment of socially validated identities was required.[5]

This framework facilitated the establishment of a social category of black people who were no longer enslaved. This societal shift required an adjustment in the hierarchical associations governing all individuals; the creation of an identity politic to address the changes in the social schematic. The transition of enslaved Africans into freed people ushered in a bifurcated black/white social schema. Subsequently, preserving the socially constructed category of "whiteness" required of whites, the categorization of "blackness" in opposition to the purity, entitlement, and moral hegemony associated with whiteness. As such, anything identified with blackness remains fixed within a contradictory and flawed notion of inherent deficiency—based primarily on the construction of the word itself.

Within this paradigm, blackness exists as oppositional to any associations of whiteness. Therefore, by default, anything marked as black lacks access to the beauty, moral justness, and purity associated with whiteness. This supposition is grounded in the deduction that while "American" men mastered Western ways, enslaved Africans struggled to find an identity within the imposition of blackness, which, as a social construct, exists within narrowly defined and contradictory notions of deviancy. Because neither blackness nor masculinity is constructed adequately enough to facilitate fluid identity construction, the continued use of flawed constructs in academic, social, and personal identity formations results in the perpetual problem discourse surrounding black masculine identity in America.

Directly related to the analysis of black men as forced to exist within fixed constructions of black male types are the psychological and sociological observances of W.E.B. Du Bois. Asserting in *The Souls of Black Folk* that the American Negro is born with "a veil: gifted with second-sight in this American world—a world which yields him *no true* self-consciousness—but only lets him see himself through the revelation of the other world,"[6] Du Bois gives voice to the problem of being both gendered and raced in a society wherein each construct exists as a separately marked, already constituted, category. In highlighting the peculiar position of black people in America, DuBois underscores the significance of existing within socially imagined but life-shaping constructs.

Matthew Frye Jacobson's *Whiteness of a Different Color* supports a reading of race as the primary constituent in the creation of the dominant discourse used to make sense of and retain stories associated with the settling of the colonies. Jacobson's contemplation of race lends itself to the discourse of masculinity, which posits that "white" and "black" exist as social constructs not unlike "masculinity." Based upon Jacobson's contention that "as races are invented categories—designations coined for the sake of grouping and separating peoples along lines of presumed difference—Caucasians are *made* not born,"[7] the assertion that black masculinity exists as a social construct, narrowly defined against existing notions of white masculinity, appears valid.

Similarly, philosopher, author, and early feminist theorist Simone de Beauvoir purports in "The Second Sex" that "one is not born a woman, but rather becomes one," pointing to a significant flaw in the deployment of gender as socially constructed. Within this quote de Beauvoir's point underscores the fragility of black masculine identity by highlighting the semantics by which one locates agency and subjectivity in the process of *becoming*. Too often, the process by which one chooses, or is chosen, to become, is lost within the finalization of being identified as something—having become a man or a sexed being. In this case, the construction of the final thing—becoming a black man—is difficult to locate because the process of becoming is assumed to occur naturally. Understanding that both race and gender are fashioned from restricted definitions and pressures to embody those definitions allows us to understand the ways in which black masculinity has been constructed.

Specific to the production of black masculinity are the ways in which the term itself was created by those in power during colonization—overwhelmingly European, protestant, land owning gentry. The ability of those in power to create, validate, and perpetuate notions of black masculinity cannot be overstated. Constructs, such as black masculinity, linguistically fixed and juridically codified as they are, have become invisible stories perpetuated throughout the history of the United States.[8] Pejorative narrative of black males as lazy, violent, and disengaged—first offered to justify slavery—continue to significantly impact the ways in which black males are understood and in many ways understand themselves.

On Becoming: How Black Men are Perceived by Others

Beyond being exclusively fashioned by its oppositional relationship to white masculinity, black masculinity has been shaped by other socially constituted groups as well.   There were several significant changes in prevailing understandings of white masculinity—such as the inclusion of Irish, Italian, Russian and Jewish men that impacted black masculine identity. Similarly, the relationships between black men and white women and black men and black women have significantly contributed to the refashioning of black male identity. Historically, black women are often regarded as one of four types: mammy, jezebel, sapphire and mule. In the social history of U.S. economy the black matriarch has single-handedly led the black household.[9] Pejorative stereotypes of black men as dispensable, inconsequential to the functioning of black households, and often only serving to complicate the lives of black women has significantly shaped dominant understandings of black masculinity over time.

To deconstruct black masculine identity it is essential to recognize the ways in which social context contributes to meanings attributed to black men. As Historian Arnold Sio states, "the concept of slavery covers a considerable variety of social phenomena, but is generally thought of as the practice of bringing strangers into a society for use in economic production and legally defining them in terms of the category of property."[10] Here Sio speaks to the social categorization imposed upon slaves as 'property' as having precluded their ability to contribute to the construction of terms that they would eventually become identified by. For black men in particular masculine identity is governed by patriarchal codes. These codes expressly dictate the ways men are expected to behave. Initially fashioned by restrictive standards initially associated with white maleness, the concept of masculinity continues to be protected by national values and perpetuated by cultural icons and images—many of which serve to re-enforce dominant images of (white) masculine identity.

Ideally, free will makes it possible for one to construct his or her identity by making choices; choices in the present that are not inextricably bound to history. Black male identity, like all other identities, is inextricably tethered to its historical production. Consequently, black males are frequently engaged in a battle between black men and those who perceive black men; both of whom struggle to re-define the construct.

Institutions and history alone do not determine the ways in which social relationships are structured or the ways in which various identity constructs are imbued with meaning. However it is important to recognize the ways in which governing structures impact ideas about identities and their implications. Since few individuals live in complete isolation, social relationships are contingent upon negotiating socially constructed boundaries designed to unite and divide individuals. The very nature of cultural recognition and rejection is reflective of the mobility and fluidity of both individual identity formation and the spirit of social relations.[11] Accordingly, the system of U.S. relations, significantly contributes to the ways in which black masculinity is fashioned.

Pejorative intersections of black and masculinity exist historically and linguistically as contradictory to anything accepted as just, equitable, right or pure as buoyed by the original fashioning of each identity construct. Juxtaposed with the construction of both whiteness and maleness, black masculine identity is incessantly subjected to the demands of validating itself against the dominant discourse: white masculine identity. For this reason the shared experience of black masculine identity—through both the personal formation of one's identity and the effects of social interaction—produces imagined notions of the ways black men should and do exist.[12] With this in mind, the contradictory nature of black masculine identity's sub-discourse, in relation to the flawed construction of masculinity, logically continues to result in portrayals of black men as "problem" people. Nevertheless, how is this problem solved?

How Black Men Perceive Themselves:
Black Male Identity According to 6th Grade Boys

In a study titled "Shadowboxing: Black Male Identity and Independent Schools," I build upon themes presented in this essay to examine how black male adolescents at elite self-selecting independent schools, manage spoiled identities.[13] that is, how do they understand and respond to perceptions and expectations of black males projected upon them by teachers in school and families at home?[14] Similar to the aim of this project, this work proposes identifying the origins of pejorative stereotypes surrounding black males as a starting point to re-imagine black masculine identity. Acknowledging the incompatibility of the diversity existing within the black male community and overly simplistic images of black men, circulated via popular discourse, literature, history, and politics, this work attempts to theorize a common phenomenon among young black male adolescents. I contend that many black male adolescents, in schools, both public and private, struggle, at some level, with pejorative images of "bad black boys."[15]

These students engage in daily shadow boxing matches that occur on many levels and in multiple contexts.[16] The voices of black male students at Immaculate[17] enable us to better understand the processes brought to bear when black male students make decisions regarding representations of self. Through my study, I sought to answer the questions: How do black males navigate through the world with their stigmatized identity? How does this stigmatization shape their perception of themselves?

Contrary to most studies of black male adolescents in schools, the black male sixth grade students at Immaculate have agency that they use strategically to not simply resist or capitulate but to shadowbox in ways that maintain their sense of self. Each of the students understood in some way the benefits of attending a school like Immaculate.[18] Although most felt they owed it to their parents to do well, they struggled to cope with the *de facto* culture of elite independent schools.[19] Some felt they had something to prove to friends and family at home but also articulated the difficulty of being in classrooms and a school where they were the minority and were frequently reminded of that fact. For the black male students in my study, being unsuccessful or returning to previous schools was not an option but being both black and male complicated life at Immaculate. In light of this, students were forced to make sense of and find ways to successfully navigate the expectations, sometimes-pejorative attitudes, and lack of culturally relevant, stimulating, and affirming experiences.

Complicating existing notions that black male students in particular simply react to their environments, often in one of two mutually exclusive ways, the students in my study tended to be clear who their allies were and conversely which teachers "had thoughts about them in their heads;" made conscious choices about self representation; and found ways, both in and outside of school, to affirm their black male identities. Left to fend for themselves, rather than simply reject notions that success is for white children, each of the student's made conscious decisions regarding the choices they exhibited inside and outside of school, the friendships they maintained, and the level at which they allowed the beliefs of others, positive or negative, to impact how they saw themselves and the possibilities for their futures.

I found that black male students at Immaculate clearly understood how teachers and school personnel perceived them. Most of the students in my study spoke of being labeled as troublemakers and felt they stood out. They know which teachers to avoid confronting directly, when possible, and conversely which adults they could turn to in moments of distress, or when in need of affirmation, or help.

When asked how he thought his teachers would describe him, Stephan had the following to say, "Dufus. . .not a dufus. . .Goofy, goofy I don't know where I got that from because dufus goofy is the same thing." When asked how he felt about teachers having that perception of him he responded:

> I just try and remember that and brush up on my behavior to don't be...don't try and make people laugh and be a comedian...but it doesn't always work. I always get in trouble, I get sent out all the time. Even when the teacher didn't see it I'm the one who has to leave the room or stay after class. . .

When asked to talk about a teacher who inspired him or one he looked up to Stephan struggled to produce a name. However, when asked about a teacher who he had a challenging or difficult relationship with he sat up in his chair and held up his hand to count on his fingers. He fired off the names of seven teachers, an administrator, and the former head of school's executive assistant. When asked what all these people had in common he replied, "...they're always watching me; they're glued to me." The sentiments of the other students corroborate Stephan's experiences. Two other students mentioned being sent out of the classroom at least once a day, the others, though sent out less frequently, were no strangers to hallways or the punishing room.

Black male students are acutely aware of their hypervisible presence at Immaculate. Many expressed awareness that they were "watched," always "on the minds of their teachers," and perceived as being "trouble" or "trouble makers." Similarly, teachers recognized, or at least, revealed existing contradictions between expectations and perceptions of black male adolescents and pedagogical and personal approaches to the students themselves.

Inconsistent with Anne Ferguson's (2001) framework of school boy versus bad boy—or the idea that black male students are often forced to identify with one of two binaristic identity types—the students in this study are acutely aware, for instance, that teachers see them as "trouble" while expressing joy for not having to attend a neighboring public school. They are incensed when they are unfairly singled out or when teachers confuse them for another black male, calling them by one another's name. Yet, at the same time, they are sure that Immaculate is where they want to and should be. These contradictory feelings and experiences, unquestionably contribute not only to the interactions the students have with teachers and other school personnel but also strongly affect the ways in which they understand and relate to these professionals.

For the black male students in my study, being in trouble or labeled a trouble maker had been such a frequent experience that it was no longer significant, or at least important, when talking about their experiences in school or their hopes for the future. For most it was as natural as saying we have lunch each day around noon. However, despite stating as much, many of them spoke in detail of disappointment and frustration with the reality that they, as black male students, were subject to expectations, perceptions, and punishments that their non-black male counterparts were not.

Many teachers at Immaculate perceived black males as trouble, without ever seeing them as individual students beyond simple classifications according to race, gender, and class. As a result, Kwame, who often finished his work and then became bored, was interpreted as being "hyper," and "in constant need of attention." For Jamaal, constantly raising his hand and calling out answers more frequently than desired was seen as "disruptive and disrespectful," rather than as excited about the subject, or the process of learning. Important to consider, are the ways that the students found to disassociate themselves with the beliefs they believed their teachers had and find empowerment in the assumption that they were not as competent as their non-black male counterparts, or simply put; trouble.

Jamaal believed that it was in part his responsibility to change the way "some people believed black people are not as good as. . .can't do well in school or become more than rappers and athletes." For him and many others, it was up to them to disprove societies controlling images. Buying into the thought that they were, in fact, troubled was not an option. Consider the thoughts of Jamaal:

> Some people are just racist. They have it in their mind that black people are bad and they don't care that you aren't. All they see is bad because in society the majority of black people are not like the upper class...they're more lower class or middle-class as opposed to being upper class. [To change that] black people especially black people with fame would have to portray themselves differently...um black people. . .have to. . .want to get. . .better.

For Jamaal the ability to portray himself differently was not only an opportunity, but also a responsibility. This is evident in his desire to become a football player so he can use his money to "send it to people in Africa." Both Jamaal and his parents talked at length about the importance of African history and the role of kinship systems both formal and informal. This became clear as Jamaal expressed the desire to "change [it so] black people care about getting a good education and they had the money and the resources to actually do it."

Data generated from this study strongly suggests the sense with which black male students at Immaculate saw it as their responsibility to change how people perceived and treated black people. Accepting the belief that black male students are uneducable, lazy, and incapable of success or the notion that acting white was a cultural form of oppression worthy of complete dismissal of the schooling process, for these black male students, is not an option. Rather, the students saw it as their responsibility to find ways to challenge, subvert, circumvent, and sometimes reify notions of positive black male identity.

It is important to recognize the aptitude with which these students saw beyond the immediate to make sense of their individual and collective struggles as black male adolescents. Far too frequently black boys and men are accused of being selfish, unable to consider themselves as a part of a community, and disinterested or incapable of making informed decisions that would likely contribute to individual and communal success. With regard to conversations about intersections of race and education, that often suggest black male students are disinterested in or incapable of success in school, black male students at Immaculate, not only understood the terms of the debate, but also, found ways to participate, on their own terms and as they saw fit.

CONCLUSIONS AND RECOMMENDATIONS

Although it is difficult to make a direct comparison between controlling images and their impact on the experiences of black male adolescents at Immaculate, students, parents, and teachers each spoke unabashedly about the burdens that black males face. Each of my research participants characterized the burden of being both black and male as "heavy," "extremely difficult," and "harder than any other students at the school."

The existence of dominant and often negative images of black males is undeniable. Frequently, a spate of articles attending to, contextualizing, or simply highlighting the litany of problems associated with and attributed to black males reignite and reify socially constructed notions of black males as beyond love.[20] The exceptional few become media darlings; the likes of super star athletes, entertainers, and hypervisible political figures. However, for far too many black males, negative conversations about the things black men are believed to do, or not do, negatively impact opportunities and shape life courses in profound ways.

The project of re-imagining black masculine identity is one that exposes various ways in which the often-sensationalized lives of black males go without being recognized, explored, or celebrated. In the absence of reflective and critical conversations, the experiences, resilience, and skills of black males go unnoticed and unrecognized. As a result, too many black males are marginalized and excluded from obtaining skills and experiences needed to participate in an increasingly global marketplace.

If we have any hope of developing the black community and saving the black family; finding solutions to the crises that continually envelop black males regardless of time and space; or finding ways to support the position of the United States as a global leader, it is critically important that we find ways to challenge, disrupt, and supplant negative and harmful images of black males. By first identifying and then continually challenging stereotypes about the things we expect from black men and the ways we interpret individual performance of masculine traits we can begin the process of re-imagining black masculine identity.

NOTES

[1] Fields, Barbra. "Slavery, Race and Ideology in the United States of America." New Left Review I/181 (1990).

[2] I do not seek to suggest black people generally and black men in particular have not had agency in the construction of their self-identification. Social identification and interaction involves reciprocal relationships and black people continue to offer up affirming and contradicting images associated with blackness. However, it is important to highlight the process of becoming to call into question and begin to re-imagine black masculinity. Identifying the ways in which the categorization of black maleness came into being through the shift in society following the formal collapse of the institution of slavery allows us to expose its flaws and reconstitute its meaning.

[3] Much has been written about the alleged mal-adaptive nature of black boys and men. Frequently labeled as immoral, lazy, violent and mentally deficient, along with being supernatural sexual icons, athletes and rapacious criminals (Hare & Hare 1984; Herrnstein & Murray 1994; Ogbu, 2003).

[4] I find it necessary to address the scope of this project, primarily the precise focus on constructions of black masculinity absent an analysis of (black) femininity as it contributes to, alters, or contests these identities. In struggling to effectively initiate and facilitate dialogue designed to address existing "problems" surrounding socially constructed identities is it critical to maintain a narrow focus or risk the imposition of additive politics. This is, the social tendency to equate or purport that the oppression, struggle, or plight of a group of individuals is tantamount to or greater than another. Consequently, attempts to investigate the nature of black men as discursive subjects warrant an analysis of black masculinity absent from the social dependence upon binary constructs, that is, the necessary juxtaposition of masculinity and femininity. Such a suggestion seemingly defies the logic of reality. In the broadest sense, this desire can be criticized as unrealistic and more pointed analyses, as chauvinistic. On the other hand, the homo-social, not to mention homo-erotic, nature of maleness within the Eurocentric paradigm persists throughout contemporary social settings and subsequently warrants a momentary isolation from the discourse of body politics and the tendency to focus on retributive methods for correcting socially produced and perpetuated flaws—as in the case of the construction of black masculinity.

[5] While this shift may not implicitly rely upon the institution of slavery, the posture of Douglass' slave narratives and his subsequent social positioning, as an early, highly visible, representative figure of black masculine identity both literally and physically, facilitates an understanding of the ways in which a black male "slave was made a man." (Blight, David W ed. Narrative of the Life of Frederick Douglass An American Slave Written by Himself, New York: Bedford Books, 1993. 73. (Emphasis Mine)

[6] Du Bois, W.E.B.. *The Souls of Black Folk.* New York: Dover Publications, 1994.

[7] Jacobson, Matthew Frye. Whiteness Of A Different Color: European Immigrants and the Alchemy of Race. Cambridge, MA: Harvard University Press, 1998.

[8] My desire here is not to be overly deterministic in discussing the role of history in shaping black masculine identity. Although it is important to understand how the term came into being it is more important to recognize that the meanings as well as their consequences can be changed. Moreover, black men specifically and black people more generally continue to challenge and change these constructs daily through words and actions.

[9] It is important to note that historically women of color, especially women of African descent, have been responsible for managing white families while also caring for their own.

[10] Sio, Arnold. "Interpretations of Slavery: The Slave Status in the America." *Comparative Studies of Society and History* 7.3 (April 1965): 289-308. MA, 1996.

[11] Kaplan, Cora. "A Cavern Opened In My Mind." Blount, Marcellus and Cunningham, George P. Representing Black Men. New York: Routledge Press, 1996.

[12] This notion speaks to the codependency of linguistic representation and structural social formation; also represented in Butler's analysis of the hegemonic construction of language and the ways in which social constructs such as gender were designed to enforce, regulate, and normalize heterosexuality. The idea that historically constructed flaws manifest themselves in cyclical discourse, in many ways, speaks to the constitution of identity and subsequent interaction through flawed language.

[13] Johns, David. "Shadowboxing: Black Male Identity and Elite Self Selecting Independent Schools." Masters Thesis. Teachers College, Columbia University. Submitted May 2006.

[14] This study is an attempt to better understand the processes brought to bear when black male adolescents make choices regarding self-presentation in school suggests an entry into (and hopefully a way out of) the crisis literature surrounding black males in education. At present, the reasons why so many black males go through school disengaged and unchallenged; graduate from

high school functionally illiterate and without basic math skills; and do not meet basic achievement standards are unknown.

[15] Ferguson's (2001) analysis of black male identity, in <u>Bad Boys: Public School in the Making of Black Masculinity</u>, highlights the ways in which dominant cultural representation of childhood for black males mirror expectations for adult males. She writes, "These [identity] types are grounded in the commonsense, taken for granted notion that existing social divisions reflect biological and natural dispositional differences among humans: so children are essentially different from adults, males from females, blacks from whites. At the intersection of this complex subjection positions are African American males who are doubly displaces: as black children, they are not seen as childlike but adultified: as black males, they are denied the masculine dispensation constituting white males as being "naturally naughty" and are discerned as willfully bad (p.80). Ferguson highlights how these expectations often negatively influence interactions between parents and teachers with black male adolescents.

Furthermore, Ferguson's use of the categories "school boy" and "bad boy," used to describe the types of black male's in her study, highlight the role of controlling images in the lives of black male adolescents. By employing mutually exclusive and exhaustive categories, Ferguson captures the binary identity types often projected upon and expected from black male adolescents. At the same time, Ferguson highlights the constraints placed upon the expression of black male identity by linking the conversation to the larger conversation about black boys and men as "naturally naughty."

[16] I introduce the term shadowboxing as a trope embodying the emotional and intellectual battle black male students engage in daily while in school spaces. The boxers are black male adolescents. These young back males are individually unique yet tied to one another by imagined notions of black male identity. Within the context of this study, socio-historically constructed stereotypes of black men cast large shadows that hover over black boys from the moment the school bell rings demanding that these students engage with socially constructed understandings of what it means to be a black male and how black boys and men should behave.

[17] The names of people and institutions in my study have been changed to preserve anonymity.

[18] Immaculate (pseudonym), is a young progressive independent school in New York City. Independent schools are not dependent upon national or local government for financing. Like private schools they operate on monies generated by tuition, gifts, and yields from investments and endowments. It desires to position itself as a model of the urban institution. Ideally, this

means granting access to those typically denied entrée, principally poor and minority students. Immaculate employs innovative educators, uses cutting edge technology in each classroom as integrated teaching and learning tools, and benefits from the many formal and informal resources available at its partner institution (money, human capital, and curriculum are but a few).

[19] Traditionally independent and private schools, which are often synonymous, serve affluent families. Attendance often provides small class sizes, progressive and challenging curricula, cutting edge technology and facilities, gifted and often innovative faculty and staff, and abundant extra curricular programs such as language, robotics, and technology. These offerings often translate into social capital used by graduates of and those affiliated with elite schools to gain entrée into previously unavailable social networks of individuals and institutions. Graduates from these schools benefit from highly valued social spaces such as Ivy-League universities and Fortune 500 companies.

[20] In " Beyond Love: A Critical Race Ethnography of the Schooling of Black Males," Garrett Albert Duncan (2002) argues that black male students are beyond love and excluded from society's economy and networks of care and thus expelled from useful participation in social life. For Duncan, and many others, because black male adolescents in particular have been constructed as a "strange" population, a group whose cultural attributes, distinctive attitudes, values, predispositions, and resulting behaviors, are fundamentally different from most students—that is, middle class, upper-middle-class white students—the challenges black males often face are understood as not only natural but also a product of their own design.

Reconnecting Young Black Men: What Policies Would Help?

by Harry J. Holzer, Ph.D.

T he term "disconnected youth" refers to young people who have been out of school and out of work for a year or more. They are not temporarily "idle" but are fully disconnected from the mainstream worlds of schooling and work. They may be incarcerated or on parole or probation; they might be aging out of foster care or still attached to their nuclear families. But, overwhelmingly, they come from low-income families and often grow up in poor and relatively segregated neighborhoods.

Of all racial and gender groups, young black men are by far the most likely to become "disconnected" from school and work. In the year 2000—when the labor market was very tight—over 17 percent of all young black men between the ages of 16 and 24 were disconnected, while the comparable percentages for other race/gender groups were much lower. Indeed, this figure implies that *one out of every six young black men was disconnected from both school and work at that time.*[1]

Employment, education and incarceration rates across different racial and gender groups tell a similar story. For instance, employment rates among less-educated young black men (ages 16 through 24) who were not enrolled in school and not institutionalized were barely over 50 percent at the end of the 1990s—nearly 30 percentage points below the employment rates of young whites and Latinos with comparable characteristics. These gaps grew even larger during the labor market downturn that began in 2001. According to recent data from the National Longitudinal Survey of Youth (NLSY97), over 30 percent of young black men drop out of high school—a higher rate than is observed for any other group—and by some estimates, the dropout rates among inner-city youth are much higher than that. On any given day, roughly 12 percent of all black men between the ages of 16 and 34 are incarcerated while roughly twice that number are on parole or probation. It is also expected that nearly one out of every three young black men will spend some time behind bars in their lifetimes. On all of these dimensions, the gaps between young black men and other groups have widened over the past few decades.[2]

What accounts for the uniquely high tendency of young black men to disconnect from school and from work, and why is this tendency actually worsening over time? What sets of policies might help reverse these trends, by preventing further disconnection among young black men and helping to "reconnect" those who have already dropped away from school and work?

Causes of the Problem: Jobs, Schools, Families and "Culture"

The employment rates of young black men have been dropping steadily since the 1960s, even though family incomes and educational attainment were rising markedly for blacks (relative to whites) at least during the earlier part of this period. Rising expectations of earnings, and perhaps some growing unwillingness to accept menial low-wage employment, might account for some of this trend, but cannot explain the steady downward trend in employment over this entire period for young black men.

What is clear is that the decline in employment for this group has largely coincided with a dramatic decline in the labor market opportunities of all less-educated men—i.e., those with a high school diploma or less. The earnings of all less-educated men, adjusted for inflation, have either stagnated or declined over much of the past 30 years; and they certainly have fallen behind relative to the earnings of more-educated workers and even less-educated women. The disappearance of well-paying blue-collar jobs in manufacturing and other industries has certainly contributed to this problem, and looms especially large in some regions (like the Midwest). In response to stagnating wages, employment and labor force activity among all groups of less-educated young men have declined somewhat.[3]

But why have the declines been far greater among young black men than other groups?

The most likely explanation is that *young black men now face greater barriers in gaining access to better-paying jobs than do those of any other group.* To the extent that better-paying jobs remain, they simply require higher levels of education and basic skills than they did in the past. And, while racial gaps in schooling and achievement (as measured by test scores) have narrowed somewhat over time, they remain disturbingly high. Gaps between blacks and whites in high school completion, college attendance, and college completion (either at the 2-year or 4-year level) have barely budged in the past 20 years. While test score gaps narrowed somewhat during the 1980s, they widened a bit during the 1990s. Very high rates of racial and economic segregation in schools and neighborhoods no doubt help perpetuate these gaps, though they start to develop well before most children set foot in kindergarten.[4]

Even relative to Hispanics, the test scores of blacks continue to lag, though they are more likely to graduate from high school. Yet, employment rates among immigrants with much lower educational attainment and language skills are much higher than those of native-born young black men. This likely occurs because the immigrants are more willing to accept low-wage jobs in much of the service sector, and also because employers prefer them and actively recruit them into many key sectors—including construction and some parts of manufacturing. Black women with skills and educational attainment comparable to their black male counterparts gain higher rates of employment than do the men in many parts of the service sector (particularly health services, child and elder care, retail trade, and related sectors), once again reflecting their own greater tendency to apply for such jobs as well as greater employer aversion to the men.[5]

Skills and education aside, young black men continue to face a number of barriers to gaining access to good jobs. These include: 1) Ongoing discrimination by employers; 2) Weakening informal networks; and 3) Ongoing "spatial mismatch" between where jobs are growing in number (usually in downtown areas of central cities or the higher-income and outlying suburbs) versus where most blacks still live (in segregated urban neighborhoods or lower-income suburbs).

Employer aversion to hiring black men, especially in service jobs in smaller establishments with mostly white customers, has been amply documented in a number of studies. In recent years, this aversion is greatest when employers suspect (rightly or wrongly) that the men in question might have criminal records. The informal networks through which less-educated young men have historically found jobs continue to weaken as older black men leave the workforce. And continuing spatial imbalances reinforce gaps not only in information about jobs but also in transportation and physical access.[6]

But can these job market factors really explain why young black boys—especially in their adolescent or teen years—often disconnect from school, and never even enter the mainstream labor market in a sustained way? Some commentators (like Bill Cosby, Juan Williams, John McWhorter and Orlando Patterson) have recently focused more attention on the *choices* made by young black men and women, rather than on the opportunities they face. To many of these critics, low rates of marriage, high rates of teen pregnancy and out-of-wedlock childbearing, and participation in crime at early ages all suggest a lack of personal responsibility and participation in an oppositional *culture*.[7]

Indeed, these critics have a point. Young people growing up in single-parent families have worse education and employment outcomes along every dimension, even after adjusting for the lower incomes of their parents. The single mothers themselves also have lower educational attainment and earnings, though this is at least partly due to their own tendencies to come from poorer families. By some accounts, the pressure to avoid "acting white" deters many lower-income black boys from seriously pursuing academics in middle and high school. And, once they engage in illegal activity and become incarcerated, their lifetime employment chances seriously diminish.

On the other hand, it is also clear that the disappearance of mainstream economic opportunity for less-educated young black men and the growth of counterproductive behaviors and "disconnection" have gone hand in hand. While many factors have contributed to falling marriage rates in different communities over time, there is little doubt that declining employment opportunities (and rising incarceration) among men have contributed to its decline in the African-American community. The rising tendency of young men to commit crime during the 1980s was certainly related to the disappearance of well-paying legal jobs, and the rise of well-paying illegal jobs (at least in the short term) in the crack trade. While the crack trade waned in the 1990s, and the terrible costs of violence and incarceration associated with it became more apparent, many young black men in low-income communities have been left without models of successful employment and marriage among their fathers, older brothers and older friends.[8] In short, young men disconnect from school and work when their options for success in the mainstream world seem to dissipate.

The failure of black men to benefit more from the enormous labor market boom of the 1990s is also troubling. While young black women were pouring into the job market during that decade—being "pulled" in by a tight labor market and growing supports for the working poor (like expanding child care benefits and a growing Earned Income Tax Credit for low-income working families) and "pushed" by welfare reform—young black men continued to drop out of the labor market.

Why did this occur? Following the dramatic rise in incarceration rates during the 1980s and early 1990s, ever-growing fractions (perhaps up to 30 percent) of young black men now have criminal records. They face great employer reluctance to give them job offers. Indeed, employers are less likely to hire young black men than white men, and those with criminal records compared to those without them; thus, black men with criminal records are much less likely than others to gain job offers, especially in sectors where state laws prohibit the hiring of ex-offenders. The poor skills and work experience, mental health problems and substance abuse that often hamper these men worsen their problems; and their poor labor market opportunities often lead to high job turnover rates and low retention, even when they become hired.[9]

In addition, many young black men are non-custodial fathers with steep child support orders, some of whom are likely to be in "arrears" due to a period of incarceration. Those in arrears are likely to face "tax rates" as high as 65 percent on their meager earnings; and, in many cases, the money may not be "passed through" to their children, further weakening their incentives to pay. As a result, many young men out of prison tend to disappear into the "underground economy," where they do not face exorbitant tax rates and where at least some tend to support their children informally, though perhaps sporadically in many cases.

Unfortunately, large fractions of young black men have criminal records and child support orders, which limit their job prospects and reduce their own incentives to remain attached to the formal labor market. At the same time, younger boys in their adolescents and teens face an economy with weaker schooling and fewer connections to the job market that give them access to good jobs. Absent some clearer mechanisms that provide hope of success and incentives to remain attached to the mainstream world of work, many opt out early and "disconnect" from both school and work. By giving up on their chances of success in these worlds, many are doomed to become non-custodial and unmarried fathers, and to run afoul of the law, as well.

What to Do: A Comprehensive Range of Policies

To reverse the negative trends in education and employment that afflict young black men, we need a comprehensive set of efforts that will improve their skills and early employment and prevent disconnection from school and work. Such a set of policies will tend to focus on schools and local communities, but will also demand responsible behavior among young men while augmenting their opportunities. For those still facing the prospects of mostly low-wage employment, their work incentives need to be strengthened. And, for young men who have become incarcerated and are also noncustodial fathers, the barriers they face to stable employment need to be reduced while their incentives to work and pay support are strengthened as well.

Improve Skills/Employment and Prevent Disconnection of Youth

Since the gaps in test scores between white and minority children open up very early in life—to a large extent, before they even set foot in kindergarten—the need for high-quality early childhood and pre-kindergarten programs is clear. Intensive interventions for very young children should be more available to the poor, as well as universally available pre-K for those aged 3 and 4 (with sliding fees based on income). Continued pressure on schools to improve the achievement of all children in the K-12 grades should remain, though also with special efforts to recruit and retain better teachers and with other supports for teacher development in these schools.[10]

Since "disconnection" is most likely to occur in the adolescent and early teen years, it is in these age groups that newer efforts for young boys should be focused. Programs that provide "positive youth development," and especially those that have been rigorously evaluated and appear to be cost-effective, should be greatly expanded at the middle school level. These programs include "Big Brother/Big Sister" programs and other mentoring efforts for young people. A variety of comprehensive "dropout prevention" programs, like the Quantum Opportunities model, need to be studied and further developed as well.

At the high school level, young people continue to need sustained relationships with adults and positive role models, as well as clear pathways to success in post-secondary education and the labor market. High-quality options for career and technical education (CTE), as provided through apprenticeships/internships and Career Academies, need to be expanded. These should not be seen as substitutes for strong academic training, but as complements to more academic approaches. The Career Academies, in particular, provide occupational training and early work experience that supplement good academic instruction. In the rigorous MDRC evaluations, those who attended the Academies did not attend college at lower rates than those in the control groups; but they did have higher employment and earnings, for at least four years beyond high school.

Thus, the best examples of career education open further doors to success, without shutting pathways to college. As Baby Boomers retire in the coming decades and many well-paying jobs open up in construction, transportation, maintenance and repair occupations and other areas, improving the access of younger black men to these jobs through appropriate combinations of career-oriented education and early work experience will become even more important.

Access to post-secondary training must also increase for young black men; along with their chances of completing college degree programs that they start (at either the 2-year or 4-year level). This will require a combination of improved financial assistance, through expanded Pell grants and state-level "merit scholarship" programs; and other supports and services, such as remedial efforts and counseling. More transparency and simplicity in the student grant and loans processes will help as well. A greater provision of on-site child care along with more flexible curricula might better enable students with parental responsibilities to attend school and complete their courses of study.[11] For those obtaining certificates rather than full degrees, the links between courses of study and local employment options need to be strengthened as well; perhaps with the assistance of "intermediaries" in key economic sectors (like construction, health care, etc.) that can work with both employers and workers to build skills and supports for lower-income young workers.

Of course, for young men "at risk" of failure or who have already failed (by dropping out and perhaps getting in trouble with the law), a range of "second-chance" options must be more readily available. Programs like the Job Corps, the Youth Service and Conservation Corps and Youth Build appear successful at raising subsequent employment while preventing further incarceration. Newer programs, like the National Guard "ChalleNGe" program, look very promising as well. These should be funded at much higher levels than currently. Alternative charter schools that seek to "recapture" high school dropouts and return them to the classroom—often on community college campuses and other nontraditional sites—deserve more exploration and support as well.

In all of these efforts, there is a real need to develop comprehensive sets of approaches at the community level. Without this, many young men will simply "fall through the cracks," and never have access to supportive arrangements that might actually be available. The most compelling private effort to date to develop a comprehensive range of supports and services for youth at the local level is the Harlem Children's Zone, developed by Geoffrey Canada with extensive foundation support. On a somewhat larger basis, the "After School Matters" program in Chicago offers an appealing model that might ultimately spread across low-income neighborhoods in the entire city. Finally, the 36 "Youth Opportunity" sites funded by the U.S. Department of Labor in 2000 and 2001 marked the first federal effort to support the development of comprehensive community-level programming for low-income youth. These efforts deserve expansion and replication in other communities, with continuing public and private support.[12]

Improve Incentives in Low-Wage Work and Reduce Barriers to Employment

The New Hope Demonstration Project in Milwaukee during the 1990s demonstrated that employment and other behaviors can be improved among low-income young men if their low wages in the labor market are supplemented with a range of benefits (as well as guaranteed public service jobs). While a dramatic expansion of health care, parental and pension benefits can only occur through a much broader political agenda than the one we present here, at least some improvements in the work incentives facing low-wage men must be considered now.

For those who will continue to face the prospect of low-wage work, higher minimum wages would help, for one. Federal efforts to raise the federal minimum wage to $7.25 over a two-year period will raise the earnings prospects of low-wage workers without dramatically lowering employers' incentives to hire these workers. Many states will likely continue to raise their own minimum wage levels, regardless of what the federal government does in this area.

Low-wage jobs also need to be further supplemented by benefits like the Earned Income Tax Credit. The EITC has been widely credited with helping to draw millions of low-earning single mothers into the labor market in the 1990s. By providing a refundable tax credit that raises low earnings by up to 40% at its peak, the EITC substantially raises incentives to work in low-wage jobs.[13]

Currently, the EITC provides maximum benefits to families with two or more children, and usually it is only families headed by single mothers that qualify (based on income). Those with just one child receive a much reduced subsidy, while childless adults—including noncustodial fathers—can receive a "childless" credit worth only about $400 per year.

The EITC available to childless adults could be expanded in two ways: 1) Noncustodial fathers who are paying their current child support orders can get some benefit, as they do now in the state of New York; or 2) Childless adults between certain ages (say 21 to 40) can receive an enhanced benefit. Marriage penalties in such a system would have to be addressed, as would various administrative difficulties. But, for fairly modest expenditures, these could be dealt with.[14]

There are also options for reducing barriers and improving attachments to work for young men whose labor market activity is curtailed by their having criminal records, child support orders (or arrearages), or both. Those with criminal records could benefit from a much wider range of supports before and at the time of release, to deal with a variety of personal needs and to strengthen ties to the workplace. The "Second Chance Act" currently under consideration in Congress would provide funding for some such supports. The activities of "intermediaries" here are crucial, since the tasks of securing employment, housing and even proper identification (not to mention getting mental health and substance abuse treatment for those who need it) are daunting to those just released from prison and on their own. Some intermediaries, like the Center for Employment Opportunity (CEO) in New York, provide each program participant with a paid "transitional job" for several months. The benefits of this approach are currently being evaluated. Work-related activities should begin even before release, to better prepare ex-offenders for a private-sector labor market much different than what they have been recently accustomed to. Indeed, mandatory work release programs that provide employment requirements as well as supports should be tried and expanded, where successful.[15]

State policies also need to play a more positive role. The Legal Action Center (2004) has documented, on a state-by-state basis, the many legal prohibitions against occupational licensure and employment that have been enacted in recent years. States should consider whether these barriers ultimately serve the public interest if they also reduce employment options to ex-offenders and raise recidivism rates. The states should also consider whether their current rates of incarceration, especially for non-violent criminal offenses, go beyond what is optimally needed to deter criminal activity and incapacitate criminals.

When it comes to low-income non-custodial fathers, a similar combination of better programs and policies is needed. States need to develop "arrearage management" options that allow the non-custodial fathers to gradually pay off arrears, without so heavily punishing those who would work and pay on their current orders. More money needs to be "passed through" to low-income families, which would help the families and also raise incentives of fathers to pay. "Fatherhood" efforts that combine labor market assistance with parenting supports might pay off.

CONCLUSIONS

Since many forces have contributed to the collapse of employment among lower-income young black men, no single policy remedy will turn the situation around. However, a comprehensive effort to improve skills and early labor market contacts, support positive youth development in communities, improve incentives to take low-wage jobs, and especially to reduce barriers and improve incentives for ex-offenders and non-custodial fathers would no doubt help. The tragedy of wasted human potential among these young men, and the enormous costs imposed on families, communities, and the nation as a whole by their low employment and huge rates of incarceration, suggest that we can do far better than we have to date.

REFERENCES

Bendor, Joshua; Jason Bordoff and Jason Furman. 2007. "An Education Strategy to Promote Opportunity, Prosperity and Growth." The Hamilton Project, Brookings Institution.

Berlin, Gordon. 2007. "Rewarding the Work of Single Adults." In *The Future of Children*, Vol. 17, No. 1, Spring.

Besharov, Douglas. 2005. "The Economic Stagnation of the Black Middle Class." Testimony before the U.S. Civil Rights Commission, Washington DC, July 15.

Bound, John and Richard Freeman. 1992. "What Went Wrong? The Erosion of Relative Earnings and Employment among Young Black Men in the 1980s." *Quarterly Journal of Economics.* Vol 107, No. 1.

Bound, John and Harry J. Holzer. 1993. "Industrial Shifts, Skill Levels, and the Employment of Black Men." *Review of Economics and Statistics*, Vol. 75, No. 3.

Blank, Rebecca and Lucie Schmidt. 2001. "Work, Wages and Welfare." In R. Blank and R. Haskins eds. *The New World of Welfare.* Washington DC: The Brookings Institution.

Blau, Francine; Lawrence Kahn and Jane Waldfogel. 2000. "Understanding Young Women's Marriage Decisions." *Industrial and Labor Relations Review.* Vol. 53, No. 4.

Edelman, Peter; Harry Holzer and Paul Offner. 2006. *Reconnecting Disadvantaged Young Men.* Washington DC: Urban Institute Press.

Freeman, Richard. 1999. "The Economics of Crime." In O. Ashenfelter and D. Card eds. *The Handbook of Labor Economics*, Vol. 3. Amsterdam: North Holland.

Fryer, Roland and Steven Levitt. 2004. "Understanding the Black-White Test Score Gap in the First Two years of Schooling." *Review of Economics and Statistics.* Vo. 86.

Fryer, Roland; Paul Heaton, Steven Levitt and Kevin Murphy. 2004. "Measuring the Impact of Crack Cocaine." National Bureau of Economic Research Working Paper.

Holzer, Harry J. 1996. *What Employers Want: Job Prospects for Less-Educated Workers.* New York: Russell Sage Foundation.

Holzer, Harry J. 2001. "Racial Differences in Labor Market Outcomes Among Men." In N. Smelser, W. Wilson and F. Mitchell eds. *America Becoming: Racial Trends and their Consequences*. Washington DC: National Academy Press.

Holzer, Harry J.; Paul Offner and Elaine Sorensen. 2005. "Declining Employment among Young Black Men: The Role of Incarceration and Child Support." *Journal of Policy Analysis and Management*. Vol. 24, No. 2.

Holzer, Harry J.; Steven Raphael and Michael Stoll. 2004. "Will Employers Hire Former Offenders?" In Mary Pattillo, David Weiman and Bruce Western eds. Imprisoning America. New York: Russell Sage Foundation.

Ludwig, Jens and Isabel Sawhill. 2007. "Success By Age 10." Washington DC: The Brookings Institution.

McWhorter, John. 2006. *Winning the Race: Beyond the Crisis in Black America*. New York: Dutton and Gotham Books.

Mead, Lawrence. 2007. "Raising Work Levels among Low-Income Men." In *The Future of Children*, Vol. 17, No. 1, Spring.

Meyer, Bruce and Daniel Rosenbaum. 2001. "Welfare, The Earned Income Tax Credit, and the Labor Supply of Single Mothers." *Quarterly Journal of Economics*. Vol. 116, No. 3.

Mishel, Lawrence and Joydeep Roy. 2006. *Rethinking High School Graduation Rates and Trends*. Washington DC: Economic Policy Institute.

Moffitt, Robert. 2001. "Welfare Benefits and Female Headship in U.S. Time Trends." In L. Wu and B. Wolfe eds. *Out of Wedlock: Causes and Consequences of Nonmarital Fertility*. New York: Russell Sage Foundation.

Pager, Devah. 2003. "The Mark of a Criminal Record." *American Journal of Sociology*. Vol. 108.

Travis, Jeremy. 2003. *But They All Come Back: Facing the Challenges of Prisoner Reentry*. Washington DC: Urban Institute Press.

Williams, Juan. 2006. *Enough: The Phony Leaders, Dead End Movements, and Culture of Failure That Are Undermining Black America*. New York: Crown Publishing.

Wilson, William J. 1996. *When Work Disappears*

NOTES

[1] See Edelman et al. (2006). Comparable numbers for young white and Latino men are 4 percent and 12 percent, respectively.

[2] See Holzer et al. (2005) for evidence on employment rates, and Mishel and Roy (2006) for discussion of high school dropout rates among young whites and minorities. Data on incarceration rates among young black men and other demographic groups are widely available at the website of the Bureau of Justice Statistics, U.S. Department of Justice.

[3] See Bound and Freeman (1992), Bound and Holzer (1993) and Juhn (1992).

[4] See Edelman et al. (2006); Besharov (2005); and Fryer and Levitt (2004).

[5] See Holzer (1996).

[6] See Holzer (2001).

[7] See McWhorter (2006) or Williams (2006).

[8] See Wilson (1996) for a general discussion about how joblessness affects personal behaviors and choices, such as marriage and crime. See Freeman (1999) for evidence on how participation in crime is affected by job market prospects; Blau et al. (200) and Moffitt (2001) on the impacts of male earnings opportunities on female headship of families; and Fryer et al. (2004) on the effects of the crack epidemic.

[9] See Pager (2003), Holzer et al. (2004), and Travis (2003).

[10] See Ludwig and Sawhill (2007) and Bendor et al. (2007) for discussions of pre-K programs and K-12 reforms respectively.

[11] See Bendor et al. (2007).

[12] See Edelman et al. (2006), especially Chapters 3 and 4.

[13] See Blank and Schmidt (2001) or Meyer and Rosenbaum (2001).

[14] See Edelman et al. (2006), Chapter 5 or Berlin (2007).

[15] See Mead (2007).

Why Should African-Americans Care About Macroeconomic Policy?

by William M. Rodgers III, Ph.D.

T he U.S. economy recently completed its 63rd month of economic expansion, yet the African American male and teenage male unemployment rates have only fallen to 7.5 and 34.4 percent, respectively.[1] More disturbing is the fact that the employment-population ratio (percent of civilian high school graduate population with a job) for African Americans age 25 and over still remains below its value at the start of the recovery in November 2001.[2]

These higher jobless rates make African Americans and their communities more susceptible to suffering from sudden macro shocks. Hurricane Katrina provided the nation with an education about natural disaster's disparate racial impacts by demonstrating the vulnerability of low-income African-American communities to such shocks. It is now well-documented that this catastrophe could have been ameliorated if prior to the storm, federal, state and local policy makers had placed greater weight, or higher priority on the welfare of these communities.

The deindustrialization of the U.S. economy, particularly in the Midwest, is an example of how structural changes in the economy can have a disparate impact on African Americans. For example, the percentage of manufacturing jobs in the Gary, IN metropolitan area fell from 23 percent in 1990 to 14 percent in 2005. During the 1990s recovery, Gary lost 1,800 manufacturing jobs. In the current recovery, Gary has lost a cumulative total of 7,800 manufacturing jobs.[3] As a result, the percentage of older and out of school young African-American men with no more than a high school degree, employed in above-average manufacturing wage jobs, fell dramatically. The erosion in Gary's manufacturing sector has also taken a toll on earnings. In 2000, the inflation-adjusted wages of Gary's African-American men remain lower than in 1980.

The National Urban League and others have identified the following as contributing factors to the high and persistent rates of African-American joblessness and greater sensitivity to macro shocks and structural change:

- Poor preparation for participation in the mainstream labor force,[4]
- A loss of jobs in low-skilled, relatively well paying industries like manufacturing and construction, compounded by spatial and/or skills mismatch for available jobs,[5]
- Disproportionately high rates of incarceration accompanied by employment discrimination against former prisoners,[6]
- Continued discrimination in a variety of markets: labor, housing and credit.[7]

The tools used by policymakers and practitioners to address these causes tend to be micro solutions: increasing the federal or state minimum wage, creating living wage ordinances, expanding the Earned Income Tax Credit, investing in education and training, expunging the criminal justice records of ex-offenders, and modifying non-custodial parent policies such that they engage rather than disengage men from their responsibilities as fathers.[8] Macro economic policies, on the other hand, are typically absent from the list of remedies for high and persistent African-American unemployment rates.[9] Macro policy is defined as the actions by state and federal governments utilizing monetary and fiscal policies to influence national consumption, investment, government expenditures, and international trade.[10] Macro policy is particularly important to African Americans because it impacts the breadth and depth of an economic expansion's (recession's) ability to lower (raise) black unemployment rates.[11] For example, because the Federal Reserve Board of Governors held off on raising the federal funds rate in the late 1990s, firms continued to hire workers and consumer spending remained strong. As a result, the macro economy's prosperity finally trickled down to the least skilled African Americans and African-American communities with weaker economies. Although African-American unemployment still remained high relative to other groups, the prolonged tightness of the labor market led to its lowest level ever recorded.

Research on the transmission mechanisms between macro economic policy and African-American outcomes is very thin. Leaders and practitioners who are concerned about these issues don't have the analytical and empirical stories at their disposal to describe macro policies' linkages to African - American outcomes. Further, macro researchers focus on the "representative agent" (average consumer and family), which minimizes the importance of diversity of experience. Both of these factors make it difficult for policymakers to utilize "fairness, equity, and efficiency" criteria in policy debates. Also, micro and macro policy analysts tend to conduct their research in separate silos, leading to policy agendas that don't complement one another, or at least are not integrated.[12]

This essay has several goals. First, create greater public understanding of and interest in macro policy's disparate racial impacts. Second, motivate policy analysts to conduct more studies that identify macro policy's distributional impacts in a way that goes beyond efforts to describe the disparate impacts of sudden shocks (e.g, Hurricane Katrina) and structural shifts (e.g., deindustrialization). Third, urge policymakers to demand the reporting of distributional impact statements and benefit-cost analyses that utilize "constituency weighting" structures that assign greater priority to the well-being of middle and lower income families. Such a shift will do a better job of addressing the short and long-term needs of African Americans as well.

MACRO POLICIES AND THEIR IMPACT ON BLACKS

Monetary Policy

One of the Federal Reserve's primary activities is to "conduct monetary policy by influencing the monetary and credit conditions with the goal of achieving maximum employment, stable prices, and moderate long-term interest rates."[13] Recently, the actions of the Federal Reserve seem to place greater weight on maintaining price stability, which implies their willingness to accept lower employment, particularly among African Americans and their communities. The rationale for this tradeoff is the following: Price stability is in the best interest of lower and middle-income families, and low inflation and stable inflationary expectations do not erode their purchasing power. This rationale is reasonable, but it is important to understand the implications of this tradeoff. Contractionary monetary policy, which has the goal of preventing the economy from overheating, has disproportionate down stream effects on African Americans. An increase in the federal funds rate raises the costs of capital, thus reducing the demand for workers and causing banks and other lending institutions to increase their mortgage and credit card rates. African American's higher unemployment rates and lower incomes place them at greater risk of financial instability as a result of these effects.

Federal Reserve economist Seth Carpenter and I have shown that increases in the federal funds rate have disparate negative impacts on African Americans. African-American unemployment rates, particularly those of teens, are more sensitive to changes in monetary policy than white unemployment rates. The unemployment rates for out-of-school teenagers and less educated out-of-school youth are the most sensitive to changes in monetary policy. More recently, I have found that lower-income counties such as those in the Lower Mississippi Delta are more sensitive to increases in the federal funds rate than the typical U.S. County.

Fiscal Policy

Fiscal policy comprises the framework that shapes government revenues and expenditures. More important, they are a reflection of society's values and priorities, indicating the weight that demographic groups and areas receive. The 2001 and 2003 federal tax cuts are a perfect example. Economist Richard Freeman and I identified the fiscal stimulus of the federal tax cuts as one of three major contributions to the historically slower job growth during the current recovery. The vast majority of the tax cuts went to wealthy families whose propensity to spend quickly is likely to be less than that of middle and lower-income families. Between 2001 and 2006, the U.S. fiscal deficit rose by 2.9 percentage points relative to potential GDP: from a surplus of 1.1 percent to a deficit of 1.8 percent. This exceeds the increase in the deficit and the size of stimulus in both the 1980s and 1990s recoveries. Yet actual GDP grew by just 15 percent between 2001 and 2006 despite the huge stimulus. This is a lower growth rate than in the two previous recoveries when fiscal stimulus was weaker. Freeman and I suspect that the larger stimulus had a smaller impact on GDP growth because the tax cuts were slanted to the super-wealthy.[14]

CHANGING THE WEIGHTS: SIX STRATEGIES FOR DISCUSSION

At the national level, African Americans comprise approximately 12 percent of the population. Even with the growth in the African-American middle class since the mid-1960s, the typical African-American family's income falls well below the typical white family's income. In 2005, the mean income of African-American families at the third fifth (41st to 60th percentiles) of their annual income distribution was $35,630, falling just below the mean income of white families at the second fifth (21st to 40th percentiles) of their income distirbution.[15] Thus, the typical African-American family is not the "representative agent" in macroeconomic models and receives less weight from macro policy makers."

One basic question needs an answer. How do we raise the "weights" that policymakers assign to middle and lower-income families and weaker local labor markets, such that they are more favorable to the well-being of African Americans?

Greater Coordination between Policymakers and Analysts

Policy researchers and policymakers must have greater collaboration and coordination when describing and measuring the disparate impacts of monetary and fiscal policy. However, greater collaboration will not be enough. Advocates for individuals and communities that are not labeled as "representative" need assistance with demonstrating how greater equity and fairness generate societal benefits that exceed societal costs.

We also need policymakers that can speak to macro policies. An example of this occurred during the latter part of the 1990s boom when the labor market tightened, creating fears of inflation. Former Labor Secretary Herman would cite three pieces of evidence to argue that the Federal Reserve needed to be patient and not raise the federal funds rate. First, productivity growth exceeded real wage growth. Employers could raise wages without generating inflation. Second, the U.S. labor market still had over 13 million Americans that comprised an untapped pool of potential. Third, just because the national unemployment rate was 4 percent that did not mean that the jobless rate was 4 percent in Newark, NJ, 4 percent in parts of the Mississippi Delta, or 4 percent among young African Americans who have no more than a high school degree.

I am encouraged by recent efforts of members of Congress. Not to make this a partisan discussion, but with the Democrats taking control of Congress, the agenda and tenor of debate since January 2007 have improved. At Federal Reserve Chairman Bernanke's February 2007 testimony to the House Financial Services Committee, many members prefaced their remarks by talking about how their districts are not experiencing the gains in prosperity seen on Wall Street.

I was encouraged by Chairman Bernanke's responses. He seems more willing to talk about distributional issues than his predecessor. Yet, he can go further. When pressed on how to address the reemergence of US inequality growth, the Chairman focused on long-run strategies such as education and training. To his credit, he did talk about how 12 regional banks provide data and input into monetary policy decisions, but he did not talk about how these decisions are made and what the "weighting" structure looks like during Federal Open Market Committee (FOMC) votes on monetary policy.[16]

Regional Federal Reserve Banks

African Americans need to have more engagement with the Federal Reserve's 12 regional banks.[17] They operate under the auspices of the Board of Governors. Each bank has a nine-member Board of Directors that oversees its operations. Five of the twelve presidents of the Federal Reserve Banks serve, along with the seven members of the Board of Governors, as members of the Federal Open Market Committee. The president of the Federal Reserve Bank of New York serves on a continuous basis; the other presidents serve one-year terms on a rotating basis. To inform their monetary policy decisions, each Bank tracks and monitors its regional economies.

Most Banks publish a monthly or quarterly journal that provides research and analysis of current economic issues in their District. The Federal Reserve's Beige Book is a fascinating data source. The report summarizes qualitative reports received from business and other contacts outside the Federal Reserve System. During my literature reviews on the disparate labor market impacts of monetary policy, the research departments of these Banks were major contributors to the literature. They conduct policy-relevant research in macroeconomics, microeconomics, financial studies and regional economics issues.

Many of the Banks have community advisory committees, whose purpose is to advise the Bank on issues of importance in the Bank's District, such as agriculture and small business.[18] They also have community affairs programs, which support the Reserve System's economic growth objectives by promoting community development and fair and impartial access to credit. So, there is a great deal of potential for collaboration.

"Follow the Money"

Several years ago, when I joined the Williamsburg-James City County School Board, one of my colleagues told me to always "follow the money". How public money is allocated and spent reflects societal values and priorities. A better job needs to be done on following budget debates, and extrapolating their potential impacts on African Americans.

I experienced a great deal of frustration during the confirmation hearings of Attorney General Ashcroft. Members asked Ashcroft if he was going to enforce the law. Instead, members should have probed as to how he would allocate his scarce resources across departments. For example, how much would be spent on enforcement? Members also need to probe deeper into the kind of appointments made at the sub-cabinet level. FEMA's recent history is a perfect example. I am not naïve of political patronage, but we must make sure that all cabinet and sub-cabinet appointments are "truly" qualified administrators.

African American-Specific Economic Forecasts

With Congress' change in leadership, documentation of the consequences of fiscal policy on African Americans should be better. Democrats now control committee agendas and set the rules of debate. An additional benefit of the change in leadership is that the Speaker of the House appoints the head of the Congressional Budget Office (CBO). Why is this important? In 2006, the CBO completed approximately 575 formal federal cost estimates as well as approximately 500 estimates of the impact of unfunded mandates on state and local governments and about 500 estimates of the impact of unfunded mandates on the private sector.[19] With the new leadership of the CBO, policy makers do not have to rely solely on the forecasts of left-of-center think tanks as a check to the Administration's macroeconomic forecasts.

Going forward, these and other fiscal impact statements should contain estimated distributional impacts of proposed legislation under a variety of assumptions. The CBO and other organizations use this approach when developing forecasts. Greater transparency in the estimated impacts will help to foster a more honest debate on what is best for the American economy.

The CBO and many of the forecasting organizations have advisory boards or committees. The CBO's Panel of Economic Advisers, which is composed of the CBO's previous directors and eminent economists, is an advisory panel that reviews and comments on CBO's preliminary economic forecasts and provides advice to further the reliability, professional quality, and transparency of CBO's work. At the time of the writing of this essay, none of the members are African Americans. Gender diversity is not much better. Only four of the 18 members are women.

CONCLUSIONS AND RECOMMENDATIONS

Don't Forget about State and Local Governments

Follow state and local governments. Increased federal fiscal constraints have had downstream effects on state and local governments. First, the Administration's tax policy has shifted more of the burden on state and local governments to finance investments in education, health and public infrastructure. This was particularly acute during the 2001 recession and the first few years of the recovery. Social services and public sector workforces were cut. African Americans in many states bore the brunt of these changes. The pressures of globalization are also seeping into pension and health care coverage of state and local employees. Many in the private sector argue that public sector workers' compensation packages are no longer affordable and too generous given what is happening in the private sector. If these arguments lead to cuts in benefits and compensation, African Americans will bear a disproportionate share of the cuts.

Educate Yourself and Your Community

As discussed earlier, African Americans and their leaders must connect the dots from macro policy's aggregate impacts to their micro impacts on families and communities. To do this, we must first have access to information. A resource that I use to track the releases of macro economic data is the yahoo business calendar (http://biz.yahoo.com/c/e.html).[20] The site provides a comprehensive list of all of the major macro indicators that are released by the government and other organizations. For each indicator, the actual outcome, market forecasts, and the previous outcomes are all reported. A link to a description of the indicator is also provided, along with their view of the indicator's importance.

Most important, we must educate our children about how the economy functions. Even before kindergarten, we must teach economic principles to our children. This investment will have long-term payoffs. Rutgers University economics Professor Yana Rodgers has developed a free website called EconKids (econkids.rutgers.edu). The website provides teachers and parents with resources to introduce economics to young children. The unique feature of the website is its use of children's literature to make economics enjoyable to teach and learn. The website's user-friendly design provides quick lesson ideas that are based on current economics and education research. Parents and teachers can click on an economics concept to get a list of the "Top Five" choices for acclaimed children's books that use enjoyable stories to teach an economics lesson. Story summaries are provided. The site's collection of over 350 books is based on objective research criteria and on direct experience in teaching with the books. The site also contains links to State Public Library Websites and State Public Library Catalog Systems, which enables the user to easily identify where in their community the books can be obtained.

I am old enough to remember the FRAM oil filter commercial's tag line. "You can pay me now, or pay me later." As a nation, if we don't shift the "relative weights" used in macro policy development, creation and implementation, we are going to have some major debts to repay.

REFERENCES

Badgett, M.V. (1994). "Rising Black Unemployment: Changes in Job Stability or in Employability?" *Review of Black Political Economy, 22*(3), 55-75.

Blank, R. & Blinder, A. (1986). "Macroeconomics, Income Distribution, and

Poverty," in S. Danziger and D. Weinberg (eds.) *Fighting Poverty: What Works and What Doesn't*, pp.108-208. Cambridge, MA: Harvard University Press.

Bound, John, Richard B. Freeman. (1992). What Went Wrong? The Erosion of Relative Earnings and Employment Among Young Black Men in the 1980s." *The Quarterly Journal of Economics* 107 (1): 201-232

Carpenter, Seth B; Rodgers, William M, III. (2004, 2005).The Disparate Labor Market Impacts of Monetary Policy. *Journal of Policy Analysis and Management*, 23(4), 813-83; *Labor History*. 46 (1): 57-77.

Cherry, Robert, William M. Rodgers III. (2000). *Prosperity for All? The Economic Boom and African Americans.* New York: Russell Sage Foundation.

Clark, K. & Summers, L. (1981). "Demographic Differences in Cyclical Employment Variation," *Journal of Human Resources* 16(1) (Winter), 61-79.

Clark, K & Summers, L. (1990). "Demographic Differences in Cyclical Employment Variation." in Lawrence Summers (ed) *Understanding Unemployment.* (Cambridge, MA: The MIT Press).

Freeman, Richard B; Rodgers, William M, III. (2005). The Weak Jobs Recovery: Whatever Happened to "The Great American Jobs Machine"? *Federal Reserve Bank of New York Economic Policy Review* 11 (1): 3-18.

Freeman, Richard B.(1991). "Employment and Earnings of Disadvantaged Young Men in a Labor Shortage Economy." In *The Urban Underclass,* Christopher Jencks and Paul Peterson, eds., Washington, DC: Urban Institute.

Freeman, Richard B. and Harry Holzer. (1986). *The Black Youth Employment Crisis,* Chicago: University of Chicago Press.

Freeman, R. & Rodgers III, W.M. (2000). "Area Economic Conditions and the Labor Market Outcomes of Young Men in the 1990s Expansion." R. Cherry and W. M. Rodgers III (eds). *Prosperity for All: The Economic Boom and African Americans.* New York: Russell Sage Foundation.

Hoynes, H. (2000). "The Employment and Earnings of Less Skilled Workers Over the Business Cycle," in R. Blank and D. Card (eds.), *Finding Jobs: Work and Welfare Reform* (pp. 23-71), New York: Russell Sage Foundation.

Hoynes, H., Hines, J. Jr., & Krueger. A. (2001)."Another Look at Whether a Rising Tide Lifts All Boats," in A. Krueger and R. Solow (eds.), *The Roaring Nineties: Can Full Employment be Sustained?* (pp. 493-537), New York: Russell Sage Foundation.

Korenman, S. & Okun, B.(1989). "Gender Differences in Cyclical Unemployment," *Structural Changes in U.S. Labor Markets: Causes and Consequences, Proceedings,* Federal Reserve Bank of Cleveland.

Krueger, Alan, Robert Solow. (2001). *The Roaring Nineties: Can Full Employment be Sustained?* New York: Russell Sage Foundation.

Milanovich, M. (2002). "How Great was the 1990s Boom," Unpublished Manuscript. Center for the Study of Equality, College of William and Mary, Williamsburg, Va.

Mincy, Ron B. (2006). Black Males Left Behind. Washington, DC: The Urban Institute Press.

Moorthy, V. (1988). "On Demographic Adjustments to Estimates of the Natural Rate of Unemployment: a note," Working Papers in Applied Economic Theory, 88-01. Federal Reserve Bank of San Francisco.

Pager, Devah. (2003). "The Mark of a Criminal Record." *American Sociology Review* 108 (5): 937-73.

Rodgers, William M. III. (2006). *Handbook on the Economics of Discrimination.* Northampton, MA: Edgar Elgar Publishing.

Rodgers, William M, III. (2006). Male White-Black Wage Gaps, 1979-1994: A Distributional Analysis. *Southern Economic Journal* 72 (4): 773-93.

Reimers, C. (2000). "The Effect of Tight Labor Markets on Unemployment of Hispanics and African Americans: The 1990s Experience," in R. Cherry & W. M. Rodgers III (eds). *Prosperity for All: The Economic Boom and African Americans.* New York: Russell Sage Foundation.

Shulman, S. (1991). "Why is the Black Unemployment Rate Always Twice as High as the White Unemployment Rate," In R. Cornwall and P. Wunnava (eds.), *New Approaches to Economics and Social Analyses of Discrimination*, New York: Praeger.

Spriggs, W. & Williams, R. (2000). "What Do We Need to Explain About African

American Unemployment?" in R. Cherry and W. M. Rodgers, III (eds) *Prosperity for All? The Economic Boom and African Americans* (pp. 188-207) New York: Russell Sage Foundation.

Wilson, F., Tienda, M. and Wu, L. (1991). "Racial Equality in the Labor

NOTES

[1] The nonpartisan National Bureau of Economic Research identified November 2001 as the start of the current economic recovery.

[2] The 2001 value was 68.4 percent compared to 66.8 percent in 2006. Even the employment-population ratio of African American college graduates has not returned to its 2001 value(81.3% in 2001 and 79.8% in 2006).

[3] In percentage terms, Gary's total cumulative employment growth in the 1990s recovery was 2.8 percent, with a 3.2 percent decline in manufacturing employment. During today's recovery, the cumulative contractions have been greater: 1.2 percent in all jobs and 17.0 percent in manufacturing.

[4] The 2000 decennial census indicates that 60 percent of African American men have no more than a high school degree, compared to 45 percent of white men. At the other end of the educational attainment spectrum, 28 percent of white men have at least a BA degree, while only 13 percent of African American men have completed at least a BA degree.

[5] After WWII, the percentage of durable manufacturing jobs range from 15 to 20 percent of total nonfarm payroll jobs. Since the late 1960s, early 1970s, the percentage of durable manufacturing jobs has trended downward: 26% in 1970, 21% in 1980, 16.3% in 1990, 13.2% in 2000, and 10.3% in 2007. All figures are for January of each year (www.bls.gov).

[6] See, for example, Pager (2003) for evidence of discrimination. The Human Rights Watch reported in 2002 that the incarceration rate for African American youth 18 years and younger was 86 and 16 for white youth 18 years an younger (Table 7, Race and Incarceration in the United States Human Rights Watch Press Backgrounder, February 27, 2002).

[7] See for example, Rodgers (2006). These bullet points come from a National Urban League Opportunity Compact letter of invitation for a roundtable series on jobs (January 2007).

[8] Currently, New Jersey Governor Corzine has tasked his Government Efficiencies and Reform Commission (NJGEAR) to identify the source of the rising expenditures on corrections. The Commission will focus on the contribution of mandatory sentencing requirements to the state's rapid growth in correctional expenditures. See Mincy (2006) for a recent discussion of micro-based policies to address the challenges that young African American face.

[9] An extensive literature exists on the empirical relationships between aggregate demand, macroeconomic policies and the economic outcomes (e.g., poverty) of various socioeconomic groups. For general studies, see, for example, Badgett (1994), Blank and Blinder (1996), Clark and Summers (1981, 1990), Hoynes (2000), Korenman and Okun (1989), Moorthy (1988), Romer and Romer (1998), Spriggs and Williams (2000), Reimers (2000), Shulman (1991), and Wilson, Tienda and Wu (1991). For studies on race and ethnicity, see, for example, Freeman (2001), Freeman and Rodgers (2000), Hoynes, Hines and Krueger (2001) and Reimers (2000). A second round of studies continues to find gains, but they have not made up the lost ground that occurred from the 1970s to 1980s (Holzer and Offner, 2001; and Milanovich, 2002).

For example, Romer and Romer (1998) find that expansionary monetary policy tends to lessen poverty. In the long run, low inflation and steady growth in aggregate demand is associated with lower poverty. More recently, several studies have identified monetary policy's differential impacts on labor market outcomes such as the employment-population ratios, unemployment rates, and labor force participation rates of minorities, less-educated and less-skilled individuals.

[10] Exchange rate policy is also a macro policy. It is an important determinant of the trade deficit/surplus. I was unable to find any studies that explicitly linked exchange policy to African American outcomes. Because of this, I do not formally discuss exchange rate policy, but urge analysts to explore its linkages to African American outcomes.

[11] See for example, Cherry and Rodgers (2000). This volume contains a collection of studies that examine the impact of the 1990s boom on the labor market prospects of African American men.

[12] Krueger and Solow (2001) is a recent exception to this practice. They purposefully linked micro economists and macroeconomists to write a series of papers that explored what needed to be done to recreate the conditions that led to the 1990s boom. See, for example, Hoynes, Hines & Krueger (2001). The economic development literature is another exception. There exist a large literature that links macro policy to poverty in developing countries.

[13] The other three roles are to supervise and regulate banking institutions to ensure the safety and soundness of the nation's banking and financial system and to protect the credit rights of consumers, to maintain the stability of the financial system and containing systemic risk that may arise in financial markets, and to provide financial services to depository institutions, the U.S. government, and foreign official institutions, including playing a major role in operating the nation's payments system. (http://www.federalreserve.gov/generalinfo/mission/default.htm)

[14] Trade policy (NAFTA and CAFTA), exchange rate and tariff policies constitute how the government relates to international markets. At first blush, one may view these goals and policy frameworks as objective approaches to promoting economic growth. They, too reflect societal values and priorities. Solely pushing for China to honor its trade agreement and to let their exchange rate float, but not for pushing for "core" labor and environmental standards only prolongs the existence of a costs advantage to China, thus a continued trade deficit and fewer U.S. jobs. At some point we have to ask ourselves, how long are we willing to accept the trade off of lower priced goods for lower employment.

[15] The average white incomes at the second and third fifths are $37,808 and $59,125, respectively.

[16] Testimony to House Financial Service Committee, February 15, 2007.

[17] The 12 banks are located in Boston, New York, Philadelphia, Cleveland, Richmond, Atlanta, Chicago, St. Louis, Minneapolis, Kansas City, Dallas, and San Francisco.

[18] For example, the Richmond Federal Reserve's Community Development Advisory Council (CDAC) consists of nine members representing the different communities in the Fifth Federal Reserve District. The purpose of the council is to serve as a discussion forum. The members are chosen with regard for the most diversified representation possible. Six members represent grassroots associations, community-based organizations, intermediaries, and consumer and labor groups and the remaining three members will represent state or local government, universities or foundations, and financial institutions. The CDAC provides a formal and systematic venue to increase communication and contact between the Federal Reserve Bank of Richmond (the Fed) and the community. The collection and assessment of a broad and balanced array of information on the performance of the various aspects of the economy are paramount to the effective conduct of policy. The CDAC keeps the Fed informed of community development issues, expresses concerns to the Bank President, provides "real world" data on community issues, and conveys information to their constituents about monetary, consumer, and banking policy. The CDAC's input is combined with other available information and plays an important role in the policy deliberations of the Fed. (http://www.richmondfed.org/community_affairs/cdac/mission/index.cfm).

[19] http://www.cbo.gov/aboutcbo/factsheet.shtml

[20] The mention of the Yahoo site is not a formal endorsement of the site. In fact there are a variety of business organizations and some non-profits that report the macro indicators and their release dates.

Still Segregated, Still Unequal: Analyzing the Impact of No Child Left Behind on African American Students

by Christopher Knaus, Ph.D.

T his article examines the impact of No Child Left Behind (NCLB) on educational experiences and opportunities for African- American children. Despite NCLB, public schools have continued to fail African Americans through separate and unequal educational opportunities, partially because the focus on educating African-American children well has not been legislated or mandated. In focusing on measuring the outcomes of racial inequalities (such as the achievement gap), NCLB avoids addressing fundamental inequalities in schooling and fails to expose the causes of such inequalities. NCLB advocates for teaching to bare minimums rather than meaningfully educating African-American students. As African Americans continue to be punished for the failures of their schools, NCLB has continued a separate and unequal educational system while shifting the debate from unequal schools to how to measure such schools.

State of Education for African-American Children

A few years ago, I invited the director of a university's Teacher Education Program to visit an urban classroom. The blatant state of disrepair was much more appalling than she had previously been led to believe, but the largely African-American student body also opened her eyes: "These kids," she exclaimed, "they are so well-spoken, articulate, and have so much passion!" I reminded her of their failing test scores, which she had a difficult time believing. "How can they be this well spoken and not pass these tests?" she asked. Her previous conceptions of these African-American youth as *not* intelligent or well-spoken reflected her lack of willingness to fault standardized tests as inadequate measures of academic achievement.

She did not believe in these students, yet did believe in their standardized assessment scores.

In a similar light, progress in lessening the achievement gap is often proclaimed without regard to whether the daily experiences of African-American students have improved. Yet, schooling for African Americans has remained structurally separate from and unequal to that of white Americans. African-American students regularly score significantly lower on almost every indicator of academic well-being than do whites and Asians[1], and many African American students attend the lowest performing schools in the country. For example, high-minority and high-poverty schools perform much lower than do low-minority and low-poverty schools, yet 71 percent of African Americans attend high minority schools and 72 percent of African Americans attend high-poverty schools.[2] Students who attend high-poverty schools are twice as likely to attend an overcrowded school as those who attend low-poverty schools. African Americans constitute disproportionately high numbers of students in special education as well, and are more than twice as likely to be designated mentally retarded than any other racial group.[3] At the same time, white students are three times more likely to enroll in Advanced Placement math and science courses than are African-American students. Standardized assessment scores reflect these disparities—the percentage of African Americans meeting proficiency in national assessments in reading and math is less than one forth of that of White students.[4]

Much of the achievement gap is mirrored by the severe gap in teacher quality provided to high-minority and high-poverty schools. Such schools have the least experienced teachers, the highest teacher turnover rates, the highest percentage of teachers teaching outside of their fields, and often have the highest student-to-teacher ratios.[5] A recent study demonstrated that high-poverty schools have three times as many uncertified or out-of-field teachers as low-poverty schools.[6]

The curricula in most public schools also fail to adequately engage black students. African-American students are often provided a curriculum that denies their historical experiences, positions racism as a thing of the past, and praises white colonial histories, writings, and ways of communicating.[7] For those who resist or show disinterest in such schooling, punishments are quickly doled out, often resulting in students moving from mainstream schools to continuation schools, alternative schools, or to the juvenile justice system.[8] Racial disparities in suspension rates have steadily been increasing because of "zero tolerance" policies which disproportionately impact African-American students. In 2000, African Americans comprised 17 percent of students nationwide, but 34 percent of the suspensions.[9] This school-to-prison pipeline often results in African-American students attending alternative district and county schools that do not even offer high school diplomas.[10] Even in predominantly white suburban schools, African Americans are often excluded from college preparatory curricula and tracked into remedial courses that teach the "basics" but do little to prepare students for the workforce or for college.[11] In short, many African-American students attend schools that, integrated or segregated, offer a less engaging education that focuses on discipline and achievement on standardized tests instead of critical thinking skills. No Child Left Behind (NCLB) continues this trend by ensuring that the least-resourced schools maintain focus on basic education.

In what follows, I outline how NCLB favors teaching methods and curricula that do not prepare African-American students attending failing Title I schools for college or meaningful employment. I then discuss the resegregation of schools, the inadequacy of NCLB's "highly qualified teacher" requirement, and analyze how NCLB fails to make a meaningful impact on African-American student achievement. I conclude with brief policy suggestions that expand rather than narrow the purpose of schools.

Concerns with No Child Left Behind

NCLB was touted as a way to address the achievement gap that separates African American, Latino, and Native American children from white and Asian students.[12] The federal legislation, a re-authorization of its precursor, the Elementary and Secondary Education Act, is based upon four pillars: 1) accountability, 2) increased local control, 3) research-based instructional approaches, and 4) parental choice.[13] NCLB controls the allocation of federal Title I funding based upon each school meeting annual set standards. Adequate Yearly Progress (AYP) requires that each school make benchmark improvements on test scores and high school graduation rates for racial and ethnic minority groups, English language learners, students with disabilities, and students from low-income families. These benchmarks are measured by states, which must compose or acquire standardized tests to assess student progress.[14] Schools that do not make progress for two years must offer parents the choice to send their child to a non-failing school in the district, and after three years, must provide supplemental services, such as free tutoring or after-school assistance. After five years of not meeting AYP, the school must make dramatic changes to how the school is run (this could entail state-takeover).[15]

Questions about the lack of academic achievement among many African-American students should focus on the severe inequalities between public schools that affect opportunities to learn. Yet, NCLB focuses instead on assessing the outcome of these inequalities—the achievement gap. The real causes behind the failure of predominantly minority schools, however, are ignored in favor of NCLB's simplistic measurements in achievement, graduation rates, and teacher certification. Rather than raise the bar on comprehensive education levels, NCLB measures only basic proficiency levels in math and reading, while replicating current national assessments. In effect, NCLB measures if students can barely read, but does not ensure adequate preparation for admission into college (though it does require increased high school graduation rates). Rather than address lower high school graduation rates among African-American students, or inadequate preparation for enrollment in four-year colleges for those who do graduate, NCLB focuses on a limited measurement of "achievement." As a result, NCLB simply measures inequality while reinforcing academic structures that repeatedly have been shown to fail African-American students. In fact, NCLB provides incentives to narrow education towards assessing only math and reading and creates a cycle of pseudo-improvement where scores improve based on increased instructional time on reading or math.[16] The additional resources provided to schools that do not meet AYP (so that they can to teach to the tests used to determine AYP) exacerbates conditions that lead African-American students (and all others attending Title I schools) to further disconnect from schooling.[17] Indeed, 71 percent of districts are spending less time on other subjects in elementary schools, and 97 percent of high-poverty districts require a specific amount of time for reading; whereas, only 55 to 59 percent of low-poverty districts require set times.[18]

Aligning the curriculum with such narrow standards ignores issues students face daily, including a context of violence, fewer accessible parents, fewer parents who have successfully navigated schooling, and historical (under) achievement levels of the student population, all of which require enhancing, rather than restricting, opportunities to learn.[19] These conditions are precisely what limit many African-American students' willingness to engage in schools. In a national context where some estimates suggest that one of two African-American students drops out before graduation,[20] further narrowing a curriculum many students already find irrelevant is hardly an incentive to stay in school. Furthermore, rather than conceive of schools as working in conjunction with other public service agencies (such as social work, juvenile justice, welfare, health, and employment sectors), NCLB operates in isolation from social services. Yet researchers have often demonstrated that educational achievement is directly tied to the social conditions in which students live.[21] NCLB ignores how the surrounding community, parental income and education levels, language and cultural barriers, teacher awareness of student cultural context, and pedagogical approaches influence academic engagement of all students.[22] As was recently argued:

> …underlying NCLB is the assumption that schools by themselves can achieve dramatic, totally unprecedented levels of educational achievement for all racial and ethnic groups as well as for children with disabilities, low-income children, and children who lack English fluency—all in a short time and without changing any of the other inequalities in their lives.[23]

Because NCLB ignores the social context that shapes opportunity for many African American youth, it shifts the conversation about educational equity away from what really matters. Federal assessments are not required for critical thinking, art, history, biology, or anything specifically related to participating in democratic society as a creative or independent thinker, and NCLB provides incentives to eliminate such curricula from "failing" schools.[24] Increasingly absent from low-income urban schools across the country are creative, flexible curricula that allow students to express themselves outside the arena of what may be on a test.[25] NCLB ultimately requires basic, rote educational strategies for failing schools; a requirement that would be rejected by elite schools as an inadequate method for engaging students in higher-level critical thinking skills valued by colleges and employers alike.[26]

Resegregation

African Americans often attend urban schools that are woefully inadequate when compared to schools attended by the majority of white students. While such race-based segregation is not new, it is increasing. Since desegregation efforts have all but formally ended, the percentage of African Americans attending predominantly minority schools nationwide has steadily increased. In 2003, 73 percent of African-American students attended a predominantly minority school, and 38 percent of African Americans attended a school that is over 90 percent minority (in 1991, those numbers were 66 percent and 34 percent).[27] In 2005, 71 percent of African-American students attended a predominantly minority school, whereas only 11 percent of white students did. This racial segregation is tied to increasing poverty—in 1996, the average African-American student attended a school where at least 43 percent of its students were poor. In 2002, that number increased to 49 percent.[28] Nationwide, 48 percent of African-American students attend schools where over 75 percent of the students are eligible for free or reduced price lunch, and 72 percent attend schools where over 51 percent of the students are eligible.[29] Segregation negatively impacts student achievement. One recent study shows that African-American students in Florida who attend segregated schools perform lower on state tests than African-American students in non-segregated schools, even after controlling for teacher quality, class size, and poverty levels.[30]

African Americans are increasingly attending schools that serve low-income and minority students and NCLB accountability provisions appear to exacerbate this segregation. Segregated predominantly African American and Latino schools are disproportionately identified as needing improvement. According to one study, schools not meeting AYP in California and Illinois serve 75 to 85 percent minority student populations, while schools meeting AYP have less than 40 percent minority students.[31] Illinois schools needing improvement have five times more African-American students as those meeting AYP, and only 1 percent of schools where the student body is 90 percent white were in need of improvement compared to 68 percent of schools where the student body was 90 percent African American.[32] Similar trends exist in Georgia, Virginia, and California, where predominantly African American or minority schools are disproportionately identified for improvement and predominantly White or Asian schools tend to meet AYP.[33]

Students not meeting proficiency are often isolated from students who are meeting proficiency and additional federal funds are often spent on after school or pull-out programs for failing minority students. While data is not readily available on the percentages of African-American students being tracked into "support" structures (that segregate), educators note that many are pushed into alternative education systems (another segregated population).[34] Therefore, instead of addressing segregation of our public schools, NCLB punishes students who attend segregated low-income minority schools.

Parental choice in school is NCLB's solution for segregated, low-performing schools. Yet while districts are required to provide transportation to another school, there is no requirement that another school actually enroll that student and no guarantee of the required transportation.[35] Thus, schools that might already be full (particularly the highest performing schools in the district) are not likely to be desegregated by NCLB's parental choice provision because they do not have to enroll students exercising their right to a non-failing school.[36] NCLB's school choice provision thus rests upon three faulty assumptions: 1) that African-American parents want their children to attend segregated predominantly white schools; 2) that such schools would readily enroll African-American children from low performing schools; and 3) that such schools would educate African-American students as well as they do white and Asian students.

Teacher Effectiveness

A recent conversation I had with several high school principals illustrated NCLB's "highly qualified" teacher provision as an arbitrary definition of good teaching. As we stood outside this well-maintained predominantly African American and Latino urban high school, dozens of White teachers hurriedly made their way from campus just 20 minutes after the end-of-school bell. Within an hour, the campus was deserted. One of the principals laughed ruefully: "Well, at least those well-certified teachers are home before 4 pm everyday." His point was simple: "good" teaching has little to do with certificates or diplomas. "Commitment to African-American students" he argued, "does not fit on these certificates."

NCLB requires a "highly qualified" teacher in every classroom, but how this relates to effectiveness at teaching African-American students is under question.[37] What is certain is that high-poverty and high-minority schools have much lower proportions of "highly qualified" teachers.[38] For example, one recent study found significant gaps between classes taught by highly qualified teachers in high- and low-poverty schools in 2003-04.[39] In California, that gap was particularly extensive—40 percent of core classes were taught by highly qualified teachers in high-poverty schools, while 60 percent were taught by highly qualified teachers in low-poverty schools.

NCLB has recently relented on its demand for highly qualified teachers in every classroom, but there is no clear evidence documenting the impact of "highly qualified" teachers on African-American learning. Because there are many factors, above and beyond certification, that lead to effective teaching (including curriculum, experience, and classroom support), many school districts are skeptical that "this requirement will improve the quality of teaching."[40] I often interact with "highly qualified" teachers in their first few years of teaching in predominantly African-American schools, and what they most often convey is their lack of preparation for dealing with the everyday context of their students. As states scramble to adhere to NCLB requirements for teachers, conversations about how to effectively teach African-American students are even further silenced. There is little mention of culturally responsive teaching or recognition of the extensive research on teaching African-American students in state plans or in federal NCLB provisions.[41]

Student Academic Performance

Because NCLB requires each state to measure its own progress on standardized assessments in math and reading, there is a limit to cross-state analysis and NCLB does not provide an understanding of the national achievement levels of African-American students. Scores on the National Assessment of Educational Progress (NAEP)—which is not connected to NCLB—measure student performance on the national level and indicate that there has been a gradual narrowing of the achievement gap as measured by the NAEP since the

1970's.[42] Despite these larger trends, several studies argue that NCLB has no clear impact on student knowledge in math or reading.[43] Most states have increased student performance on their NCLB elementary assessments, but in a handful of states, African-American student scores have decreased (and achievement gaps widened) since NCLB.[44] At the middle and high school levels, few states have seen a change in the achievement gap, while in some states African-American student scores increased, albeit at lower rates than did white scores. Overall, mean national scores on the NAEP have not increased, suggesting that NCLB progress may be due to teachers learning to teach to the test.[45]

According to the NAEP's assessment of urban school districts, the majority of African-American students are not meeting even basic performance levels.[46] In 2005, almost 60 percent of African-American students in urban districts did not meet basic proficiency in 4th grade reading, while 1 in 2 did not meet basic reading proficiency in 8th grade. The corresponding percentages for white students in urban districts were 25 percent in 4th grade, and 20 percent in 8th grade. In terms of basic math proficiency, 40 percent of 4th grade African-American students in urban districts did not perform at the basic grade level and almost 60 percent of 8th graders did not.[47] This compares to just over 10 percent of white students in these districts not meeting basic levels in 4th grade math, and 20 percent not meeting basic levels in 8th grade.

Disparities in the percentage of students meeting proficiency on the NAEP in all school districts are just as startling. Only 13 percent of African American students met basic proficiency in 4th grade reading, whereas 41 percent of White students did. In math, only 15 percent of African-American students were proficient in 4th grade math, while almost 50 percent of white students were. The results in 8th grade are similarly illustrative of the achievement gap. Twelve percent of African-American 8th graders were proficient in reading and only 9 percent were proficient in math. Thirty-nine percent of white 8th graders were proficient in reading, while 37 percent were proficient in math. These results show that, regardless of the progress being made, there continues to be a major gap between the academic performance of African-American students and that of white students.

According to national graduation statistics, in 2003, less than half of all African-American students graduated high school in four years with a

diploma.[48] And while NCLB purports to create incentives to increase graduation rates, many states are relying upon high stakes exit exams to determine
diploma eligibility, despite data that show their exclusive use may lower graduation rates.[49] Perhaps because of such requirements, the African
American/White graduation gap has been increasing: in 1999, 48.4 percent of
African Americans graduated high school nationwide (compared to 72 percent of white students). In 2003, the African-American high school graduation
rate had increased by 3 percent, while the white student graduation rates
increased 4 percent.[50] While the conversation about NCLB centers on achievement on standardized tests, the overall graduation rates of African Americans
remain paltry. The increased reliance upon state exit exams for graduation
spells particular trouble for the next generation of African-American students
whose increasing attendance in segregated low-income, high-minority schools
limits their chances of earning a high school diploma. Through the chance of
birth, such students suffer from inadequate opportunities to learn while the
nation debates policy about how to measure their inadequacies.

CONCLUSIONS AND RECOMMENDATIONS

NCLB has not only failed (and promises to continue to fail) African-
American students, but has also shifted the debate from unequal schooling to
monitoring failing schools. Because of this shift, the American public increasingly focuses on superficial measurements that hide the reality of segregated
public schools. In order for federal policies such as NCLB to be successful, the
conversation must shift from measuring achievement gaps to educating
African-American students. NCLB claimed to bring in a new era of parental
accountability leading to the right to take children out of failing schools; however, the overall approach to mending the achievement gap is misguided and
far removed from the difficult questions about how best to educate African-
American students within the context of racism, violence, incarceration and
increasingly irrelevant, segregated schools that are more concerned with
assessment than education.

Given the lack of improvement in the achievement gap, according to its
own measures, NCLB appears to have failed in its first five years. NCLB lacks
the capacity to prepare African-American students for critical engagement in
shaping democratic society, encourages segregated schools, pushes students

out of mainstream schools, narrows a curriculum that many African-American students already find alienating, and ignores high drop out rates. Despite the rhetoric of NCLB, schools in which a majority of students are African American are still in disrepair, are still staffed by less experienced teachers, and generally do not provide a college preparatory curriculum. But NCLB has provided a forum through which advocates of African-American students can offer meaningful policy recommendations for strengthening educational opportunities and improving educational outcomes for African-American students. Current policy conversation should concentrate on three primary concerns:

- Expanding definitions of academic skills beyond math and reading. A central pillar of NCLB is relevant research; however, much of the research about the skills needed for meaningful participation in democratic society is being ignored. Important subjects such as art, music, history, biology, speech, and social studies must be included in the fabric of schooling.

- Reengaging African-American students in the educational process. Conversations with students, educators, policy makers, and communities about how to best educate African-American students should be informed by research on culturally relevant and responsive pedagogy, curricula, and school structures.[51]

- Expansion of assessment to include multiple measures of academic success. Research has shown that in order for assessment to effectively guide school efforts, it must reflect a wide range of student skills and provide a foundation from which to teach.[52] Multiple measures include portfolios, teacher assessments, problem solving, diagnostic feedback for students, project management, essays, oral exams, and public performance.[53]

Essential feedback and comments provided by Marcos Pizarro, San José State University and Cyndy Snyder, Office of Educational Assessment, University of Washington.

NOTES

[1] Children's Defense Fund: *State of America's Children, 2005.*; Holzman, M. (2006). *Public Education and Black Male Students: The 2006 State Report Card.* Schott Educational Inequality Index, Cambridge, MA: The Schott Foundation for Public Education.; Smith, R. A. (2004). "Saving Black Boys." *The American Prospect, 15*(2).

[2] High-minority and high-poverty schools are defined here as more than 50 percent minority or students on the free and reduced lunch program. See U.S. Department of Education, National Center for Educational Statistics (2006). *The Condition of Education 2006*, NCES 2006-071. Washington, D.C: U.S. Government Printing Office.

[3] U.S. Department of Education, National Center for Educational Statistics (2006). *The Condition of Education 2006*, NCES 2006-071. Washington, D.C: U.S. Government Printing Office.

[4] U.S. Department of Education: *The Condition of Education 2006.*

[5] See Darling-Hammond, L. & Sykes, G. (2003). *Creating a National Manpower Policy for Education: The Right Way to Meet the 'Highly Qualified Teacher' Challenge.*; Hawley, W. D. & Wayne, A. J. (2003). Good Teaching, Good Schools. In G. Orfield & E. DeBray (eds.), *Hard Work for Good Schools: Facts Not Fads in Education Title I Reform.* Century Foundation Press.; Strauss, R. & Sawyer, E. A. (1986). Some New Evidence on Teacher and Student Competencies. *Economics of Education Review*, 41.

[6] *Educate*, Jan. 3, 2005. p. 4.

[7] Brock, R. (2005). *Sista Talk: The Personal and the Pedagogical.* New York, NY: Peter Lang. Gay, G. (2000). Culturally Responsive Teaching: Theory, Research, and Practice. New York: Teachers College Press; Knaus, C. B. (2006). *Race, Racism and Multiraciality in American Education.* Bethesda, MD: Academica.; Ladson-Billings, G. (1994). *The Dreamkeepers: Successful Teachers of African American Children.* San Francisco, CA: Jossey-Bass.

[8] Casella, R. (2001). *At Zero Tolerance: Punishment, Prevention, and School Violence.* New York: Peter Lang.; Lipman, *Cracking Down.*

[9] Wald, J., & Losen, D. (2003). Defining and Redirecting a School-to-Prison Pipeline. In Wald, J. & Losen, D. (eds.), *Deconstructing the School to Prison Pipeline: New Directions for Youth Development, No. 99*, 1-7.

[10] Many instead offer G.E.D. options; see Wald & Losen: *Deconstructing the School-to-Prison Pipeline.*

[11] Connor, M H., & Boskin, J. (2001). Overrepresentation of Bilingual and Poor Children in Special Education Classes: A Continuing Problem. *Journal of Children & Poverty*, 7, 23-32.; Kozol, J. (1991). *Savage Inequalities: Children in America's Schools*. New York: HarperPerennial.; Oakes, J. (1985). *Keeping track: How schools structure inequality*. New Haven, CT: Yale University Press. Slavin, R. E., Karwiet, N. L., & Madden, N. A. (1989). *Effective Programs for Students at Risk*. Boston, MA: Allyn and Bacon.

[12] See Hess, F. M., & Petrilli, M. J. (2006). *No Child Left Behind Primer*. New York: Peter Lang; Peterson, P.E., & West, M. R. (2003). *No Child Left Behind? The Politics and Practice of School Accountability*. Washington, D.C.: Brookings Institution Press.

[13] Hess & Petrilli: *No Child Left Behind Primer*.

[14] 95 percent of all students must take the state-instituted assessment tests.

[15] Peterson and West: *No Child Left Behind?*

[16] Neill, M., Guisbond, L., & Schaeffer, B. (2004). *Failing Our Children: How "No Child Left Behind" Undermines Quality and Equity in Education*. Cambridge, MA: FairTest.

[17] Lynch: *Closing the Achievement Gap*.

[18] Jennings, J. & Rentner, D. S. (2006). Ten Big Effects of the No Child Left Behind Act on Public Schools. *Phi Delta Kappan*.

[19] See Gay: *Culturally Responsive Teaching*; Lee, J. (2006). *Tracking Achievement Gaps and Assessing the Impact of NCLB on the Gaps: An In-Depth Look into National and State Reading and Math Outcomes Trends*. Cambridge, MA: The Civil Rights Project at Harvard University.

[20] Bridgeland, J. M., DiIulio, J.J., & Morrison, K.B. (2006). *The Silent Epidemic: Perspectives of High School Dropouts*. Civic Enterprises, Peter Hart Research Associates.; National Association for the Advancement of Colored People (2006). *Equity Matters: Ensuring Access to Quality Education for Minority Students.*; Orfield: *Dropouts in America*.

[21] Bourdieu, P. (1990). *Reproduction in Education, Society, and Culture*. Newbury Park, CA: Sage.; Foster, M. (2001). Education and Socialization: A Review of the Literature. In Watkins, W. H., Lewis, J. H., & Chou, V. (eds)., *Race and Education: The Roles of History and Society in Educating African American Students*. Boston, MA: Allyn and Bacon.; Perry, T., Steele, C., & Hilliard, A. G. (2003). Young, Gifted and Black: *Promoting High Achievement Among African-American Students*. Boston, MA: Beacon Press.

[22] See Davidson, A. L. (1996). *Making and Molding Identity in Schools: Student Narratives on Race, Gender, and Academic Achievement*. Albany, NY: SUNY Press.; Foster, M. (1997). *Black Teachers on Teaching*. New York, NY: New Press.; Gay: *Culturally Responsive Teaching*; Nieto, S. (1996). *Affirming Diversity: The Sociopolitical Context of Multicultural Education*. White Plains, NY: Longman.; Noguera, P. (2003). *City Schools and the American Dream: Reclaiming the Promise of Public Education*. New York: Teachers College Press.; Perry, T., & Delpit, L. (1998). *The Real Ebonics Debate: Power, Language, and the Education of African American Children*. Boston, MA: Beacon Press.; Pizarro, M. (2005). *Chicanas and Chicanos in School: Racial Profiling, Identity Battles, and Empowerment*. Austin, TX: University of Texas Press.; Valdés, G. (1996). *Con Respeto: Bridging the Distances Between Culturally Diverse Families and Schools*. New York, NY: Teachers College Press.

[23] Sunderman, G.L., Kim, J.S., & Orfield, G. (2005). *NCLB meets school realities: Lessons from the field*. Thousand Oaks, CA: Corwin Press.

[24] See Kornhaber, M. L. (2006). *Beyond Standardization in School Accountability*. Paper presented to Roundtable Discussion on Reauthorization of NCLB, Washington, D.C.; Neill, M., Guisbond, L., & Schaeffer, B. (2004). *Failing Our Children: How "No Child Left Behind" Undermines Quality and Equity in Education*. Cambridge, MA: FairTest.

[25] See Koretz, D. (2006). *The Pending Reauthorization of NCLB: An Opportunity to Rethink Basic Strategy*. Paper presented to Roundtable Discussion on Reauthorization of NCLB, Washington, D.C.; Linn, R. L. (2006). *Toward a More Effective Definition of Adequate Yearly Progress*. Paper presented to Roundtable Discussion on Reauthorization of NCLB, Washington, D.C.

[26] Brantlinger, E. (2003). *Dividing Classes: How the Middle Class Negotiates and Rationalized School Advantage*. New York: RoutledgeFarmer.; McDonough, P. M. (1997). *Choosing Colleges: How Social Class and Schools Structure Opportunity*. Albany, NY: SUNY Press.

[27] Orfield, G., & Lee, C. (2006). *Racial Transformation and the Changing Nature of Segregation*. Cambridge, MA: Civil Rights Project at Harvard University.

[28] Orfield, G., & Lee, C. (2005). *Why Segregation Matters: Poverty and Educational Inequality*. Cambridge, MA: Civil Rights Project at Harvard University.

[29] Only 5 percent of this nation's White students attend schools in which 75 percent of the students are on the free and reduced lunch program. See U.S. Department of Education, National Center for Educational Statistics (2006). *The Condition of Education 2006*, NCES 2006-071. Washington, D.C: U.S. Government Printing Office.

[30] Borman, K.M., Eitle, T. M., Michael, D., Eitle, D.J., Lee, R., Johnson, L., Cobb-Roberts, D., Dorn, S., & Shircliffe, B. (2004). Accountability in a Postdesegregation Era: The Continuing Significance of Racial Segregation in Florida's Schools. *American Educational Research Journal, 41*(3), p 605-631.

[31] Owens, A., & Sunderman, G. L. (2006). *School Accountability under NCLB: Aid or Obstacle for Measuring Racial Equity?* Cambridge, MA: Civil Rights Project at Harvard University.; Novak, J. & Fuller, B. (2004). Penalizing Diverse Schools? Similar Test Scores, But Different Students Bring Federal Sanctions. In K. Goodman and Y. Goodman (Eds)., <u>Saving our schools: The case for public education</u>, p. 218-222. Berkeley, CA: RDR Books.

[32] Owens and Sunderman: *School Accountability under NCLB.*

[33] *Id.*

[34] Allensworth, E. M. (2004). Graduation and Dropout Rates after Implementation of High-Stakes Testing in Chicago's Elementary Schools: A Close Look at Students Most Vulnerable to Dropping Out. In G. Orfield (Ed.), *Dropouts in America: Confronting the Graduation Rate Crisis,* 157-179. Harvard Education Press.; Meier, D.., Kohn, A., Darling-Hammond, L., Sizer, R. R., & Wood, G. (2004). *Many Children Left Behind: How the No Child Left Behind Act is Damaging Our Children and Our Schools.* Boston, MA: Beacon Press.; Wald and Losen: *Deconstructing the School-to-Prison Pipeline.*

[35] Schools not meeting Adequate Yearly Progress for the third year are required to provide transportation to another school within the district, but schools are not required to admit students because another school is not meeting AYP.

[36] Data on how many African American parents taking advantage of the school choice provision is not readily available. In 2003-04, according to the Department of Education, only 38,000 students took advantage of this option.

[37] This goal has been pushed back to the start of the 2007-08 year because many districts are struggling to meet this requirement in special education, math, science, and in rural areas. California provides an example of efforts to meet the requirement that have not received adequate federal support – see Guha, R., Campbell, A., Humphrey, D., Shields, P., Tiffany-Morales, J., & Wechsler, M. (2006). *California's Teaching Force 2006: Key Issues and Trends.* Santa Cruz, CA: Center for the Future of Teaching and Learning.; Jennings and Rentner: *Ten Big Effects of the No Child Left Behind Act on Public Schools.* Regarding teaching African American students, see: Darling-Hammond, L. & Sykes, G. (2003). *Creating a National Manpower Policy for Education: The Right Way to Meet the 'Highly Qualified Teacher' Challenge.*; Darling-Hammond, L. (2005). *A Good Teacher in Every Classroom: Preparing the Highly Qualified*

Teachers our Children Deserve. San Francisco: Jossey-Bass.; Foster, M. (1997). *Black Teachers on Teaching*. New York, NY: New Press.

[38] Peske and Haycock: *Teaching Inequality*.

[39] Sunderman, G. L. (2006). *The Unraveling of No Child Left Behind: How Negotiated Changes Transform the Law*. Cambridge, MA: Civil Rights Project at Harvard University.

[40] See; Jennings and Rentner: *Ten Big Effects of the No Child Left Behind Act on Public Schools*.; Peske, H. G., & Haycock, K. (2006). *Teaching Inequality: How Poor and Minority Students are Shortchanged on Teacher Quality*. Washington, D.C.: Education Trust.

[41] Ladson-Billings: *Strengthening the African American Educational Pipeline*.

[42] U.S. Department of Education, Institute of Education Sciences, National Center for Education Statistics (2006). *National Assessment of Educational Progress, Selected Years, 1971-2004 Long Term Tread Reading and Math Assessments*.

[43] Fuller, B., Gesicki, K., Kang, E., & Wright, J. (2006). *Is the No Child Left Behind Act Working? The Reliability of How States Track Achievement*. Berkeley, CA: Policy Analysis for California, University of California, Berkeley.; Lee, J. (2006). *Tracking Achievement Gaps and Assessing the Impact of NCLB on the Gaps: An In-depth Look into National and State Reading and Math Outcome Trends*. Cambridge, MA: Civil Rights Project at Harvard University.; Owens and Sunderman: *School Accountability under NCLB*.

[44] *Stalled in Secondary: A Look at Student Achievement Since the No Child Left Behind Act* (2005). Washington, D.C.: Education Trust.

[45] Fuller, Gesicki, Kang, and Wright.: *Is the No Child Left Behind Act Working?*; Lee: *Tracking Achievement Gaps and Assessing the Impact of NCLB on the Gaps*; Jennings and Rentner: *Ten Big Effects of the No Child Left Behind Act on Public Schools*.; Owens and Sunderman: *School Accountability under NCLB.*; Public Education Network (2004). *Open to the Public: Students Speak Out on "No Child Left Behind."*

[46] See *2005 Trial Urban District Results*. Nation's Report Card, National Center for Education Statistics.

[47] *2005 Trial Urban District Results*. Nation's Report Card, National Center for Education Statistics.

[48] Some research demonstrates higher graduation rates for African Americans but most

calculations are based on incoming seniors (12th graders) rather than those who might drop out before ninth, tenth, or eleventh grades. Many states therefore present a more appealing picture of graduation rates in the 70 percent range – yet these ignore students who have dropped out prior to their senior year. The Cumulative Promotion Index incorporates a more comprehensive measure by counting all high school students who drop out against the overall graduation rate. For more information, see Diplomas Count: An Essential Guide to Graduation Policy and Rates. *Education Week*, June, 22, 2006.

[49] Darling-Hammond, L., Rustique-Forrester, E., & Pecheone, R. L. (2005). *Multiple Measures Approaches to High School Graduation.* Stanford, CA: School Redesign Network.

[50] Statistics from Education Week: Editorial Projects in Education Research Center. For more on the Cumulative Promotion Index, see *Diplomas Count: An Essential Guide to Graduation Policy and Rates.*

[51] See Gay: *Culturally Responsive Teaching*; and Ladson-Billings: *The Dreamkeepers.*

[52] Kornhaber, M. L. (2006). *Beyond Standardization in School Accountability.* Paper presented to Roundtable Discussion on Reauthorization of NCLB, Washington, D.C.;

[53] Darling-Hammond, et al.: Multiple Measures Approaches to High School Graduation.

ESSAY 5

On Equal Ground: Causes and Solutions for Lower College Completion Rates Among Black Males

by Valerie Rawlston Wilson, Ph.D.

R egardless of race, ethnicity, gender, or social class, all parents dream of a bright future for their children. For most, the path to this future follows a well-established pattern—graduate from high school, complete at least four years of college and secure a good job. Prior to the Civil Rights Movement of the 1960s, this path to success was extremely narrow and traveled by few African Americans who for over 200 years after arriving in this country had been prohibited from receiving any kind of formal education, much less attending institutions of higher learning. With the help of religious organizations and the Freedmen's Bureau, African Americans responded to these restrictions by opening the first "colleges" for blacks as early as 1837 when Cheyney University was founded in Pennsylvania. These early "colleges" served primarily as high schools for blacks and offered instruction in industrial or agricultural trades and teacher training. They ultimately evolved into what we know today as Historically Black Colleges and Universities (HBCUs). At either the graduate or undergraduate level, HBCUs have educated some 75% of all African-American Ph.D.s, 46% of all African-American business executives, 50% of African-American engineers, 80% of African-American federal judges, and 65% of African-American doctors. The *Brown v. Topeka Board of Education* decision and affirmative action policies helped to further widen the path to upward mobility by allowing African Americans greater access to all American colleges and universities, resulting in tremendous strides in educational attainment. In 1960 only 3.5 percent of African-American adults age 25 or older had completed four years of college or more. By 2005, this number had grown to 18 percent.[1]

The relationship between educational attainment and earnings is well established. According to 2005 estimates from the Bureau of Labor Statistics, individuals with a bachelor's degree earn more than one and a half times as much as high school graduates and more than twice as much as those without a high school diploma. Also, the black-white earnings gap narrows considerably when you compare median earnings of blacks and whites with a bachelor's degree or higher.[2] Yet, high rates of joblessness and high school dropout among black males indicate that the benefits of higher education are yet to be fully realized by many of these young men.

According to the 2005 *Digest of Education Statistics*, total undergraduate enrollment in degree-granting institutions[3] increased by 24 percent between 1990 and 2004. Over this same period of time, the proportion of those students who were African American increased from 10 percent to 13 percent. African-American males represented less than one third of this growth. A look at degree completion statistics indicate that less than half (43 percent) of all African-American students who enrolled in a 4-year college as first-time freshmen in 1995-96 had completed a bachelor's degree by 2001, compared to 63 percent of white students. College completion rates for black males (36 percent) are roughly ten percentage points lower than for black females (47 percent) , reflecting in part the greater number of women relative to men enrolled in college since the 1980s.

While much can and has been said about the failure of the public education system to adequately engage and prepare young black men to enter college or the workforce, there tends to be less discussion about the educational experiences of those who actually do make it into college. By observing the factors that contribute to success (or failure) in college, policymakers can begin to create policies and programs that not only help those already enrolled, but also better prepare students before they enter college. Aggregate enrollment and completion statistics give us a snapshot of students at the beginning and end of the college education process, but fail to address the specific dynamics at work in the decision to remain enrolled and complete a college degree. A meaningful discussion of the black male college experience must go beyond a simple statement of the facts to an analysis of how differences in socioeconomic status, family background, educational preparation and even college environment contribute to different educational outcomes. The historical significance of HBCUs adds another dimension to the analysis of the black male college experience.

Historically Black Colleges and Universities have served a unique role in educating and graduating a significant portion of economically (and often otherwise) disadvantaged, college-aged African Americans. With typically lower tuition rates and more flexible admission policies, they are credited with providing a college education to many for whom it would have been out of reach otherwise. Smaller class sizes and a sense of shared racial history and identity have also been said to cultivate a more supportive and nurturing environment for students to flourish in. The Higher Education Act of 1965 defines HBCUs as institutions of higher learning established before 1964 whose principal mission was then, as is now, the [higher] education of black Americans. All institutions classified as HBCUs are accredited or making reasonable progress toward accreditation by an approved accrediting body. Currently there are 105 institutions classified as HBCUs, representing three percent of all institutions of higher education in the United States. In 2004, HBCUs enrolled 13% of all black college students and produced roughly one fifth of all black college graduates.[4] While the graduation rate at HBCUs tends to be much lower than the graduation rate for black students at the nation's highest-ranked institutions, the graduation rate at a number of HBCUs is well above the average for black students nationwide and at least twenty-one HBCUs have seen an improvement in their graduation rate between 1998 and 2005. The flip side is that for a significant number of the nation's HBCUs, two thirds or more of all entering black students do not go on to earn a degree.[5]

Identifying Factors that Influence Persistence & Graduation Outcomes

What role do HBCUs play in educating young black men? Are these institutions more successful at retaining and graduating African-American students than traditionally white institutions (TWIs) and do these outcomes vary for males and females? Aggregate statistics can be misleading because they mask underlying differences across students and institutions that affect persistence and completion outcomes. For example, lower graduation rates at HBCUs can be partially explained by the fact that most HBCUs are small, have a relatively high percentage of disadvantaged students, and lack many of the resources available at mainstream institutions. Empirical analysis is necessary to disentagle some of the many factors affecting the decision to attend (or not to attend) an HBCU in the first place, as well as how these factors affect four-year persistence rates and six-year graduation rates for African American students at HBCUs and TWIs.[6]

In order to perform such an analysis I use data from the Beginning Postsecondary Students (BPS) Longitudinal Study. BPS was implemented by the National Center of Educational Statistics (NCES) to improve nationally representative data on participants in postsecondary education. Information is collected on first-time students as they begin their postsecondary education and their progress is updated at 2-year intervals for up to six years. The most recently available data is from the cohort of students who began their postsecondary education in 1995 with data collection commencing in 2001. From this group of students I draw a sample of 469 African-American students (146 attend an HBCU) between the ages of 17 and 21 who enrolled for the first time at a four-year postsecondary institution at the start of the 1995 fall semester.[7]

The first question that must be addressed is whether African-American students who attend HBCUs are inherently different from thost who attend TWIs. For the sample of students used in this analysis, the two groups were demographically very similar, except for a few notable differences. First, the male-female ratio for African-American students at TWIs (0.37) was higher than at HBCUs (0.29). Aggressive recruitment of black male athletes at major colleges and universities is a possible explanation for this difference. Second, average family income was higher for those who attended TWIs ($44,000) than for those at HBCUs ($37,000). Finally, African-American students who attended TWIs were more likely to be top students in high school than their counterparts at HBCUs, but it is important to keep in mind that top students are more likely to attend the country's elite universities, all of which are classified as TWIs.

Taking account of individual characteristics, family background, high school academic performance and local labor market conditions in the student's home state, I estimated the probability that a student would choose to attend an HBCU as opposed to a TWI, given that they had already decided to attend college. The estimates suggest first of all that despite a relatively low male-female ratio, gender alone was not a significant determinant of

HBCU attendance for college bound African-American males and females. They further suggest that students who live in states with a greater number of HBCUs, as well as students from single parent or broken homes and those with lower SAT scores were more likely to attend HBCUs. However, the largest single factor in determining the likelihood that a student would attend an HBCU was whether their mother attended college. Those whose mothers attended college were 24.7 to 34.8 percentage points more likely to attend an HBCU than those whose mothers had less education. This is what can be called a "legacy effect" as the parents of those attending college in the nineties would have been college students in the 1960s before integration became widespread. As a result, many of these mothers could have attended HBCUs and may encourage their children to do so, as well.

Proponents of HBCUs often argue that the absence of racism on these campuses along with smaller, more intimate social and academic settings help to promote academic success among African-American students. One dimension along which this success can be measured is student persistence. Persistence refers to the decision a student makes to remain enrolled in college. In addition to individual characteristics, family background, high school academic performance and local labor market conditions, persistence is likely to also be influenced by previous investments of time and resources. After controlling for each of these factors, I found that African-American students who attended HBCUs were no more likely to leave college before completing a degree than similar students at TWIs. Differences in persistence rates between males and females also diminished once student characteristics were controlled for. Rather, persistence was most strongly affected by academic preparation. Compared to students with a cumulative high school grade average of 85 – 100 (A to B), the chances of stopping out were 5.6 percentage points higher for students with a 75 – 84 (B- to C) high school grade average. The difference was nearly twice that for students with less than a C high school grade average (10.7 percentage points). Students who scored higher on the SAT were also less likely to withdraw from college. A 200 point difference in the SAT scores of otherwise similar students was associated with a 1.5 percentage point difference in the probability of stopout. Family background also has significant effects on persistence. Students from single parent or broken homes were 4.5 percentage points more likely to stopout. Holding all other characteristics constant, students in the lowest income category (less than \$16,100) were 4.4 percentage points less likely to stop out in any given term than those with family income above \$53,750. This suggests more determination to remain in school and complete their college education among lower income students.

Additionally, most students who stopped out chose to do so before the beginning of a new academic year (which begins in the fall) as opposed to the middle of the year. Though not very pronounced, there was also some evidence that the chances a student will stop out at any point in time decreases the longer a student has been enrolled.

Since the ultimate goal of college attendance is degree completion, the final indicator of success is how well this goal is accomplished among African-American students at HBCUs and TWIs. Again individual characteristics, family background, academic performance and local labor market conditions are used to estimate the probability of completing a bachelor's degree within six years. And again, holding all of these factors constant, there is no evidence that degree completion rates differ significantly for African-American students at HBCUs or TWIs, nor were there significant differences between African-American males and females. Not surprisingly, academic performance is the strongest determinant of college completion as well. For example, students who had a B to C (75 to 84) high school grade average were 20 percentage points less likely to graduate within six years than those with an A or B (85 to 100) high school grade average. Similarly, the probability of graduating within six years increases by 6.8 percentage points per 100 point difference in SAT score.

Graduation outcomes for African-American students do, however, vary by family income. Students in the lowest income quartile, as well as those in the second highest income quartile were more likely to graduate than those in the highest income quartile by at least 35 percentage points. This again tends to indicate that lower and middle-income students are more driven to complete their college education than otherwise similar upper-income students.

CONCLUSIONS AND RECOMMENDATIONS

Ultimately, the question is what, if anything, does the absence of a distinct HBCU effect really mean? The answer to that question is determined by the basis upon which we choose to evaluate what matters. On one hand, if students with similar educational and family backgrounds are just as likely to persist and complete a degree at an HBCU as they would be at a TWI, then there is some advantage to be gained (at least economically) in attending an HBCU at a fraction of the cost of attendance at a comparable TWI. On the other hand, although degree attainment is the primary reason why colleges and universities exist, the observation of this outcome alone gives no consideration to the quality of education, prestige of the school, or the personal satisfaction and pride derived from the educational experience; all of which help to shape future aspirations and post-baccalaureate outcomes.

The most important point to take away from this analysis is that success in college begins long before students ever enroll. In fact, a student's performance in the higher education arena is intricately linked to his or her ability to develop the skills necessary to compete and meet the demands of college before they arrive. Observed differences in persistence and completion statistics across schools as well as between African-American males and females exist largely because of differences in academic preparation and performance. Inadequate academic preparation is also a major barrier to initial college enrollment, affecting observed differences in enrollment rates between African- American males and females. Contributing also to differences in enrollment is the fact that 15 percent of young black males (age 18-24) are high school dropouts, compared to 11 percent of young black females. A major revamping of the American educational system—including quality and type of instruction as well as re-integration of schools along racial and socioeconomic lines—is necessary. Better access to college preparatory and advanced placement classes are needed for all African-American students at the high school level. Since achievement gaps appear even before kindergarten, early childhood education is important. Furthermore, the preparation necessary to complete more challenging high school curricula must begin at the middle and elementary school levels. At the college level, remedial courses are needed to help disadvantaged students get up to speed.

A second major determinant of persistence behavior is the student's family or support structure. In fact, students from single parent or broken homes—meaning parents were either divorced, separated or never married—were five percentage points more likely to stopout than students from two parent homes, even after controlling for family income. This is especially relevant since nearly two-thirds (64 percent) of African-American children live in single parent homes. While additional analysis would be needed to discover exactly how college outcomes and the student's home environment are related, it seems apparent that the family structure has important implications for well-being beyond the childhood years. Mentoring programs and other means of offering additional support to African-American students, be it through parents, teachers, or others concerned adults, could be effective ways to improve college persistence. Also, since students are most likely to stop out between the second and third year of college, the earlier college administrators can identify problems and offer appropriate interventions the more likely students are to persist.

While money does not appear to be as big a barrier to persistence and completion as it is for initial enrollment, need-based aid programs, like the Pell grant should be expanded to insure that students with a desire to complete college have the means to do so.

Finally, without adequate information, even well-inteded policies are misguided. Due to the scarcity of data on African-American students attending HBCUs, the sample sizes used in empirical analysis tend to be small and often represent only a fraction of the 105 HBCUs in this country. Availability of data is tantamount to the ability of researchers to produce precise and reliable results that inform public policy. If we as a country are serious about strengthening the nation's historically black colleges and universities and addressing the challenges faced by African-American males at these and other postsecondary institutions, a detailed, longitudinal HBCU database is needed.

REFERENCES

Anonymous. 2007. "Black Student College Graduation Rates Inch Higher But a Large Racial Gap Persists." *Journal of Blacks in Higher Education*, no. 54. http://www.jbhe.com/preview/winter07preview.html

Wilson, Valerie R. 2006. "The Effect of Attending an HBCU on Persistence and Graduation Outcomes for African-American College Students." *The Review of Black Political Economy* 33(4): 11-52.

NOTES

[1] Source: U.S. Department of Commerce, Bureau of the Census, U.S. Census of Population, 1960; U.S. Census Bureau, *Current Population Survey*, March 2005.

[2] Source: http://nces.ed.gov/programs/coe/2006/section2/table.asp?tableID=475

[3] Degree-granting institutions are defined by the National Center for Education Statistics as postsecondary institutions that grant an associate's degree or higher and are eligible for Title IV federal financial aid.

[4] Source: U.S. Department of Education, National Center of Education Statistics, Integrated Postsecondary Education Data System (IPEDS), 2004.

[5] Source: Journal of Blacks in Higher Education (Winter 2006/07).

[6] A discrete time hazard model is used to estimate the probability that a student will stop out of college for the first time in any semester, given that they have been enrolled for each previous semester. An instrumental variable estimator is used to identify the "pure" effect of attending an HBCU apart from other factors associated with both HBCU attendance and persistence behavior. Complete tables including the estimates discussed in this essay are presented in the Appendix to this chapter. The reference for the full analysis is Wilson (2006).

[7] While this is a small sample size, the nature of the population and question being analyzed automatically limits the number of observations available from nationally representative samples. Ehrenberg & Rothstein (1994) only had a sample size of 638, with 298 coming from HBCUs.

Table 1

Means of Explanatory Variables for Fall 1995
(Standard Errors in Parentheses)

VARIABLES	Total (N = 469)	TWI (N = 323)	HBCU (N = 146)
Male	0.35	0.37	0.29
Family Income	$41,495	$43,552	$36,943
	(51,477)	(58,144)	(31,859)
Father's Education			
Less than High School	0.04	0.04	0.04
High School Graduate	0.40	0.40	0.40
Some College (Less than Bachelor's Degree)	0.15	0.14	0.16
Bachelor's Degree or Beyond	0.33	0.34	0.33
Single Parent/Broken Home	0.45	0.41	0.51
Mother's Education			
Less than High School	0.03	0.03	0.02
High School Graduate	0.41	0.43	0.38
Some College (Less than Bachelor's Degree)	0.20	0.20	0.21
Bachelor's Degree or Beyond	0.34	0.32	0.39
Took the SAT	0.97	0.98	0.94
SAT Score	792	813	741
	(187)	(186)	(181)
High School Grades Available	0.90	0.92	0.87
High School Grades			
A to A- (100 - 90)	0.20	0.24	0.12
A- to B (89 - 85)	0.36	0.35	0.40
B to B- (84 - 80)	0.16	0.18	0.11
B- to C (79 -75)	0.14	0.11	0.21
C to C- (74 - 70)	0.03	0.03	0.03
C- to D- (69 -60)	0.01	0.01	

Table 2

Probability of HBCU Attendance
(Marginal Effects)

	Linear Probability)
Male	-0.043
	(0.046)
Family Income: 25th Percentile (<$16,100)	0.004
	(0.075)
Family Income: 50th Percentile ($16,100 - $31,500)	-0.099
	(0.069)
Family Income: 75th Percentile ($31,500 - $53,750)	-0.043
	(0.064)
Father High School Grad	-0.136
	(0.112)
Father has Some College (No Bachelor's Degree)	-0.102
	(0.123)
Father has Bachelor's Degree or Higher	-0.131
	(0.118)
Single Parent/Broken Home	0.116
	(0.046)*
Mother High School Grad	0.156
	(0.084)
Mother has Some College (No Bachelor's Degree)	0.247
	(0.091)**
Mother has Bachelor's Degree or Higher	0.348
	(0.094)**
SAT Score/100	-0.043
	(0.014)**
Didn't take SAT or ACT	0.043
	(0.191)
High School GPA: 84 to 75	0.020
	(0.060)
High School GPA: 74 to 60	-0.220
	(0.127)
State Weekly Earnings in Mfg. Sector/1,000	0.320
	(0.361)
State Unemployment Rate	0.027
	(0.023)
Number of HBCUs in Home State	0.222
	(0.055)**
(Number of HBCUs in Home State)^2	-0.052
	(0.015)**
(Number of HBCUs in Home State)^3	0.003
	(0.001)**
Constant	0.062
	(0.344)
Person-Spell Records	2590
R-Squared	0.18
P-Value for Test of Joint Significance of Instruments	0.00

Robust Standard Errors in parentheses.
*Significant at 5%; ** Significant at 1%.

Full regression includes a constant term, and dummy variables for missing parental education, and missing
high school GPA.

Table 3

Probability of First Stopout
(Marginal Effects)

HBCU	-0.093
	(0.078)
Spring 1996	0.093
	(0.020)**
Fall 1996	0.005
	(0.016)
Spring 1997	0.073
	(0.021)**
Fall 1997	-0.009
	(0.015)
Spring 1998	0.029
	(0.019)
Fall 1998	-0.026
	(0.013)*
Male	-0.034
	(0.031)
HBCU * Male	0.129
	(0.097)
Family Income: 25th Percentile (<$16,100)	-0.044
	(0.021)*
Family Income: 50th Percentile ($16,100 - $31,500)	-0.023
	(0.020)
Family Income: 75th Percentile ($31,500 - $53,750)	-0.036
	(0.018)*
Father High School Grad	-0.038
	(0.041)
Father has Some College (No Bachelor's Degree)	-0.064
	(0.044)
Father has Bachelor's Degree or Higher	-0.072
	(0.043)
Single Parent/Broken Home	0.045
	(0.016)**
Mother High School Grad	-0.035
	(0.060)
Mother has Some College (No Bachelor's Degree)	0.015
	(0.063)
Mother has Bachelor's Degree or Higher	-0.024
	(0.066)
SAT Score/100	-0.015
	(0.005)**
Didn't take SAT or ACT	0.013
	(0.073)
High School GPA: 84 to 75	0.056
	(0.018)**
High School GPA: 74 to 60	0.107
	(0.048)*
State Weekly Earnings in Mfg. Sector/1,000	-0.079
	(0.080)
State Unemployment Rate	0.009
	(0.006)
Person-term Records	2,590
N	469
R-squared	0.05

Robust Standard Errors in parentheses.
*Significant at 5%; ** Significant at 1%.

Full regression includes a constant term, and dummy variables for missing parental education, and missing high school GPA.

Table 4

Probability of Degree Completion Within Six Years
(Marginal Effects)

HBCU	0.883
	(0.543)
Male	0.016
	(0.102)
Male * HBCU	-0.165
	(0.276)
Family Income: 25th Percentile (<$16,100)	0.351
	(0.174)*
Family Income: 50th Percentile ($16,100 - $31,500)	0.236
	(0.173)
Family Income: 75th Percentile ($31,500 - $53,750)	0.383
	(0.174)*
HBCU * Family Income: 25th Percentile (<$16,100)	-0.833
	(0.547)
HBCU * Family Income: 50th Percentile ($16,100 - $31,500)	-0.639
	(0.595)
HBCU * Family Income: 75th Percentile ($31,500 - $53,750)	-1.137
	(0.589)
Father High School Grad	0.098
	(0.111)
Father has Some College (No Bachelor's Degree)	0.198
	(0.127)
Father has Bachelor's Degree or Higher	0.188
	(0.127)
Single Parent/Broken Home	-0.051
	(0.059)
Mother High School Grad	0.087
	(0.135)
Mother has Some College (No Bachelor's Degree)	-0.055
	(0.144)
Mother has Bachelor's Degree or Higher	0.090
	(0.149)
SAT Score/100	0.068
	(0.020)**
Didn't take SAT or ACT	0.216
	(0.195)
High School GPA: 84 to 75	-0.200
	(0.058)**
High School GPA: 74 to 60	-0.167
	(0.116)
State Weekly Earnings in Mfg. sector/1,000	0.305
	(0.350)
State Unemployment Rate	-0.015
	(0.024)
N	469
R-squared	0.04

Robust Standard Errors in parentheses.
*Significant at 5%; ** Significant at 1%.

Full regression includes a constant term, and dummy variables for missing parental education, and missing high school GPA.

ESSAY 6

Black Male Life Expectancy in the United States: A Multi-level Exploration of Causes

by Mercedes R. Carnethon, Ph.D.

A s one of the richest nations in the world, the United States enjoys many comforts, including a stable government and economy, a robust education system, and access to technology and health care. Not surprisingly, a nation's wealth is positively correlated with the life expectancy of its residents. Demographers project that a baby born today in the US can expect to live 77.85 years. Predictably, our ranking falls behind that of Luxemburg (78.9 years) and Norway (79.5 years), the two countries with a gross domestic product higher than ours.[1, 2] However, life expectancy estimations in the United States exemplify the "ecologic fallacy"—the belief that an association observed at the aggregate level applies to individuals.

Disparities in life expectancy along racial and socioeconomic lines are the result of complex social factors in our otherwise low mortality country. By highlighting the relatively shorter life expectancy of black men in our country, I advance the hypothesis that our social environment is a component, though not the sole cause, of shortened life expectancy in black men. In this essay, I describe the life expectancy of black men relative to white men, present data on disease-specific causes of the life expectancy disparity, and place the causes of these diseases on their broader social context.

WHICH U.S. RESIDENTS EXPERIENCE LONG LIVES?

Unfortunately, that question can easily be answered—not black men. Black men born in 2004 are projected to die six years sooner than their white counterparts, and seven years sooner than black women (Figure 1). In an analysis comparing years of potential life lost by black and white men with low (0 to 8 years) and high (13+ years) levels of education to that of black women with high levels of education, highly educated black men lost 8.1 years of life and white men lost an estimated 5.2 years of life. By comparison, black men with low levels of education lost 19.9 years of life, while white men lost 11.9 potential years of life.[3]

Black men have higher mortality rates than white men at every age (Table 1). It is only among adults older than age 65, where this disparity begins to decline. This "survivor effect", demonstrates that if one can survive to old age, the mortality rate is roughly equivalent. According to estimates generated in 2004, white and black men who live to age 65 can be expected to live 17.1 and 15.3 years longer, respectively.[4] While this observation is encouraging for a segment of our society, by definition this phenomenon only applies to that relatively small proportion of black men who exceed their life expectancy projections and live into older age.

Over time, life expectancy has increased for all persons living in the U.S. (Figure 2). Despite life expectancy gains in the aggregate, the gap in life expectancy between blacks and whites has not narrowed with time. Between 1940 and 1998 excess mortality in blacks (men and women combined) as compared with whites has ranged between 50,000 and 103,900. The greatest discrepancies of 103,900 and 96,800 were in 1990 and 1998, respectively.[5] Shifting the course of this public health crisis requires that we understand the causes of the disparity.

CAUSES OF THE LIFE EXPECTANCY DIFFERENTIAL

In 1991, *Time* magazine featured an article titled, "Why do blacks die young?"[6] Sixteen years later that question generates identical answers. On the macro level, our society is still plagued by subtle and overt discrimination that leads to unequal access to education, economic opportunity, housing, and health care. On a micro- or individual level, black men still engage in adverse health behaviors and have lifestyle characteristics associated with higher mortality. However, some proportion of the adverse health behaviors and lifestyle characteristics is influenced by socioeconomic opportunity and other macro-level correlates. Despite knowing that the causes and consequences of the

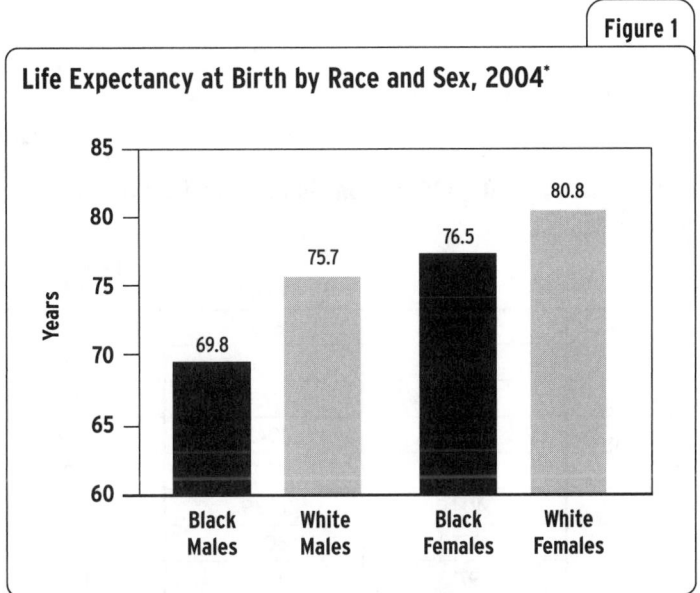

Figure 1

Life Expectancy at Birth by Race and Sex, 2004*

*Adapted from Minino, AM et al. Deaths: Preliminary Data for 2004.
National Vital Statistics Reports, 2006; 54: 1-49.

Table 1

Mortality Rates per 100,000 persons in Black and White Males by Age, 2004[*]

Age	Black	White	Ratio Black to White
<1	1404.1	629.1	2.23
1-4	50.4	28.8	1.75
5-14	26.4	17.9	1.47
15-24	165.8	104.2	1.59
25-34	259.7	129.1	2.01
35-44	404.0	232.9	1.73
45-54	967.3	507.2	1.91
55-64	1971.3	1072.1	1.84
65-74	3858.2	2624.0	1.47
75-84	7757.0	6484.0	1.20
Total[†]	**1281.7**	**949.9**	

[*]Adapted from Minino, AM et al. Deaths: Preliminary Data for 2004. *National Vital Statistics Reports*, 2006; 54: 1-49.
[†]Age-adjusted rate per 100,000.

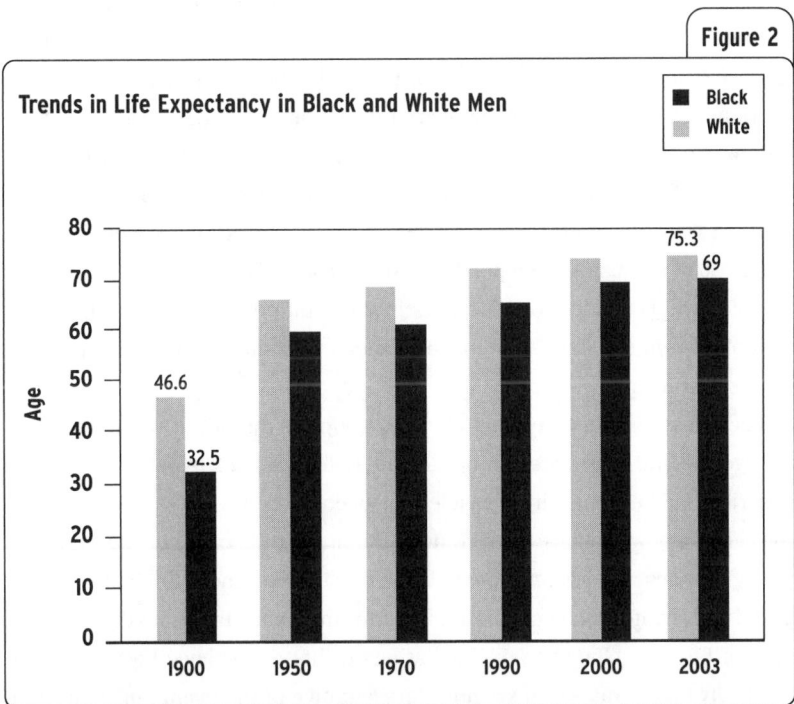

Figure 2

Trends in Life Expectancy in Black and White Men

■ Black
▨ White

Sources: Center for Disease Control and Prevention, National Center for Health Statistics, National Vital Statistics System, Grove RD. Vital Statistics Rate in the United States, 1940-1960. Washington, DC: US Government Printing Office, 1968. Hoyert DL, Heron M, Murphy SL, Kung HC. Deaths: Final Data for 2003. National Vital Statistics Reports. Vol 54 no. 13. Hyattsville, MD: National Center for Health Statistics, 2006.

black male life expectancy gap "then" and "now" have not changed, a renewed exploration is warranted, if only to call attention to the persistent disparity.

Leading Causes of Mortality

As an industrialized country, the U.S. has undergone the "epidemiologic transition" from infectious diseases and injuries as leading causes of death to chronic diseases causing the most overall deaths. Four out of five leading causes of death for all age, sex, and race groups in 2004 are chronic diseases (Table 2). In absolute numbers, the age-standardized death rates from heart disease and cancer (217.5 and 184.6 per 100,000 persons, respectively) account for half (50.1%) of the overall death rate of 801.1 per 100,000.[4] Of course the leading causes of death varies by age group, with accidents (36.4 per 100,000) and assaults (11.7 per 100,000) comprising 61% of mortality in 15 to 24 year olds and 28% of mortality in 25 to 44 year olds (accidents 33.6 per 100,000 and assault 8.5 per 100,000). Causes of death in older age (over age 65) largely reflects the numbers in the total population (with the addition of alzheimer's disease in place of accidents) since 73% of deaths occur in this age group.

These leading causes of death by age group are important when we examine age-specific death rates for black men. Referring back to Table 1 where we described higher mortality in black men as compared with white men across the age range, we can also see (column 3) that the ratio of the black: white disparity changes with age. Although the greatest excess mortality in black compared with white men is most prominent for infant mortality, death in the first year of life is excluded from calculations of life expectancy because of the markedly higher rates that are not representative of the overall life expectancy experience. After the first year, the life expectancy difference is most pronounced for men aged 25 to 34 and 45 to 64 years old. Investigating the leading causes of death by race and age can shed light on the role of specific causes of death on the life expectancy differential.

Violence in the black community receives considerable media attention. Homicide is estimated to account for 0.9 years (14%) of the life expectancy difference between black and white men,[7] occurring predominately in the younger ages. Even when sociodemographic factors such as age, employment status, income, education, and marital status held constant (through statisti-

Table 2

Leading Causes of Death, All Races and both Sexes, 2004*

TOP 5 CAUSES OF DEATH	AGE CATEGORY			
	All Ages	15 to 24	25 to 44	45 to 64
1	Heart Disease	Accidents	Accidents	Cancer
2	Cancer	Assault (Homicide)	Cancer	Heart Disease
3	Stroke	Suicide	Heart Disease	Accidents
4	Chronic Lower Respiratory Disease	Cancer	Suicide	Diabetes
5	Accidents	Heart Disease	Assault(Homicide)	Stroke

*Adapted from Minino, AM et al. Deaths: Preliminary Data for 2004.
National Vital Statistics Reports, 2006; 54: 1-49.

cal adjustment) between black and white men, black men are over five times more likely to be victims of homicide than white men.[8] Homicide accounts for 31 to 51 percent of mortality in 15 to 34 year old black men; corresponding proportions among white men are seven to ten percent. While homicide drops out of the top ten causes of death for white men older than 44 years, it remains in the top ten for another decade of life in black men, ending up as the fifth leading cause of death for black men of all ages.[9]

Heart disease and cancer are the two leading causes of death in all race-sex strata, and are disproportionately responsible for death in the middle and older ages. Unlike homicide, however, non-fatal heart disease occurs in roughly equivalent proportion in black and white men. According to the National Health and Nutrition Examination Survey conducted from 1988 to 1994, the age adjusted prevalence of self-reported heart disease was approximately 12% in black men and 14% in white men over age 40 years.[10] Nevertheless, the life expectancy differential attributable to heart disease is the largest of all at 1.2 years (19%).[7] By contrast, age-adjusted rates of cancer at the three most common sites—prostate, lung, and colorectal are more common among black men (Figure 3). The greatest disparity in cancer development is for prostate cancer. Prostate cancer is a benign disease in older white men, but an aggressive and deadly disease in black men who are often afflicted at younger ages and are diagnosed at later stages.[11] Thus, it is plausible that the one year life expectancy differential due to cancer (16%) is largely attributable to prostate cancer. Mortality differences, in the absence of varying rates of illness, suggest one of the following: more deadly (virulent) disease, later stage of diagnosis or less aggressive therapies to treat disease.

THE SOCIAL ENVIRONMENT

When asked to speculate about why black men have shorter life expectancy than other race-sex groups, most people quickly respond that violence is the root of the problem. Upon continued probing, some identify higher mortality rates from heart disease and cancer in black men. Each answer is correct and applies directly to the mortality experience at extreme ends of the

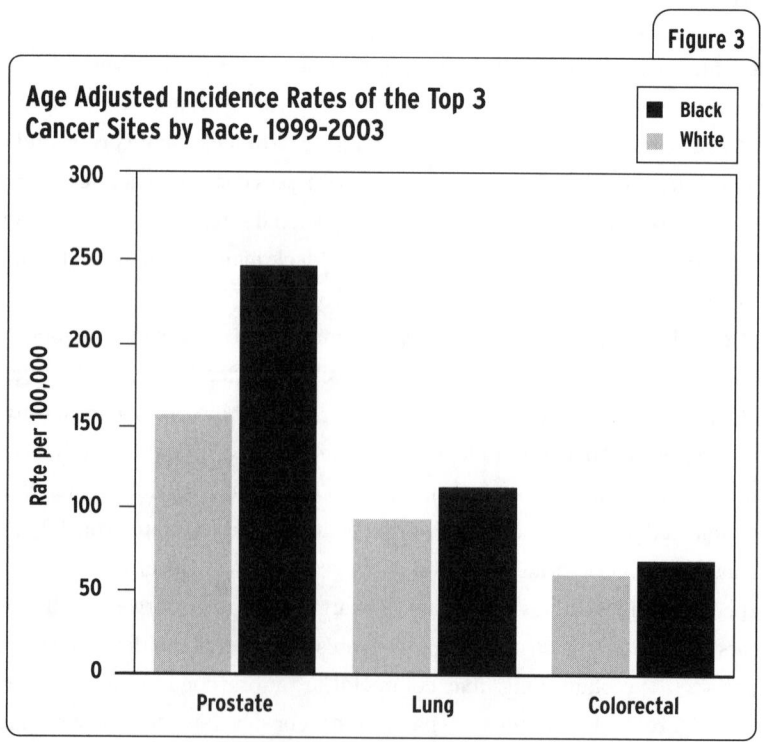

Figure 3

Age Adjusted Incidence Rates of the Top 3 Cancer Sites by Race, 1999-2003

■ Black
░ White

age spectrum. However, both answers ignore the contribution of the broader social environment to this mortality disparity. Using the examples of violence and heart disease, I will make the case for the undeniable role of the social environment on the life expectancy differential.

Violence: Contribution of the Social Environment

The February 5, 2007 headline in the New York Times reads: "In New Orleans, Dysfunction Fuels Cycle of Killing".[12] This article is a striking commentary on the upheaval in New Orleans stemming from the devastation caused by Hurricane Katrina. Certainly, New Orleans had problems prior to the storm's arrival in September 2005, but in the 17 months since, the city experienced 161 homicides in 2006 and an additional 18 before the end of February 2007. Based on these statistics, New Orleans has the nation's highest per capita murder rate.

The acute situation in the aftermath of Hurricane Katrina is a microcosm of the social experience of many black men in the United States. Beginning with instability in the family, many young black men lack role models in their home. Instead of modeling themselves after men who are adequately employed and able to provide support for their families, these young men turn outside the home and emulate men who have the trappings of success and who are able to promise them similar spoils. An example cited in New Orleans is that young boys can earn $30 for serving as bicycle lookouts during drug transactions or up to $1000 for helping transport drugs. New Orleans is no different from other cities where the violence often surrounds the drug trade. Apathy towards the violence is exemplified in the opening quote of the article: "When the body was brought out, the two little boys did not stop chewing their sticky blue candy or swigging from their pop bottles."[12] These scenes play out in urban centers nationwide where violence is commonplace and residents feel powerless to react.

A prevailing theory is that neighborhood characteristics such as economic deprivation and social disorganization, including racial/ethnic segregation, explain homicide differentials across race groups. The influence of economic deprivation and the lack of access to material goods and the desperation this breeds is clear. But I argue that the more salient concern is low education, which can influence health and safety in a number of ways. Education buys economic opportunity through access to higher paying jobs. With a better job and more money one can hope to move out of from the economically and socially segregated high crime neighborhoods. Educated persons are able to make informed decisions about their health and welfare, a requirement for reducing mortality from chronic diseases. Unfortunately, segregated neighborhoods often have poorer performing schools with fewer resources available to motivate and educate students.

As bleak as the social situation is, it would be a disservice to our community to suggest that the problem of homicide cannot be overcome, and that life expectancy will forever lag behind white men. There are examples of low income communities where crime rates are low or have gone down. For example, in Hispanic communities with a large proportion of foreign born residents, cultural norms that promote strong social relationships between residents and regulate the activities of youth can successfully limit access to alcohol and illegal drugs.[8] Those same norms could be adopted by a cohesive black community committed to protecting the future of its youth. Other equally insurmountable tasks, such as earning equal rights and the right to vote have been achieved through the leadership of a handful of charismatic activists.

Heart Disease: A Disease of Lifestyle

In recent decades, the medical establishment has made considerable advancements identifying the causes of cardiovascular disease. As a result, persons with heart disease are living longer and deaths rates have declined. Campaigns to educate the public about eliminating or controlling risk factors for heart disease have been successful. Further, the development of prevention and treatment guidelines for health providers has resulted in more aggressive efforts to treat the risk factors underlying heart disease. Not surprisingly, these measures have not reached all segments of the population.

Four major risk factors, cigarette smoking, diabetes, high cholesterol and high blood pressure (i.e., hypertension) are present in nearly 90% of cases of fatal and non-fatal coronary heart disease.[13] Some factors, such as levels of "good" cholesterol (i.e., high-density lipoprotein) are more favorable in black men as compared with white men. However, others, namely hypertension, are over-represented among black men and account for an estimated 15% of the life expectancy differential between blacks and whites of both sexes.[14] Based on reports indicating that these risk factors are similarly associated with fatal heart disease in black and white men,[15] reducing or controlling these risk factors should be a primary strategy to reduce the development of disease and subsequent mortality.

Referring to heart disease as a "lifestyle" disease implies that it can be controlled and reduced through the adoption of healthy behaviors. Decades of research have shown us that men (and women) who do not smoke, are more physically active, leaner, and have diets rich in vegetables, fruits, and lean meats have better health profiles than their sedentary and oftentimes overweight counterparts. Not only do healthy lifestyles protect against the development of disease, but a healthy lifestyle can mitigate complications from existing disease. The protective benefits of the lifestyle factors extend beyond heart disease, but are also hypothesized to protect against the development of certain cancers, and may boost the immune systems of persons suffering from human immunodeficiency virus (HIV) and other chronic conditions. Given the undeniable health benefits, why hasn't everyone adopted these lifestyle measures?

To begin, incorporating recommended health behaviors into one's lifestyle often assumes socioeconomic resources. Physical activity, for example, has far reaching benefits for a number of health conditions, but let's considers who is physically active and where they undertake their activity. A simple activity like walking is easier to engage in for persons living in neighborhoods where sidewalks and walking trails are present, maintained, and safe. Communities that are designed to be walkable—with accessible retail stores and public transportation, encourage residents to incorporate activity into their daily lifestyle. For persons with financial resources, flexible work schedules and childcare, joining an exercise facility is another option. There are many examples of predominately black communities that either do not have such physical resources or whose residents do not have the personal resources needed to join an exercise facility. Similar constraints apply to the adoption of other healthy lifestyle behaviors such as purchasing and preparing healthier foods. So, unfortunately, the most cost effective and palatable measures to reduce illness and death from heart disease (and other conditions) are not equally accessible in all neighborhoods.

Dr. Martin Luther King, Jr.'s oft-cited observation that "Of all forms of injustice, injustice in health care is the most shocking and inhumane",[16] can most clearly be illustrated by the disparity in mortality from heart disease. As stated earlier, the prevalence of heart disease does not differ in black and white men; but, it is more clearly fatal in black men. Consider the socioeconomic constraints on health care access experienced by many black men in the form of lack of private health insurance or insufficient insurance. Even when a black man enters our health care system for heart disease, research indicates that he is less likely to be offered a coronary bypass operation—a proven therapy for treating heart disease.[17]

Two sources of this disparity in procedures have been proposed. One, doctors offered this invasive surgery less often in blacks, possibly because blacks have more extensive co-existing disease such as diabetes or hypertension, which when poorly controlled could adversely influence the outcome of the bypass operation. It is equally likely that blacks are less likely to agree to undergo the procedure, due to mistrust of the medical care system or simply the uncertainty of the benefits of such a procedure. Neither possibility lays blame on maliciously "biased" physicians, but it does emphasize that in order for technological advancements to be enjoyed by all, efforts must be undertaken to control heart disease risk factors and to educate about the availability of aggressive, but proven treatments.

Preventive medicine is one of the most under-utilized tools we have to reduce and eliminate illness in the population. The individual can prevent disease by adopting healthy lifestyles and even greater success can be achieved if our health care system shifts its reimbursement strategies to pay for preventive health care.

In summary, unequal opportunity and treatment in our country has a long history that was not completely eliminated with the abolition of slavery or the civil rights movement. Tentacles of our history reach into the 20th century influencing not only blacks, but other minority groups, women, and those with lower socioeconomic status. Those factors most salient to the disparity in life expectancy include socioeconomic constraints on education and economic opportunity, the health care environment, and housing disparities experienced by black residents. Each of these factors is intertwined and contributes directly to the mortality experience in black men.

CONCLUSIONS AND RECOMMENDATIONS

While the underlying causes of the life expectancy differential between black and white men are rooted in our social environment, the problem is too complex to place blame solely on society or the individual. In that same vein, no single agency can solve the problem. Rather, collaboration from a number of disciplines is required. Led by academia and government, epidemiologists and demographers should identify and describe the problem and sociologists and other social scientists should place the disparity in its proper social context. Social workers, educators, and the medical establishment should use this information to propose and initiate novel solutions. Once we work together to generate multi-faceted solutions, we can begin to close the gap in life expectancy between black and white men. Perhaps our goal over the next few decades should be to disprove the "ecologic fallacy" that currently exists for life expectancy, and ensure that all segments of our society experience the long, healthy lives enjoyed by the U.S. as a whole.

Views expressed in this article are those of the author and do not reflect Northwestern University.

REFERENCES

1.Wikipedia. List of countries by GDP (PPP) per capita: Found at: http://en.wikipedia.org/wiki/List_of_countries_by_GDP_(PPP)_per_capita.

2.Rank Order-Life Expectancy at Birth. 2007 vol: Found at: https://www.cia.gov/cia/publications/factbook/rankorder/2102rank.html.

3.Crimmins EM, Saito Y. Trends in healthy life expectancy in the United States, 1970-1990: gender, racial, and educational differences. *Soc Sci Med* 2001;52:1629-41.

4.Minino AM, Heron MP, Smith BL. Deaths: preliminary data for 2004. *Natl Vital Stat Rep* 2006;54:1-49.

5.Hoyert DL, Anderson RN. Age-adjusted death rates: trend data based on the year 2000 standard population. *Natl Vital Stat Rep* 2001;49:1-6.

6.Gorman C. Why do blacks die young? *Time* 1991;138:50-52.

7.Influence of homicide on racial disparity in life expectancy—United States, 1998. *MMWR Morb Mortal Wkly Rep* 2001;50:780-3.

8.Krueger PM, Bond Huie SA, Rogers RG, Hummer RA. Neighbourhoods and homicide mortality: an analysis of race/ethnic differences. *J Epidemiol Community Health* 2004;58:223-30.

9.Anderson RN, Smith BL. Deaths: leading causes for 2002. *Natl Vital Stat Rep* 2005;53:1-89.

10.Ford ES, Giles WH, Croft JB. Prevalence of nonfatal coronary heart disease among American adults. *American Heart Journal* 2000;139:371-377.

11.Odedina FT, Ogunbiyi JO, Ukoli FA. Roots of prostate cancer in African-American men. *J Natl Med Assoc* 2006;98:539-43.

12.Nossiter A, Drew C. In New Orleans, Dysfunctoin Fuels Cycle of Killing. *New York Times*. National Desk Late Edition ed. New York; 2007:1.

13.Greenland P, Knoll MD, Stamler J et al. Major risk factors as antecedents of fatal and nonfatal coronary heart disease events. *Jama* 2003;290:891-7.

14.Wong MD, Shapiro MF, Boscardin WJ, Ettner SL. Contribution of major diseases to disparities in mortality. *N Engl J Med* 2002;347:1585-92.

15.Carnethon MR, Lynch EB, Dyer AR et al. Comparison of risk factors for cardiovascular mortality in black and white adults. *Arch Intern Med* 2006;166:1196-202.

16.Smith SC, Jr, Clark LT, Cooper RS et al. Discovering the Full Spectrum of Cardiovascular Disease: Minority Health Summit 2003: Report of the Obesity, Metabolic Syndrome, and Hypertension Writing Group. *Circulation* 2005;111:e134-139.

17.Lucas FL, DeLorenzo MA, Siewers AE, Wennberg DE. Temporal Trends in the Utilization of Diagnostic Testing and Treatments for Cardiovascular Disease in the United States, 1993-2001. *Circulation* 2006;113:374-379.

How are the Children?
Foster Care and African-American Boys

by William C. Bell

"The test of the morality of a society is what it does for its children."

– *Dietrich Bonhoeffer*

A new report from the United Nations and UNICEF recently ranked the United States and Great Britain as number 20 and 21 respectively out of 21 countries in the industrialized world with regards to the quality of life and well-being of its children and youth. UNICEF examined 40 factors, such as poverty, deprivation, education, health, relationships and risky behavior and placed the U.S. and Great Britain at the bottom of a list of 21 developed nations. In almost all categories, poorer nations such as Poland and the Czech Republic fared better than the United States.[1]

"I think we know from history in the U.S.," says David Parker, of UNICEF, "that it's not necessarily how the welfare is provided but the nature of the support. One of the key things is that the role of government is important, but the entire society must have at its heart the idea of improving child well-being." [2]

We know that in almost all categories of well-being, poor children and children of color tend to do worse than their counterparts in the general population. Therefore, one question that we must consider in America is, how are children of color faring, specifically young black males?

In a 2006 article in the *Journal of Adolescence*, authors Scott & Davis summarized what it means to be young, black and male in American society today:

"It means to be a member of a group who is the disproportionate victim of homicide. It means to be a member of a group whose rate of suicide is increasing astronomically in comparison to other populations. It means to be a member of a group whose labor force status is declining enormously as evidenced by high rates of joblessness. And for those in foster care, it means being a member of a group with poorer life outcomes (e.g. incarceration, education, employment)." [3]

Clearly, being a young, black male in America today means facing significant challenges as well as daunting odds. As we explore these issues as a society and try to identify solutions, one of the critical questions to ask ourselves is: "How are we preparing our nation's children, especially those in most need, to be productive participants in the process of helping America regain its place of prominence in the world?"

The Most Vulnerable

One of the most vulnerable child populations in this country is children who are in foster care. Each year approximately 300,000 children are removed from their birth parents and placed in the child welfare system due to harmful conditions (i.e. neglect, abuse, or parental substance abuse, incarceration and/or death). Every year in America, over 500,000 children live in foster care in the United States. Of those, 57% are children of color.[4] What is especially concerning is that: (1) there is an increasingly disproportionate number of children, youth and families of color in the child welfare system; and (2) there is substantial evidence that minority children who enter the child welfare system are at greater risk for poorer outcomes than their white counterparts. In nearly every state, African-American children are represented in foster care in higher percentages than in the state's general population. A review of all the studies conducted over the last fifteen years found that "children of color and their families experience poorer outcomes and receive fewer services than their Caucasian counterparts". [5]

Disproportionate representation among children of color continues to be a chronic problem despite studies that report no significant differences in maltreatment rates between different racial and ethnic groups.[6] Nationally and in 46 states, the percentage of the foster care population that is comprised by children of African heritage is between 1 ½ times to 3 ½ times more than the percentage of African-American children in the overall population.[7]

"Being African American presents a threefold set of challenges for children in foster care. First, they suffer the racial disparities that still linger in our society. Second, they traverse through childhood with little appropriate guidance and support. And third, they do not always have a clear connection to the functional knowledge, understanding and appreciation of their African-American culture and heritage.

The Foster Care Reality

On average, once a child enters foster care, he or she experiences one or two placement changes every year. Understandably, moving from home to home without a permanent family takes a toll on a child's emotional well-being and overall health. The majority of children who stay in foster care until they "age out" at 18 years of age, are unprepared to enter society and lack the necessary family and community supports and life skills for long-term stability and success.

In 2004, Casey Family Programs, the largest operating foundation focused on foster care in America, completed a comprehensive study of foster care alumni in the Northwest and found that over 54% of alumni had experienced one or more mental health disorders, such as depression, social phobia or panic syndrome. In addition, over 25% of alumni had post-traumatic stress disorder within the last year, which is *twice* the rate of U.S. war veterans. [8]

In addition to increased mental health issues, children in foster care also experience additional challenges with educational achievement – especially when changing schools once or twice every year. The Chapin Hall study of Chicago Public School youth found that 15-year old students in foster care were half as likely to graduate than their peers, and 55% were likely to drop out and 10% to be incarcerated prior to graduation from high school.[9] For those youth in foster care who do graduate from high school and go on to college, only 3% graduate from college.[10]

Upon leaving foster care without permanent family connections and community supports, youth struggle to establish stability in their adult lives. The Northwest Alumni Study reported that one-third of alumni had household incomes at or below the poverty level, which is three times the national poverty rate. One-third also had no health insurance, which is double the national rate, and one in five experienced homelessness.[11]

Black Males In Foster Care

Given the poor overall outcomes for children in foster care, black males seem to be among the most vulnerable within that population, but there is limited national data available by ethnicity. We do know that for those youth who age out of foster care when they reach 18 or 21 years old, many become involved with the criminal justice system. For example, in one study of three states in the Midwest where 57% of the participants were African-American, 28% of the young adults reported being arrested, 12% reported being convicted of a crime, and nearly one-fifth reported being incarcerated subsequent to their first interview.[12]

One study conducted on the outcomes of black males transitioning from foster care highlighted the negative social situations they experienced. Over 40% of the black male participants responded "almost always" or "always" concerning the frequency to which police, people they did not know and white people thought they were "doing something wrong." Over 60% of participants responded "sometimes" or "almost always" concerning the frequency to which white people locked their car doors when they passed and sales people followed them when entering a store.

What Can We Do?

The majority of American citizens are not aware of the current challenges that some of our most vulnerable children face, especially African American male children in foster care. But we must begin to recognize that the challenges that these youth face are merely a window into the bigger problem we need to confront in order to more effectively support all children in this country.

As we look ahead, we know there is no silver bullet, but across time and history, when confronted with inequality, American families and communities have proven that by joining together, positive, national change is possible.

To help catalyze and support this national change, the Alliance for Racial Equity which was created by the Casey foundations and the Center for the Study of Social Policy, recently joined with national experts to examine and develop a "theory of change" for America's child welfare system. The six critical levers of this theory of change include: (1) Policy change and finance reform; (2) Research, evaluation and data-driven decision making; (3) Youth, parent and community partnership; (4) Building public will and strategic communications; (5) Human service workforce development; and (6) Practice change (site-based implementation). Moving forward, Casey Family Programs, together with our partners, will continue to lead change through a relentless national effort to improve outcomes for children and families of color in foster care in this country.

But perhaps more importantly, as citizens, we need to ask ourselves some profound questions about how our children are being treated and demand change for the future. Child well-being is a community and societal concern that requires shared responsibility. Protecting and ensuring a better life for every vulnerable child in America must become this nation's top priority.

As we consider the findings from reports such as the UNICEF Child Well-Being Report, we must not simply get lost in the notion that other countries are more serious about the health and well-being of their most vulnerable children than we are here in America. We must see this as a call to action to change the standard that we apply to caring for vulnerable children.

There is really only one standard that will produce lasting change in the lives of America's most vulnerable children and that is "the standard of your own". Simply put, "If it is not good enough for your own children, then it is not good enough for any vulnerable child in America".

SOURCES

Quote: Dietrich Bonhoeffer

(February 4, 1906 – April 9, 1945) German Lutheran pastor, theologian and leader in the German resistance movement against Nazism. For his anti-Hitler protests, he was arrested in March 1943, imprisoned and eventually hanged, just before the end of the Second World War in Europe.

Casey-CSSP Alliance for Racial Equity, *Race Matters Toolkit, Fact Sheet*: Racial Disproportionality in the Child Welfare System: An Analysis of Embedded Inequities" (Baltimore: Annie E. Casey Foundation).

Courtney, M.E., Barth, R.P., Berrick, J.D. Brooks, D., Needell, B., & Park, L. (1996). Race and child welfare services; Past research and future directions. *Child Welfare*, p.75, 99-137.

Harvey, A.R., Loughney, G.K. & Moore, J. (2002). A Model Program for African American Children in the Foster Care System *Journal of Health & Social Policy* (The Hayworth Press, Inc.) 16(1-2), p. 195-206

National Center on Child Abuse and Neglect, Children's Bureau. (1981). *Study Findings: National Study of the Incidence and Severity of Child Abuse and Neglect.* Washington, DC: U.S. Department of Health and Human Services.

Pecora, P. J., Kessler, R. K., Williams, J., O'Brien, K., Downs, A. C., English, D., White, C.R., Hiripi, E., Wiggins, T. & Holmes, K. (2005). *Improving family foster care: Findings from the Northwest Foster Care Alumni Study.* Seattle, WA: Casey Family Programs. www.casey.org

Scott, L.D., & Davis, L.E. (2006). Young, black and male in foster care: Relationship of negative social contextual experiences to factors relevant to mental health service delivery. *Journal of Adolescence,* 29(5): 721-736

Sedlak, Andrea J. (1991). *National Incidence and Prevalence of Child Abuse and Neglect: 1988.* (revised report) Rockville, MD: Westat.

Sedlak, Andrea J. and Broadhurst, Diane D. (1996).*Third National Incidence Study of Child Abuse and Neglect.* Rockville, MD: Westat.

Smithgall, C.L., Gladden, R.M., Howard, E., Goerge, R.M., & Courtney, M.C. (2004). *Educational experiences of children in out-of-home care.* Chicago, IL: University of Chicago, Chapin Hall Center for Children, p.28.

UNICEF Innocenti Research Centre Report Card 7 (2007). *An Overview of Child Well Being in Rich Countries.*p 2-34. Gifford, Rob (February 15, 2007). National Public Radio summary "UNICEF's Worst Countries for Kids." http://www.npr.org/templates/story/story.php?storyID=7407245

U.S. Department of Health and Human Services, Administration for Children and Families, Children's Bureau. (2006). *The AFCARS report No. 13: Preliminary FY 2005 esti-mates as of September 2006.* Washington DC: U.S. Department of Health and Human Services, 2005.

NOTES

[1] UNICEF Innocenti Research Centre Report Card 7 (2007). *An Overview of Child Well Being in Rich Countries.*p 2-34.

[2] Gifford, Rob (February 15, 2007). National Public Radio summary "UNICEF's Worst Countries for Kids." http://www.npr.org/templates/story/story.php?storyID=7407245

[3] Scott, L.D., & Davis, L.E. (2006). Young, black and male in foster care: Relationship of negative social contextual experiences to factors relevant to mental health service delivery. Journal of Adolescence, 29(5): 721-736

[4] U.S. Department of Health and Human Services, Administration for Children and Families, Children's Bureau. (2006). The AFCARS report No. 13: Preliminary FY 2005 estimates as of September 2006. Washington DC: U.S. Department of Health and Human Services, 2005.

[5] Courtney, M.E., Barth, R.P., Berrick, J.D. Brooks, D., Needell, B., & Park, L. (1996). Race and child welfare services; Past research and future directions. Child Welfare, p.75, 99-137.

[6] Hill, R. B. (2006). *Synthesis of Research on Disproportionality in Child Welfare: An Update.* Washington, DC: The Casey-CSSP Alliance for Racial Equity and the Center for the Study of Social Policy. http://www.cssp.org/major_initiatives/racialEquity; National Center on Child Abuse and Neglect, Children's Bureau. (1981). *Study Findings: National Study of the Incidence and Severity of Child Abuse and Neglect.* Washington, DC: U.S. Department of Health and Human Services. Sedlak, Andrea J. (1991). *National Incidence and Prevalence of Child Abuse and Neglect: 1988.* (revised report) Rockville, MD: Westat,.; Sedlak, Andrea J. and Broadhurst, Diane D. (1996).*Third National Incidence Study of Child Abuse and Neglect.* Rockville, MD: Westat.

[7] Casey-CSSP Alliance for Racial Equity, *Race Matters Toolkit, Fact Sheet*: Racial Disproportionality in the Child Welfare System: An Analysis of Embedded Inequities" (Baltimore: Annie E. Casey Foundation).

[8] Pecora, P. J., Kessler, R. K., Williams, J., O'Brien, K., Downs, A. C., English, D., White, C.R., Hiripi, E., Wiggins, T. & Holmes, K. (2005). *Improving family foster care: Findings from the Northwest Foster Care Alumni Study.* Seattle, WA: Casey Family Programs. www.casey.org

[9] Smithgall et al.(2004), p.28

[10] Pecora, et al. (2005). The Casey Family Programs NW Alumni Study.

[11] *Id.*

[12] Gender but not ethnic breakdowns were reported. See Courtney, M. E., Dworsky, A., Ruth, G., Keller, T., Havlicek, J., and Bost, N. (2005). *Midwest Evaluation of the Adult Functioning of Former Foster Youth: Outcomes at Age 19.* Chicago: Chapin Hall Center for Children at the University of Chicago, pp. 60-61.

The Battle Over Affirmative Action: Legal Challenges and Outlook

by Barbara R. Arnwine, J.D.[1]

"There are those who say we can stop now, America is a color-blind society. But it isn't there yet. There are those who say we have a level playing field, but we don't yet. There are those who say that all you need is to climb up on your bootstraps, but there are too many Americans who don't have boots, much less bootstraps."

Colin Powell, May 25, 1996

I n 1964, Dr. Martin Luther King, Jr. called on a nation to unite against oppression and injustice. His message of collaborative problem-solving reminded Americans that racism is a societal ill, shared equally by all members of a nation. Honoring his vision, large segments of society came together to promote legislation and initiatives designed to end discrimination and to strive for true inclusiveness. In this environment, affirmative action was born.[2] Affirmative action was meant to survive only so long as needed to right the wrongs of the past and create a truly equal society. Thirty years later, Colin Powell reminded us that we are far still from accomplishing that goal.

THE HISTORY OF AFFIRMATIVE ACTION

President Lyndon Johnson was the first to use the term "affirmative action" in a 1965 Executive Order requiring federal contractors to "take *affirmative action* to ensure that applicants are employed, and that employees are treated during employment, without regard to their race, creed, color, or national origin."[3] In a historic commencement speech at Howard University in that same year, President Johnson explained why affirmative action is imperative for achieving a free and equal society:

> Freedom is the right to share, share fully and equally, in American society—to vote, to hold a job, to enter a public place, to go to school. It is the right to be treated in every part of our national life as a person equal in dignity and promise to all others. But freedom is not enough. You do not wipe away the scars of centuries by saying: Now you are free to go where you want, and do as you desire, and choose the leaders you please. You do not take a person who, for years, has been hobbled by chains and liberate him, bring him up to the starting line in a race and then say, "you are free to compete with all the others," and still justly believe that you have been completely fair. *Thus it is not enough just to open the gates of opportunity. All our citizens must have the ability to walk through those gates.* This is the next and the more profound stage of the battle for civil rights. We seek not just freedom but opportunity. We seek not just legal equity but human ability, not just equality as a right and a theory but equality as a fact and equality as a result.[4]

In the forty years since that historic speech, civil rights legislation, court decisions and an evolving national commitment to equality have begun to open the gates of opportunity to all, and affirmative action programs have helped many citizens walk through those gates. Both private and public institutions have implemented various types of race-conscious affirmative action measures, primarily in the contexts of education, employment, and government contracting. Some of these programs are intended to remedy past discrimination, while others are aimed at promoting diversity and inclusiveness. Across the board, these measures have brought our nation closer to realizing the freedom envisioned by President Johnson and idealized in our Constitution.

For decades, however, these affirmative action programs have been the subject of controversy. Opponents argue that these measures are tantamount to unlawful preferences, quotas, and reverse discrimination. Traditionally, opponents waged the battle over affirmative action in the courts, challenging publicly-sponsored race-conscious measures as antithetical to Constitutional equal rights principles. The U.S. Supreme Court has settled on a middle ground, approving many forms of government affirmative action, but evaluating the validity of specific programs with a "strict scrutiny" test.[5] In practical terms, this means that a government-sponsored, race-conscious affirmative action program will survive only if it is absolutely necessary to further a "compelling interest" of the state—usually, an interest in promoting diversity or righting past discrimination. In addition, it has to be "narrowly tailored," meaning, for example, that it is flexible, contains an end or renewal date and does not overburden the rights of third parties. Despite such strict limitation on race-conscious diversity measures, opponents of affirmative action are not satisfied, and, over the past decade, they have sought to move the battle from the courtroom into the court of public opinion.

One of the now-favored tools of these opposition groups is the ballot referendum. In California, Washington, and Michigan, opponents took the battle directly to the voters and succeeded in passing ballot initiatives that outlaw certain forms of affirmative action. At the helm of this anti-affirmative action movement is Ward Connerly, a well-funded and politically-connected former member of the University of California's Board of Regents, who is widely recognized as the architect of the three successful state ballot initiatives.[6]

Connerly spearheaded the first state constitutional campaign to outlaw affirmative action in his home state of California. In 1996, 54 percent of the voters approved California's Proposition 209, the so-called "California Civil Rights Initiative" that amended the state constitution to provide that "[t]he state shall not discriminate against, or grant preferential treatment to any individual or group on the basis of race, sex, color, ethnicity, or national origin in the operation of public employment, public education, or public contracting."[7] This deceptively equalizing language appears innocuous—even positive—at first glance, yet, in practice its supporters have argued that it prohibits California state and local schools, colleges, universities, employers, and contracting agencies from engaging in almost all types of race-conscious affirmative action designed to promote diversity and redress past discrimination.

Following Proposition 209's success, Connerly formed the self-styled "American Civil Rights Coalition" to take his cause nationwide.[8] The ACRC moved on to Washington and Michigan to promote substantially similar ballot initiatives that would end government-sponsored affirmative action in those states.[9] In 1998, Washington voters passed Initiative 200,[10] which was modeled after California's Proposition 209. Most recently, in November 2006, Michigan voters passed Proposal 2006-02, also modeled after Proposition 209.[11] A group of Michigan citizens have since mounted a challenge to Proposal 2, asserting that it "run[s] afoul of core Fourteenth Amendment principles."[12] Emboldened by his successes, Ward Connerly has announced that ACRC is forming "exploratory committees in Arizona, Colorado, Missouri, Nebraska, Nevada, Oregon, South Dakota, Utah and Wyoming" to determine whether to launch ballot measure campaigns in those states as well.[13]

Even where voters have not attempted to ban affirmative action through ballot initiatives, the courts have constrained government's ability to redress past discrimination and promote diversity through race-conscious measures. In this article, we examine the impact of anti-affirmative action ballot initiatives in the targeted states and conclude with recommendations for what can be done to protect a vital tool in the struggle for equality.

IMPACT OF BALLOT REFERENDA BANNING AFFIRMATIVE ACTION

While the Michigan initiative is still in its development stage, the California and Washington bans on affirmative action have been around long enough to exhibit their pernicious effects. In some respects, the application of these initiatives remains an open question. Some argue that these ballot initiatives prohibit any kind of race-conscious activity by government entities in these states. However, many programs that expand opportunities for minorities without disadvantaging any group—such as data collection, targeted outreach efforts, recruitment and funding—should remain permissible despite these initiatives.[14] Furthermore, all of these ballot initiatives allow affirmative action plans that are required by federal law. The initiatives also do not bar preferences based on religion, age, economic disadvantage, sexual orienta-tion, or disability. Incorporating race-neutral and gender-neutral means to increase diversity in a student body or public workforce may be achieved by focusing on neutral factors such as socioeconomic or geographic indicators.[15] Lastly, these initiatives do not restrict *private* affirmative action plans; private schools and employers are still free to promote diversity through race-con-scious measures. Despite these limits on their reach, the initiatives have had devastating effects.

Real-World Effects In Contracting

When California's Proposition 209 went into effect, most affirmative action programs in public contracting simply required prime contractors either to make good faith efforts to meet goals for subcontracting to women- or minor-ity-owned businesses or to demonstrate that they had made outreach efforts to notify those businesses of bidding opportunities. After Proposition 209 was implemented, subcontracting opportunities were no longer distributed to the directory of registered women- and minority- owned businesses, leading to a sharp decline in the opportunities publicized to disadvantaged business enter-prises. Only a third of the certified minority businesses in California's trans-portation construction industry at the time of Proposition 209's passage in 1996 remain in business today.[16]

According to one report, "[c]ontract dollars awarded to businesses owned by minorities and women fell by 22% following the repeal of affirmative action programs in California," resulting "in a loss of at least $94.5 million per year to these businesses."[17] An August 2006 report by the Discrimination Research Center found that minority businesses experienced over a 50 percent reduc-tion of total awards and contracts from the California Department of Transportation after passage of Proposition 209.[18] The greatest impact was felt by African-American- and women-owned businesses.[19] In addition, the percentage of women who were registered, active apprentices in the skilled trades fell 40 percent after rising for several years before the passage of Proposition 209. Similarly, the percentage of African-American apprentices, which had also been increasing, dropped by 25 percent in 2004, and the per-centage of Native American apprentices dropped by 35 percent in 1996.[20]

Proposition 209 has prompted a series of lawsuits in California that have severely limited affirmative action efforts in public contracting. The first, *Hi-Voltage Wire Works, Inc. v. City of San Jose,* banned not only diversity goals but also outreach efforts targeted to minorities or women.[21] Although that decision applied only to contracting, it has been considered indicative of the courts' likely interpretation of similar programs in employment and education; accordingly, many California public entities have eliminated targeted outreach programs in those contexts as well. Another lawsuit has eliminated affirmative action in public contracting in Sacramento,[22] and challenges to San Francisco's contracting program are still being decided by the courts.[23]

Following Prop. 209's passage in California, voters in Washington followed suit and banned preferential treatment or discrimination based on race or gender. Consequently, Washington's Initiative 200 has limited the state's affirmative action efforts in public contracting. Efforts such as mandatory participation goals, price preferences or selection, and award of contracts or purchases based on race or gender are not allowed. However, outreach and recruitment of minority- and women-owned businesses (M/WBEs), voluntary participation goals, as well as monitoring and reporting of M/WBE utilization is permitted. Although some of the state's affirmative action efforts remain viable, in the past, the state consistently failed to meet its race- and gender-conscious contracting goals.[24] In fiscal year 1995, the state achieved its race and gender contracting goals in only two of the eight assessment areas, falling short in the remaining six. It was estimated that an additional $107,865,644 in state spending would have been directed to minority- and women-owned firms if state agencies had met all of their race- and gender-contracting goals.[25] One would expect that this trend has continued after the passage of I-200 and that M/WBEs are still facing obstacles competing for and winning contracts with the state.

These data underscore the benefits and necessity of ensuring the survival of minority-owned businesses, as they contribute both to their surrounding communities and to the American marketplace. It has been shown that minority-owned businesses are more likely to hire minority employees and reinvest in minority communities than nonminority-owned businesses.[26] Finally, in urban areas, an increase in the number of minority-owned businesses can lead to the renewal of previously blighted areas.[27]

Real-World Effects in Education

While the citizens of Florida and Texas have not yet voted to ban affirmative action, other actions have curtailed the use of race-conscious measures in those states. In 1999, Florida's Governor Jeb Bush issued an Executive Order to eliminate state-sponsored affirmative action programs. In 1996, the Fifth Circuit Court of Appeals declared that a Texas law school could not use race as a factor in admissions. While the Supreme Court later overruled *Hopwood v. Texas* in the 2003 Michigan cases, in the interim years, Texas responded to the case by reinstating new race-conscious measures at the option of state universities and maintaining the ten-percent plan. In response to the abandonment of affirmative action programs, California, Texas, and Florida—among the nation's most populous and diverse states—adopted "percent plans" for college admissions in an attempt to foster diversity in public higher education institutions.[28]

In 1999, the California Board of Regents approved a 4 percent plan that guarantees admission in the UC system to the top 4 percent of high school students who have successfully completed specific college preparatory coursework. Although the plan guarantees admission into one of the UC system's eight campuses, it does not ensure admission into the campus of the applicant's choice, nor does this and other "percent plans" apply to graduate and professional schools.

Since taking effect in 2001, California's 4 percent plan has resulted in "small increases in applications and admissions from racial minorities compared to when the race ban was initially imposed in 1997."[29] However, these modest increases do not make up for the proportionally higher number of racial minorities who applied and enrolled in the UC system before 1995, when the race ban was first announced.[30]

Several studies have found an alarming decline in the number of African-American, Hispanic, and Native American students enrolled in the UC system's premier flagship campuses. A recent Harvard study found that from 1995 to 2001, African-American enrollment at UC-Berkeley went from 6.7 percent to 3.9 percent.[31] At UCLA, black enrollment went from 7.4 percent to 3.4 percent during this same time period. Despite the implementation of California's percent plan, there has been no effective increase in the numbers of students of color at these premier institutions.

Unlike California, the Texas ten-percent plan, instituted in 1998 by the state legislature, automatically admits high school seniors in the top ten percent of their class into the public university of their choice. Despite the ability of these top ten percent students to attend the state's flagship campuses, studies suggest that these campuses would have admitted a majority of these students without any percent program in place.[32] Nevertheless, studies reveal that both the University of Texas-Austin and Texas A&M have experienced a decline in the number of minority students admitted and enrolled. According to a report by the U.S. Commission on Civil Rights, only 38 percent of black applicants were admitted to UT-Austin in 2001.[33] African-American admissions at Texas A&M went from an average of 4.7 percent from 1992-1996 to just 2.8 percent in 1998; there was a slight increase in 2001 of 3.5 percent.

Florida's adoption of a Talented 20 Program (the "T20 Program") has also failed to achieve diversity within the state's premier universities. Introduced in 1999, by Governor Jeb Bush, the T20 Program guarantees admission to one of Florida's 11 public institutions for students graduating in the top 20 percent of their high school class. Similar to California, the T20 Program does not ensure admission to a student's school of choice.[34]

A U.S. Civil Rights Commission study found that the T20 Program places black students at a severe disadvantage from the outset, because "blacks have the smallest percentage of high school graduates qualifying as T20 students."[35] The ramifications of this finding are evident from enrollment data from the University of Florida which reveal that before the T20 Program, the proportion of black enrolled students was increasing. However, in 2001, the first full year of the T20 Program, black enrollment experienced a dramatic decline from 11.8 percent to 7.2 percent.[36]

Due to racial and ethnic segregation in housing patterns that causes segregation in the K-12 grade schools, these three states guarantee that a certain percentage of minority high school graduates in the top 4-20% of the class will be admitted to one of the state universities. Moreover, the race-neutral percentage plans have been so effectively shielded from constitutional attack that no one has really challenged them in court. Thus, while race-neutral admission plans for the top percentage of minority high school graduates to attend state universities are better than no special measures, they produce fewer minorities in higher education than race-conscious plans.

Real-World Effects in Employment

California's experience with Proposition 209 provided an opportunity to examine the effect on minorities of eliminating affirmative action programs in employment. Researchers compared California's experience with that of the rest of the country to determine the effect on the labor force of removing affirmative action programs.[37] Between 1995 and 1999, the rate of employment of minorities in California, relative to those of the rest of the country, where affirmative action programs were not removed, fell by 2.8 percent. Between 1995 and 2000, the rate of non-participation in the labor force among minorities rose by 2.2 percent (the non-participation rate, as opposed to the unemployment rate, measures the number of people who have left the workforce entirely). These results suggest that Proposition 209 removed significant numbers of women and minorities from the labor force.[38]

The statistics also emphasized the importance of access to education in securing employment: the more education a minority individual had, the less likely they were to leave the labor force after Proposition 209 was passed.[39] For minorities with less than a high school degree, non participation in the labor force rose by 3.5 percent after Proposition 209 was passed.[40] For those with a high school degree, the number was 2.8.[41] For those with education beyond a high school degree, the number was 2.5.[42] In addition, non participation in the labor force rose more for younger workers than for older ones.[43]

CONCLUSIONS AND RECOMMENDATIONS

The road to equal opportunities in education, employment, and contracting is paved with the blood, sweat and tears of civil rights leaders. Today, affirmative action opponents deceptively use phrases like "equal access" and "colorblind society" to erect barriers on that road. Although these opponents claim to support equal access, they combat efforts designed to promote inclusiveness.

The experiences in Michigan, Washington, Florida, Texas, and California are at best a warning, at worst a harbinger of things to come. Therefore, it is imperative that we respond immediately to this open hostility to affirmative action by utilizing all of our intellectual and financial resources to counter these appalling set-backs. Supporters of equal access and diversity must join forces to develop counter strategies to combat the well-organized and well-funded attacks on affirmative action.

Regardless whether a challenge is imminent in your state or not, ongoing targeted and strategic public education campaigns about the benefits of affirmative action, diversity, and inclusiveness are necessary at the local, state, and national levels. It is critical to note that promoting these policies is not a "zero sum" game—we are all winners when all of our talents and skills are engaged in employment, education, and contracting.

In states where anti-affirmative action measures have been adopted, all is not foreclosed, as there are still tools legally available to promote diversity and equal opportunity. Expanded outreach and recruitment efforts to ensure that minorities, as well as non-minorities, are encouraged to apply remain permissible. Moreover, states may still use non-racial characteristics—like socioeconomic status and geographic considerations—as factors in decision-making to promote diversity. Supporters of inclusiveness efforts should not assume that a successful ballot initiative is the end of our struggle. Instead, efforts should be explored to modify or repeal these harmful initiatives by sponsoring future pro-affirmative action initiatives in the affected states.

Conversely, we must think proactively about advancing programs, policies, and ballot initiatives that facilitate inclusion. An "Equity Agenda" has to be advocated to redress the continuing inequities in our society. Affirmative action is but one very important strategy in achieving a more just and equal society.

If you live in a state where an anti-affirmative action movement is brewing, form a local campaign to spread the word about the deleterious effects of these initiatives. The anti-affirmative movement is attempting to co-opt the open voting process to push through measures that promote exclusivity. A well-organized, energized, and informed campaign to educate the public and to "get out the vote" is needed to expose the dangers of these initiatives. It is not enough to identify this issue.

Take action now.

[1] *Thanks to Kimberley Alton, John Brittain, Sarah Crawford, Michael Foreman, Tricia Jefferson, Ellen Medlin, Zoe Segal-Reichlin, Adam Stofsky, and Audrey Wiggins for their contribution and collaboration.*

NOTES

[2] Affirmative action has been defined as "any measure, beyond simple termination of a discriminatory practice, adopted to correct or compensate for past or present discrimination or to prevent discrimination from recurring in the future." *See* Citizens Research Council of Michigan, Statewide Issues on the November General Election Ballot, Proposal 2006-02: Michigan Civil Rights Initiative, Report 343, Page 3 (Summer 2006). The terms affirmative action, inclusiveness, and diversity are used interchangeably in this essay. The author recognizes that subtle distinctions exist among these terms.

[3] *See* Executive Order 11246 (emphasis added).

[4] President Lyndon B. Johnson, "To Fulfill These Rights," Commencement Address at Howard University, June 4, 1965.

[5] *Regents of the University of California v. Bakke*, 438 U.S. 265 (1978).

[6] *See e.g.* AFFIRMATIVE ACTION COMPLIANCE MANUAL FOR FEDERAL CONTRACTORs, The Bureau of National Affairs, December 29, 2006, Number 334.

[7] Cal. Prop. 209, *adding* Cal. Const., Art. I, § 31.

[8] *See* American Civil Rights Coalition Website, *at* http://www.acrc1.org/ (last visited February 22, 2007).

[9] ACRC also launched a campaign in Florida in 1999, culminating with Governor Jeb Bush's voluntarily eliminating *state-sponsored* affirmative action programs through an Executive Order.

[10] Wash. I-200, *amending* Rev. Code Wash. (ARCW) § 49.60.

[11] Michigan's Proposal 2006-02, *amending* MLCS Const. Art. I, § 26.

[12]*Cantrell v. Granholm*, Complaint filed December 19, 2006, E.D. Mich., Case 2:06-cv-15637. Initially, a Detroit federal judge granted three Michigan state universities permission to continue use of race-conscious admissions procedures through the current admissions cycle. *Cantrell v. Granholm*, Complaint filed December 19, 2006, E.D. Mich., Case 2:06-cv-15637. The Sixth Circuit then stayed that order, and in January 2007 the Supreme Court denied an application to lift the Sixth Circuit's stay. *Coalition to Defend Affirmative Action v. Granholm*, 473 F.3d 237 (6th Cir. 2006), 2007 U.S. LEXIS 1157 (U.S. 2007). At that point, the University of Michigan elected to resume consideration of applications without taking race into account,

based on the concern that "[the university could not] sustain any further delay in our admissions process without harming [its] ability to enroll a class of students for the 2007-8 academic year." *Michigan Resumes Admissions and Says It Is Complying With Proposal 2*, CHRONICLE OF HIGHER EDUCATION, January 10, 2007, http://chronicle.com/news/article/1502/michigan-resumes-admissions-and-says-it-is-complying-withproposal-2.

[13] *See e.g.* AFFIRMATIVE ACTION COMPLIANCE MANUAL FOR FEDERAL CONTRACTORS, The Bureau of National Affairs, December 29, 2006, Number 334.

[14] The Supreme Court has approved programs that are race-neutral in nature even when they may have a racially disproportionate effect, and some lower courts have suggested that race-neutral outreach programs may be permissible. *See generally Croson*, 488 U.S. at 507, 526; *see also, Monterey Mech. Co. v. Wilson*, 125 F.3d 702, 711 (9th Cir. 1997); *Hi-Voltage Wire Works, Inc. v. City of San Jose*, 12 P.3d 1068, 1106 (Cal. 2000).

[15] *See* Synnott, Marcia G., *The Evolving Diversity Rationale In University Admissions: From Regents V. Bakke To The University Of Michigan Cases*, 90 CORNELL L. REV. 463, 501 (2005).

[16] Morris, Monique W., Thanasombat, Sirithon, Sumner, Michael D., Pierre, Sara, and Borja, Jessica Z., *Free to Compete?: Measuring the Impact of Proposition 209 on Minority Business Enterprises*, Discrimination Research Center, August 2006, at 21.

[17] Kaufmann, Susan W., *The Potential Impact of the Michigan Civil Rights Initiative on Employment, Education and Contracting*, Center for the Education of Women, University of Michigan, September 2006, at 6.

[18] Morris, Monique W., Thanasombat, Sirithon, Sumner, Michael D., Pierre, Sara, and Borja, Jessica Z., *Free to Compete?: Measuring the Impact of Proposition 209 on Minority Business Enterprises*, Discrimination Research Center, August 2006, at 2.

[19] *Id.*, pp. 24, 31-32.

[20] Kaufmann, Susan W., *The Potential Impact of the Michigan Civil Rights Initiative on Employment, Education and Contracting*, Center for the Education of Women, University of Michigan, September 2006, at 6.

[21] *See Hi-Voltage Wire Works, Inc. v. City of San Jose*, 12 P.3d 1068, 1106 (Cal. 2000).

[22] *C&C Construction v. Sacramento Municipal Utility District*, 18 Cal. Rptr. 3d 715 (Cal. Ct. App. 2004).

[23] *Coral Construction v. San Francisco*, 10 Cal. Rptr. 3d 65 (Cal. Ct. App. 2004).

[24] Paul Guppy, *A Citizen's Guide to Initiative 200: The Washington State Civil Rights Initiative*, Washington Policy Center, September 1998, http://www.washingtonpolicy.org/ECP/PBGuppyECPGuidetoI200.html.

[25] *Id.*

[26] Timothy Bates, *The Urban Development Potential of Black-Owned Businesses*, 72 JOURNAL OF THE AMERICAN PLANNING ASSOCIATION 227 (2006).

[27] *Id.*

[28] *Hopwood v. Texas*, 78 F.3d 932 (5th Cir. 1996).

[29] U.S. Commission on Civil Rights, *Beyond Percentage Plans: The Challenge of Equal Opportunity in Higher Education*, November 2002, at v.

[30] *Id.*

[31] The Harvard Civil Rights Project, *Percent Plans in College Admissions: A Comparative Analysis of Three States' Experiences*, March 2003, at 49.

[32] *Id.* at 59.

[33] U.S. Commission on Civil Rights, *Beyond Percentage Plans: The Challenge of Equal Opportunity in Higher Education*, November 2002, at i.

[34] The Harvard Civil Rights Project, *Percent Plans in College Admissions: A Comparative Analysis of Three States' Experiences*, March 2003, at 22.

[35] U.S. Commission on Civil Rights, *Beyond Percentage Plans: The Challenge of Equal Opportunity in Higher Education*, November 2002, at vii.

[36] The Harvard Civil Rights Project, *Percent Plans in College Admissions: A Comparative Analysis of Three States' Experiences*, March 2003, at 50.

[37] Caitlin Knowles Myers, *A Cure for Discrimination? Affirmative Action and the Case of California Proposition 209*, Middlebury College Economics Discussion Paper No. 05–25, September 2005.

[38] *Id.* at 17.

[39] *Id.* at 19.

[40] *Id.*

[41] *Id.*

[42] *Id.*

[43] *Id.* at 20.

The State of Civil Rights

by Theodore M. Shaw, J.D.

T he status of African Americans, more than any other group in the United States, has been defined and impacted by law. Although the days of Jim Crow, sanctioned by law, are long gone, black Americans, by experience, continue to look to the law for protection against discriminatory treatment and for the elusive ideal of equal justice. *The State of Black America 2006* Report defined the state of civil rights as "most precarious."[1] Sadly, a year later, the state of civil rights is as precarious as ever.

Supreme Court Shift

In 2005, with the retirement of Associate Justice Sandra Day O'Connor and the death of Chief Justice William Rehnquist, African Americans joined the rest of the nation in anticipating the replacements for the new vacancies. Appellate Judge John Roberts was first nominated to replace Justice O'Connor, but upon the death of his mentor, Chief Justice William Rehnquist, Judge Roberts was nominated to fill the Court's top seat. President Bush then nominated White House Counsel Harriet Miers to the O'Connor seat, but her nomination provoked strong opposition among conservatives and she quickly withdrew. Third Circuit Court of Appeals Judge Samuel Alito was then nominated for Justice O'Connor's seat.

Judge Roberts' nomination was opposed by virtually every civil rights organizations representing African Americans based on his long record of opposing the Voting Rights Act and other civil rights remedies. Nevertheless, Judge Roberts was confirmed by the Senate as Chief Justice of the United States by a 78-22 vote on September 29, 2005.

Judge Alito was also opposed by leading civil rights organizations based on his extensive record as an appellate court judge in civil rights cases. He was confirmed as Associate Justice of the United States Supreme Court on January 31, 2006 by a 58-42 vote. Supreme Court observers and practitioners agree that the addition of Chief Justice Roberts and Associate Justice Alito pushes the Court even further into the conservative camp. While the late Chief Justice was staunchly conservative, Justice O'Connor was often the center—,or "swing vote"—of the Court. For example, Justice O'Connor joined with Justices John Paul Stevens and David Souter, Stephen Breyer and Ruth Bader Ginsberg, to uphold the University of Michigan's affirmative action plan in 2003.[2] The new Chief Justice and Justice Alito are likely to vote with the conservative wing of the Court, thereby guaranteeing it a narrow majority and shifting the balance.

With the ascension of these new justices to the Supreme Court, it appears that the United States has entered into a period of time in which the long-standing role of the law as a force for continued progress by African Americans has changed.

School Desegregation Revisited

While school desegregation appears to many Americans to be yesterday's issue, it is under threat today. Two cases that could significantly impede voluntary school integration efforts were argued in the U.S. Supreme Court in December of 2006. These cases are important not just on their own terms, but also because of their potential reach. The days of mandatory desegregation – born as a result of *Brown v. Board of Education*[3] - are all but over. The Supreme Court has not only made it easier for school districts to end their voluntary school desegregation efforts, it has allowed school districts to re-segregate under "neighborhood school" assessment plans.

In the case currently pending in the Supreme Court, school boards in Louisville, Kentucky and in Seattle, Washington determined that they desired to maintain some measure of integrated schools on a voluntary basis. In order to do so, each school district denied assignments if they increase racial imbalance. However, white plaintiffs filed lawsuits Lawsuits against each district alleging that the consideration of race—a necessary component in any attempt to maintain integrated schools—constitutes racial discrimination.

The ideological underpinnings of the Seattle and Louisville cases are the same as recent decisions by the U.S. Supreme Court upholding the limited use of race by colleges and universities seeking diversity in student enrollment. However, as in these previous cases, those challenging the desegregation/diversity efforts contend that any consideration of race for a non-remedial purpose is unconstitutional or otherwise illegal. Thus, all voluntary and conscious efforts to address racial inequality—scholarships, mentoring, outreach, and other programs targeted at African Americans—are in the crosshairs. Plainly stated, programs that encourage more blacks to pursue PhD's, mathematics and science degrees, that create "pipelines" into corporate America, that counter crises among black men or create scholarships programs (public and private) for black students, or otherwise help blacks overcome our long history of inequality rooted in the legacy of slavery and Jim Crow segregation, will be illegal if our adversaries prevail.

While the Supreme Court's affirmative action decisions should not be up for reconsideration in the Louisville and Seattle cases, affirmative action foes nonetheless hope that this case will help to erode and eventually lead to their reversal.

Meanwhile, they do not await Supreme Court action. In Michigan, Proposition 2, a ballot initiative parroting California's Proposition 209, which banned affirmative action in education, employment and contracting, passed in November 2006. As a result, the victory in the *Grutter* case no longer has any force in Michigan, the very state in which it arose. Ward Connerly, the African-American business man who promoted Proposition 209, joined with Jennifer Gratz, a plaintiff in the University of Michigan cases, to act as the public face of Proposition 2. Voters were told that the proposition requires "color-blindness" and prohibits discrimination, a seductively idealistic message. However, the truth is that the measure's sole purpose was to ban affirmative action programs that have provided opportunities for African-Americans and other people of color, and women. Connerly has vowed to take the anti-affirmative action ballot initiative across the country.[4]

These measures—and those who support them—ignore the plain fact that massive segregation and educational inequality persist. As we watch the federal courts abandon their protection of school desegregation efforts, we continue to face the challenge of how to improve the quality of education for African American students, the vast majority of whom attend public schools. Facial re-segregation and concentrations of poverty make this task considerably more difficult. Although escape hatches in the form of vouchers and charter schools are available for a relative few, we remain challenged to reform public school education for the many.

The No Child Left Behind Act, the centerpiece of the Bush Administration's education policy, is due to be reauthorized in 2006 and, thus, looms large in the political debate. The outcome of the reauthorization effort could have a substantial impact on black children particularly and educational equality in general. Ironically, while the Justice Department's office of Civil Rights claims to oppose race-conscious measures, the No Child Left Behind Act itself is the very essence of race-conscious legislation; it requires the collection of disaggregated data by race to measure student performance on standardized tests.

Voting Rights

In August of 2006, President Bush signed the Fannie Lou Hamer, Rosa Parks, and Coretta Scott King Voting Rights Act Reauthorization and Amendments Act, which renewed the expiring provisions of the Voting Rights Act. These provisions included Section 5, which required certain jurisdictions with a history of discrimination and low minority voter participation to seek approval for changes in electoral processes either from the Justice Department or from the federal district court in Washington, D.C. The law has been a powerful deterrent to schemes to dilute minority voting strength. Section 203 of the Act, which provided for language assistance in designated jurisdictions, was also renewed, as were provisions providing for election monitors. The reauthorization also included two legislative fixes for Supreme Court decisions that had limited the Voting Rights Act's effectiveness. For example, the Supreme Court had ruled in *Reno v. Bossier Parish School Board*[5] that a school board election plan that made it virtually impossible for black voters to elect their preferred candidates to a school board that never had black representation did not violate Section 5 because it was not retrogressive. In other words the Court appeared to say, "If you never had anything, and the electoral plan was rigged to make sure you never get anything, you are not worse off than you were before." The amended Act makes clear that Section 5 of the Voting Rights Act was intended to protect against attempts to keep minority voters from gaining strength. The second legislative fix addressed *Georgia v. Ashcroft*, a Supreme Court case that weakened Section 5. [6] The Voting Rights Act has been called "the crown jewel of civil rights litigation", and its extension was nominally supported by the Republicans and Democrats. Media coverage, for the most part, treated extension as a *fait accompli*. Behind the scenes, however, there were intense battles over the language of the Act that went to the core question of its constitutionality and effectiveness. The battle over the 2006 extension of the Voting Rights Act was fought below the surface while media and most elected officials predicted smooth sailing. Right up to the moment the Act was signed into law, there were attempts to drop time bombs into the legislative history that would explode during post-enactment litigation. Those attempts were thwarted and the legislative history presents a strong and overwhelming case for re-authorization. The Act was signed into law and extended for an additional twenty-five years. Not surprisingly, however, the newly-enacted law was attacked almost immediately. In a lawsuit filed against a small municipal utility district in the Austin, Texas area, plaintiffs challenged the constitutionality of the newly extended Act, claiming that it is an unwarranted and intrusion into local governmental affairs by the federal government. Black and Latino voters, represented by the NAACP Legal Defense Fund, the Mexican American Legal Defense and Educational Fund (MALDEF), the Lawyers Committee for Civil Rights Under Law, American Civil Liberties Union (ACLU), League of United Latin American Citizens (LULAC) among others, have intervened to defend the Act.

Housing

Housing segregation remains a hallmark of American life, with black Americans the most highly, segregated group, even adjusting for economic status.[7] Housing strongly defines other opportunities—the schools our children attend, the jobs we seek and hold, where we vote, the economic conditions in which we live, etc. As the gap between the wealthy and the poor continues to widen in the United States, affordable housing is becoming more difficult to find. Fair Housing Act enforcement, while alone insuffi-cient to address the growing crisis of the unavailability of affordable hous-ing, is an indispensable tool in the quest to improve the life conditions of African Americans.

Criminal Justice

Perhaps in no other area are the statistics and the conditions of black Americans more compelling than in the arena of criminal justice. According to the 2007 National Urban League Equality Index, African Americans are seven times more likely to be imprisoned as whites. One in 8 black males in their twenties is incarcerated on any given day. [8] These conditions are sim-ply not sustainable without serious cost to the society at large. As dire as current conditions are, they could get worse: according to the Sentencing Project, if current trends continue, one of every three black males born today will be imprisoned at some point in their lifetime.[9]

The collateral effects of the massive incarceration of African American men and women are devastating to their lives, and to the lives of their fami-lies and communities. For example, a felony conviction can bar an individ-ual from public housing, federal education loan programs, employment, and from exercising the right to vote. In short, those who are convicted of a felony experience what Columbia University Professor Manning Marable has called "civic death"[10].

Legislators are loathe to change drug laws for fear of being portrayed as soft on drugs and crime. We remain trapped in a criminal justice system that struggles to overcome an apparently insatiable appetite for illegal drugs on the part of a significant part of the population, regardless of race, with law enforcement concentrating its efforts disproportionately on black and brown communities in a manner that defines its relationship with these communities.

While tensions between law enforcement officials and the black commu-nities they patrol have existed for decades, the "War on Drugs" that has resulted in the explosion in incarceration during the last quarter of a centu-ry has come to largely define their relationship.

Too often, this 'war" has transformed all of the people of those communi-ties into suspects, sometimes with deadly results. In some communities it has resulted in excessive stops and frisk programs that have engendered widespread resentment of law enforcement among many black men and women, and in the disproportionate arrest and conviction of young black people for minor drug violations, usually marijuana, for which white users are being neither arrested nor prosecuted.

In poor black and brown communities, drug transactions tend to take place in public spaces. In more affluent and white communities, drug transactions transpire in private spaces, e.g. in the home or at the work place. Law enforcement officials seeking results in the "War on Drugs" patrol the spaces in black and brown communities with a mentality and approach that differs from law enforcement in white, middle class or affluent communities. It is likely, if not probable, that it is this difference that accounts, at least in part, for the repeated instances in black communities across the nation, in which black people, often unarmed, and sometimes entirely innocent of any crime, are beaten or shot, often with fatal results.

For example, in 2006, an elderly black woman, 92 years old, in Atlanta Georgia, was shot to death in her home when she used a gun to protect herself from a police team that forcefully invaded her in a drug raid on the wrong location.[11] In New York City, undercover police investigating prostitution and drugs at a Queens' nightclub fatally shot an unarmed young black man on his wedding day and wounded two of his acquaintances.[12] Such incidents rarely, if ever, occur in white communities.

These incidences often involve white law enforcement officers and black victims - but not exclusively. Whatever the race of law enforcement officers serving in black and brown communities, they serve in police forces whose relationship with the communities which they work is defined in large part by the "War on Drugs." The job is inherently dangerous, training is sometimes inadequate, and the threat of deadly force is always moment away. "Wars" are violent, whether foreign or domestic.

Even where deadly force is not at issue, the "War on Drugs" invites opportunities for destructive interactions between law enforcement and black communities. The infamous Tulia, Texas drug sting a few years ago was an example. There, fresh with federal funds for the "War on Drugs", state and local officials set up a drug sting which resulted in the arrest of 10% of the population of Tulia's black residents who were charged with narcotics trafficking. Convictions and pleas yielded sentences of one year's probation to 434 year's incarceration. No drugs, no weapons, no money were found. The convictions rested solely on the testimony of one undercover police officer later demonstrated to be racist and corrupt. [13] While the NAACP Legal Defense Fund lawyers working in concert with law firms were eventually able to win the release of those incarcerated, they served four years for crimes they did not commit.

Felon disfranchisement laws similarly impact the lives of black Americans with felony convictions, and the communities from which they come. Between 4.5 and 5 Million Americans are not permitted to vote because of felony convictions, including more than 2 Million African Americans. In 48 states and the District of Columbia, persons incarcerated for felonies cannot vote. In 33 of the states, persons on probation or parole are ineligible to vote. In 14 states a felony conviction can result in loss of the right to vote for life.[14]

In 2006, a number of court challenges to felon disfranchisement laws were working their way through the courts. In *Hayden v. Pataki* and *Muntaqim v. Coombe*, convicted felons incarcerated and on parole, challenged New York State's felon disfranchisement laws. The U.S. Court of Appeals for the Second Circuit, sitting *en banc* (*i.e.* with all of its judges hearing the case instead of the usual panel of three), ruled in a narrowly divided opinion that New York's disfranchisement law could not be challenged under the Voting Rights Act.[15] A similar case, *Farrakhan v. Gregoire*, arose in the Ninth Circuit, in which the Court found compelling evidence of Washington State's felon disfranchisement law. And in Alabama, a state with a long and protracted history of discrimination, LDF filed *Gooden v. Worley* challenging the manner in which the Jefferson County registrar illegally barred Mr. Gooden from voting because of a felony conviction even though the felony did not involve moral turpitude.

The effects of felon disfranchisement on black and brown communities are widespread, if not always readily apparent. For example, the U.S. Census Bureau counts persons in the jurisdiction in which they are represented, not from which they come.[16] Consequently, rural, largely white areas with penal institutions in their midst, get the benefit of a larger population count in the form of increased representation, even though those incarcerated (disproportionately and often overwhelmingly are black and brown) cannot vote. These communities also get the benefit of increased federal funding in programs that use a population formula based upon census figures. Consequently, the communicates from which those who are incarcerated come, lose voting strength, political representation and federal dollars.[17]

CONCLUSION

Law continues to define the status of African Americans in the United States in a powerful fashion. However, the law is shifting from an instrument of social change to a tool for obstruction and impediment. The state of civil rights in 2007 is indeed precarious. But it is not too late. More now than ever, we must do everything possible to ensure that the rights of African-Americans are protected. This is the least that we owe to those who stood up when standing up wasn't easy.

NOTES

1 Jones, Nathaniel R., "The State of Civil Rights," *The State of Black America 2006* Report, p. 165.

2 *Grutter v. Bollinger* ,539 U.S. 306 (2003); *Gratz v. Bollinger,* 539 U.S. 244 (2003). In this case, big business, including such household names as Pfizer, Inc., The Coca-Cola Company, Shell Oil Company, and General Electric Company joined law school deans, U.S. senators and universities in filing *amicus* briefs supporting affirmative action.

3 347 U.S. 483 (1954).

4 For further discussion on the Affirmative Action, *see,* "*The Battle Over Affirmative Action: Legal Challenges and Outlook," supra, pp. 159-172*

5 520 U.S. 471 (1997).

6 539 U.S. 461 (2003).

7 Freeman, Lance, "Black Homeownership: A Dream No Longer Deferred?," *The State of Black America 2006* Report, pp. 63–75.

8 Mauer, Marc, "Incarceration Nation," *Tompaine.com,* December 11, 2006.

9 *Id.*

10 Marable, Manning, "Race-ing Justice, Disenfranchising Lives: African Americans, Criminal Justice and the New Racial Domain,"*The Black Commentator*, December 10, 2006.

11 "Woman, 92, Dies in Shootout with Cops," *Atlanta Journal-Constitution*, November 22, 2006.

12 "50 Bullets, One Dead, and Many Questions," *The New York Times*, December 11, 2006.

13 "Texas Frees 12 on Bond After Drug Sweep Inquiry," *The New York Times*, June 17, 2003.

14 "Felony Disenfranchisement Laws In The United States," The Sentencing Project, November 2006.

15 *Muntaqim v. Coombe*, 366 F.3d 102, 107-08 (2d Cir. 2004).

16"Ending the Prison Windfall," *The New York Times*, January 17, 2007.

17 While perhaps purely coincidental, viewing the similarity between the present day effect of felon disfranchisement on political arrangements through the prism of race and the historical political arrangement enshrined in our Constitution as originally drafted and ratified is irresistible. Article I §2 counted for enumeration purposes, by euphemistic and tortured indirection, slaves as "three fifths of all other persons". Thus black people held in slavery could not vote but were counted for purposes of increasing political and economic power of the slave holding states. Incarcerated persons in early Twenty-First Century United States, while not exclusively black, are disproportionately black and brown. They are counted in way that increase the political and economic empowerment of heavily white communities, even though they cannot vote.

Who's Going to Take the Weight?
African Americans and Civic Engagement
in the 21st Century

by Silas Lee, Ph.D.

A threatening disease is trying to gain momentum as it penetrates the black community. It is not a health-related disease or a new epidemic, but the growing belief that our participation in the electoral process is futile because some perceive politics as tarnished by greed, deceit, lack of communication and inertia. What is contributing to the potential for black voters to drop out of the democratic process and civic engagement at accelerating rates? How can this hemorrhaging be stopped? In the remaining pages, I will attempt to explore some of the reasons for voter discontent in the black community and the potential consequences.

For the past twenty years I have conducted polls and focus groups domestically and internationally for institutions, elected officials and companies, and since the mid-nineties, I have heard the voices of discontent erupting with the fury of a volcano from a multitude of black voters, especially those under the age of thirty.

With intense emotional frustration and their voices advocating the gospel of non-participation, the chorus of apathy and distrust with the electoral process has the potential to infect the very foundation of democracy and the mission of progressive civil rights organizations such as the National Urban League. From voting rights to affirmative action, the fragile social and economic gains of the past three decades function in a constellation of protection from extinction, as social progressives aggressively work to protect these policies whenever they are targeted by those who want to reverse the wheels of equality.

A cursory review of the media headlines quickly reveals that the progress that African Americans and other people of color have made over the past forty years is in constant jeopardy of elimination. However, the urgency to protect those gains is not shared by all voters. In 2004, more than 9 million eligible African-American voters did not vote in the 2004 presidential election.[1] A higher black turnout could have very well reversed the outcome of this election—President Bush's margin of victory over John Kerry was 3 million votes.[2] Interestingly, there has also been a decline in voting in the general population and political scientists are confounded as they witness an increasing number of people dropping out from the democratic process. In an era of on-demand access to information and mobile technology, why are voters, in particular African Americans, disheartened with the political process? An abundance of theories attempt to explain the decline in voting in the general population as a reflection of elected officials and governmental leaders losing touch with the cultural dynamics of voters.

In the past, the conventional wisdom among many political operatives has been to motivate African-American voters through one of two strategies:

1. A Sacrifice-Privilege strategy highlighting how the right to vote has been won through blood, death and tears.

2. A Losing Ground strategy designed to motivate black voters into the voting booth to protect the gains recently accomplished through programs or policies.

Regardless of the strategies used to motivate voters, we have heard an increasing level of discontent among black voters about the political establishment. African-American voters, over the age of 40 are more responsive to the Sacrifice-Privilege strategy, but express frustration with the lack of communication from some elected officials and government itself. Conversely, for voters born twenty years after the passage of the Voting Rights Act (in the 1980s), the Losing Ground strategy is not an effective motivating tool because their social equilibrium is balanced less through historical reflection and relevance and more through a self-analysis of how they see their lives and experiences in the language of political policies and the messages crafted to motivate them. Consequently, their voting rate is less predictable and more inconsistent than voters who reached adulthood in the 1960s and 1970s. Regardless of the demographic group, the political establishment has been issued the equivalent of a "vote of non-effectiveness" by black voters citing them guilty of the following offenses:

1. Taking us for granted—inconsistent communication and outreach in the black community and attempting to mobilize the black community four weeks before an election. Because mainstream corporations with strong name recognition and customer loyalty spend billions of dollars to promote their products and stimulate their customer base, voters have now been conditioned to expect the same level of nurturing and outreach from elected officials, candidates and governmental agencies.

2. One stop messaging—since voters can customize what they hear, see and wear, they expect elected officials to tailor their messages to reflect their experiences, concerns and expectations. Simply having a slogan and endorsements from celebrities and other elected officials will not earn candidates credibility with voters.

3. Failing to be a "Look Us in the Eyes, Leader"—"We've heard it all before. No one is willing to look us in the eyes and be honest with us," is a common refrain heard in focus groups and recorded by interviewers in hundreds of polls. Black voters, like all voters are tired of "soft shoe or two-step political rhetoric," witnessing election officials retreating from taking a position or responding with vacuous answers. Instead, voters embrace the type of candidate or elected official who has the courage to admit their mistakes, who is willing to forewarn them about the limitations of governmental powers and resources and articulate a realistic vision for the future.

These deficient strategies have precipitated a sense that black voters are dispensable and can be resuscitated when necessary.

The 2002 Florida Vote Controversy and the Katrina Effect

During the first five years of the 21st century, voters have observed two events which have shaken their confidence in voting and politics. The first was the 2002 presidential campaign whereby thousands of ballots cast by black voters were disqualified in Florida, fueling suspicion that the electoral process lacks integrity and accountability. Compounded with numerous reports of voting irregularities and disenfranchisement, the residual stench of distrust in the electoral process still permeates the psyches of many African-American voters.

Three years later, on August 29, 2005, Hurricane Katrina devastated New Orleans and parts of the Mississippi Gulf Coast. For five agonizing days, America watched as thousands of mostly African American citizens remained stranded in the Louisiana Superdome and at the Morial Convention Center without food and water. As former FEMA Director Michael Brown fretted about his grooming for the television cameras, citizens of the Gulf Coast waited for governmental assistance, while the world questioned, "Where is the federal government?"

No other event in the first decade of the 21st century has forced Americans to hold a mirror to governmental accountability more than Hurricane Katrina. This issue re-ignited a sense that the federal government is insensitive when it comes to responding to the needs of the poor and African Americans. In an unusual alignment of opinions, blacks and whites shared their consternation with the slow response of the federal government in lending assistance to distressed citizens.

A Decline In Confidence

As the November mid-term elections approached in 2006, America was reeling with frustration. From the war in Iraq, to ethical breeches by elected officials, citizens were frustrated with the direction of the country and its leadership. Although the level of dissatisfaction with Congress transcended demographic and racial boundaries, political operatives in both political parties monitored turnout in the black community as it was considered essential to influencing the outcome in many important state and national races.

On the heels of Pew Research Center's poll citing erosion in confidence among black voters (from 47% feeling "Very confident" about accurate vote counts in 2004 to 30% in 2006)[3], many civil rights organizations mobilized their resources to stimulate black turnout.

Table 1

Blacks' Confidence in Accurate Vote Count Declines

Confident Your Vote Will Be Accurately Counted?	October 2004 (%)	October 2006 (%)
Very	47	30
Somewhat	36	37
Not too	11	24
Not at all	4	5
Don't Know	2	4
Total	**100**	**100**
Based on Registered Voters.	(N=120)	(N=161)

Source: Pew Research Center Poll, 2006.

A post-election analysis by Dr. David Bositis, a senior research associate at the Joint Center for Political and Economic Studies concluded:

> While black turnout nationally increased only modestly, black turnout in 2006 was strategically effective in several places, although not enough in others. There were significant increases in black turnout in Florida, Michigan, Missouri, Ohio, Pennsylvania, Tennessee, and Virginia, and probably a slight increase in Maryland. Black voters were important in electing a Democratic governor (Ohio) and re-electing three Democratic governors (Michigan, Pennsylvania, and Tennessee) and two Democratic U.S. Senators (Florida and Michigan).

Dr. Bositis also observes that in senatorial races in Maryland, Virginia, Michigan and Virginia, as well as House of Representative seats in Georgia and

Kentucky, black voters were essential to Democrats defeating Republican challengers.

A Time to Reconstitute Voting Strategy

As we acknowledge the turnout of black voters in the 2006 midterm elections, we must be conscious of the fact that there is a tremendous need for greater participation in the electoral process. To be analytically fair, social and political analysts must be cautious about stigmatizing the low turnout of black voters (as well as general population voters) simply as a sign of voter disgust. Rather, it is more a reflection of the evolving maturity of the political appetite of African-American voters. For the past decade, voters have lamented over the political establishment's procrastination in accommodating the new rules of political engagement—less hierarchy, more issue customization and continuous interaction with voters—calling for a restructuring of the political communications strategy.

The sometimes loose cohesion between blacks and the political system has also been attributed to the collaborative roles played by legal and political institutions during the civil rights movement. In their book, *Participation in America: Political Democracy and Social Equity*, political scientists Sidney Verba and Norman Nie explain that the dynamic between blacks and politics is still evolving.

> Until very recently, blacks have usually had to seek basic citizenship rights from outside the nation's electoral institutions. Thus, the frequent designation of political participation as voting, campaigning and lobbying of elected and other officials have not generally applied to black politics. For blacks, the struggle for basic citizenship rights—protection of person and property, equal treatment in the courts, the right to vote and hold public office, and equal treatment when seeking education and employment—has frequently involved litigation and protest. Through litigation and protest, black political participation has been primarily a collective process.

In America's highly individualistic culture, the traditional analysis of blacks through civil, democratic and allocational indicators (e.g., social and economic status) is not universally employed by individuals in the evaluation of their personal status. Having attained some components of civil and democratic equality through participation in the governing process and legal protection of civil liberties, today more blacks evaluate their status from a balance sheet perspective; asking whether or not they see politics contributing to positive change in their lives. Confronting poverty, racism, lack of educational resources, absence of health care providers and crime, black voters ask, *"What's improved for me and my community? I don't see any change."* The more black voters are unable to relate positive change in their community to social engagement, the less likely they are motivated and obligated to vote.

My fear for the future of democracy is that it is in jeopardy, not only from a lack of civic engagement and participation, but from the strangulation of equality resulting from the emergence of a controlling oligarchy that will be more engaged in the political process than African Americans are willing to be. Social and economic progress are never permanent achievements; they require diligent monitoring and protection. Now more than ever, voting and civic participation are essential to achieving equality, prosperity and power for African Americans. To those who believe that their vote, one vote out of many, will not make a difference, I cite the following examples of the power of one vote:

- One vote in 1920 gave women the right to vote

- One vote made Adolph Hitler the leader of Germany's Nazi Party

- John F. Kennedy defeated Richard M. Nixon in 1960 by a margin of less than one vote per precinct nationwide

In summary, this crisis in participation can only be resolved through more effective communication strategies that are realistic, continuous and honest. While it is easy for many to resort to complaining and distrust about the political establishment and its leaders, that will not change our circumstances. We cannot cross the goal line of equality by being cynical or disconnecting from participating in the political process. Vote. Engage. Participate.

REFERENCES

Bositis, David: 2006. *Blacks and the 2006 Midterm Election.* Washington: Joint Center for Political and Economic Studies.

Federal Election Committee. 2004. Presidential Election Results.

The Pew Research Center. 2006. *November Turnout May Be High.*

http://people-press.org/reports/display.php3?ReportID=291

Verba, Sidney and Nie, Norman H. 1972. *Participation in America: Political Democracy and Social Equity.* Chicago: The University of Chicago Press.

NOTES

[1] Federal Election Commission and U.S. Bureau of the Census.

[2] Ibid.

[3] Given the larger sample size in 2006, the actual number of responses provides further insight into the shifting opinions. For example, 53 people selected "Very confident" in 2004 compared to 48 in 2006. The biggest changes actually occurred in the "Somewhat confident" category (43 people in 2004 compared to nearly 60 in 2006) and the "Not too confident" category (13 in 2004 and 39 in 2006).

....

A Way Out: Creating Partners for Our Nation's Prosperity By Expanding Life Paths for Young Men of Color

Final Report of the Dellums Commission[1]

JOINT CENTER FOR POLITICAL AND ECONOMIC STUDIES HEALTH POLICY INSTITUTE

The impact was so sudden, and the casualties so severe, that America's first response was equally swift and fearsome: run from it, hide it, lock it away. Yet there were some who returned to sift through the fallout of these seismic social and economic upheavals. We sought to find out why young men of color, more than any other group, were feeling every blow. The more we uncovered, the more we realized that for the most part, the disaster was man-made. With that realization came immeasurable sorrow for the lives needlessly lost and a new sense of responsibility—and hope—for today's children who are still searching for a way out.

—Dr. Gail C. Christopher, Joint Center Vice President for Health, Women & Families and Director of the Joint Center Health Policy Institute

Over the course of the last quarter of a century, the lives and fortunes of young men of color have been caught in a tail-spin. By nearly every comparative measure—income, education, incarceration, health—the reality is stark. Yet in truth, there is one measure above all that calls the human family to respond: the measure of a life. In today's America, many young men of color are less likely to simply *live*, to fulfill their potential, enrich their communities, and be part of the progress of our nation.[1]

The diminished life options and outcomes for young men of color can be understood as the starting point for the Dellums Commission's central inquiry: *What must we do now so that young men of color may have life?*

With this approach, the Commission has charted new ground in two ways. The first part of the approach—*what must be done*—directs our attention to the way forward. The plight of young men of color has come under increased scrutiny in recent years,[2] and the Commission engaged important related research with its series of Dellums Commission background papers.[3] However, the Commission's work advances beyond diagnosis and marshaling ideas and policies to form an urgent agenda.

The second part of the approach—*so that they may have life*—encompasses a novel focus on the social determinants of health for young men of color. Adopted by the World Health Organization and various national governments, including those of Canada, Chile, Brazil, Sweden, and Kenya, social determinant theory explains that the traditional disease-centered model of health care misses the vast majority of what truly determines how and when a person lives, thrives, and dies.[4] Rather, the social conditions in which a person lives create the largest impact on his/her health. Vast and predictable disparities in health outcomes among people of different races, ethnicities, and socioeconomic status across the world testify to the power of social determinants.[5] Thus, to truly address the life options and health issues facing young men of color in America, the Commission sought policies to heal the social body in which they live.

In America, citizens living in communities of color experience poverty, exclusion and discrimination, poor housing and inferior schools, disparate treatment by the justice system, environmental toxicity, and inadequate access to health care. For young men of color and their communities, these are the social determinants of health.

A LOOK BACK: THE IMPACT OF FAILED POLICIES

Some of the events that have devastated communities of color since the 1970s are commonly understood to have been beyond the reach of public policy to prevent or mitigate. Primary among these are economic globalization and its effects at home—rapid de-industrialization, de-unionization, and a steep decline in jobs and real wages for working-class men of all colors. Our history of racial oppression made communities of color more vulnerable to such events, and we need not look far for current policies that worsened the impact of these events on communities of color. These include, but are by no means limited to, punitive and ineffective drug laws, educational inequities, anti-union government interventions, regressive tax policies, stagnation of the minimum wage, disinvestment in social and legal services, and discriminatory housing policies, including the abandonment of public housing.

The social costs of such policies for families of color have been enormous. Family-supporting jobs disappeared from the urban communities in which people of color remained, isolated in the wake of increasing residential segregation.[6] Where jobs were absent, drugs moved in, with their dangerous but irrepressible economy. Many of the nation's policy responses served to exacerbate the exclusion of men in the community, particularly mass incarceration and a welfare system that made male participation a liability instead of an asset.[7]

The Toll on Children and Youth

The youth in communities of color bore the brunt of these policies and developments. High school dropout rates have increased for young men of color and college enrollment levels have declined, while incarceration rates have grown. A report published by the Urban Institute indicated the following male high school graduation rates, by racial/ethnic group, for 2001: African Americans (42.8 percent), American Indian/Alaska Natives (47 percent), Hispanics (48 percent), and whites (70.8 percent).[8] More than 29 percent of African American males who are 15 years old today are likely to go to prison at some point in their lives, compared to 4.4 percent of white males of the same age.[9] Health outcomes are also troubling. For example, the mortality rate from homicide for African American males ages 15-17 is 34.4 per 100,000, compared to a rate of 2.4 per 100,000 for non-Hispanic white males ages 15-17.[10]

Yet again, policy responses to troubled youth of color compound the problem. Misguided policies force schools, police, courts, and juvenile authorities to adopt practices that result in marginalization, exclusion, confinement, and punishment instead of constructive solutions. Counterproductive laws and programs are systemic restraints on young men of color, and the lack of health care and diminishing educational and occupational opportunities are resulting in wasted human potential.

The impact of mass incarceration on young men of color cannot be overstated. Youth has become "a minefield of trip wires" for males of color.[11] As a result, whether innocent or guilty of an offense, a majority of youth of color will have been arrested before the age of 21.[12] Youth of color are disproportionately represented in the juvenile justice systems: African Americans (1,004 per 100,000), American Indians (632 per 100,000), and Latinos (485 per 100,000) each had higher custody rates than whites (212 per 100,000) in 1999.[13]

The mass institutionalization of young men of color has a direct and preventable effect on their health. Prison exposes young men to physical and sexual assault by other inmates and guards, substance abuse, mental trauma, as well as a host of communicable diseases, including HIV/AIDS.[14] Incarceration also limits the life options of young men of color upon release, as they struggle to re-enter society and the workforce with limited skills and resources.

Perpetuating a Matrix of Exclusion

To even a casual observer, the harsh conditions of, and often harsher policy responses to, so many of America's children—young men of color constitute more than 40 percent of American males under 25[15]—signal a profound lack of empathy for these youth. The Commission found that an unconscious yet pervasively reinforced bias against young minority males subtly guides both policy decisions and individual outcome-determinative interactions in policing, employment, housing, and education.[16]

The Dellums Commission examined the impact of this array of policies in an attempt to guarantee that neither ignorance nor malice is allowed to govern our decision making in the future. What follows is a new agenda that envisions America's young men of color as healthy, engaged partners in the nation's prosperity.

THE WAY FORWARD: THE DELLUMS COMMISSION POLICY AGENDA

Beyond the disturbing demographic statistics, there is now a large and growing body of knowledge and expertise about what works to combat this growing blight on America. The authors of the Commission's background papers have distilled their wisdom into extensive and thoughtful reports on public policy and grassroots strategies, and point to existing models for strengthening communities. This final report and its accompanying background papers serve as a guidebook for legislators, community wellness advocates, concerned citizens, and the private sector.

—Mayor Ronald V. Dellums, Chairman of the Dellums Commission

The Dellums Commission's work is unique in that it studies the full range of factors determining health outcomes and recommends policy solutions for all levels of government and the private sector. The Commission's recommendations are based on the view that systemic problems must be addressed with systemic solutions. The Commission analyzed national, state, and local policies in the areas of health and mental health services, education, juvenile justice and criminal justice, family support and child welfare, and the media. Its recommended solutions could serve to replace or reform laws, policies, and practices that are endangering increasingly large portions of the minority youth population.

The Commission was formed by the Joint Center for Political and Economic Studies Health Policy Institute, which is directed by Dr. Gail C. Christopher. The Commission is chaired by Oakland Mayor Ronald V. Dellums, a social worker by training who served with distinction as a member of the U.S. House of Representatives from 1971 to 1998. The other 24 members of the Commission are rich in expertise and experience, as well. The diverse group includes state legislators, judges, educators, human rights activists, corporate executives, and religious leaders, and is representative of African American, Latino, American Indian, and Asian American communities.

The recommendations in this report are particularly useful to policymakers and policy influentials because they are grounded in extensive research by prominent scholars and incorporate effective real-life models of reform and innovation. To be sure, public policy proposals are not the only means with which to address these problems. Many of the Commission's solutions contain strategies and approaches that empower young men and their families to address challenges and the needs of communities of color. Other recommendations were prepared by the Youth Task Force, which was convened by the Joint Center Health Policy Institute to add voices of minority youth to the Dellums Commission's work. In sum, the Commission's policy agenda is designed to ignite reforms that would enhance the well-being of ailing American communities and demonstrate that government, business, communities, and individuals can apply commitment and logic to solve even the most intractable social problems.

KEY RECOMMENDATIONS OF THE DELLUMS COMMISSION

The following is a broad overview of the Dellums Commission's final recommendations. A complete summary, including examples of models of innovation and reform, is provided in the Commission's final report, released on November 15, 2006 (see Appendix).

Health Policy

- Fund school-based healthcare programs, extend coverage to all uninsured children, and establish universal coverage.
- Provide adequate mental health and substance abuse services and include care for mental illness and substance abuse in any universal medical care legislation.
- Ensure access to culturally competent medical professionals.
- Ensure access to services for health promotion, prevention, and early intervention, including establishing a U.S. Office of Men's Health.
- Without compromising public safety, treat disorders that have manifested in antisocial behaviors outside incarceration, accurately profile the health status and unmet needs of incarcerated youth and adults, finance and monitor strategies to reform correctional health care, and redirect some correctional funds to community-based post-correctional health care and support services.
- Require that foster care caseworkers be properly trained to regularly monitor health status and finance programs that will ensure that children in foster care will receive early and periodic assessment and treatment of physical, mental, and oral health.
- Employ models of innovation that successfully address health disparities, such as a community-based empowerment model that enables minority youth to assume personal responsibility for wellness.

Education Policy

- Aggressively and creatively stem dropout rates among young men of color; narrow the application of zero tolerance to only serious threats; collect and report demographic data as they relate to suspensions, arrests, and expulsions; and properly test non-English-speaking students before placing them in special education.
- Authorize studies to determine the benchmarks for establishing excellence at underperforming schools, determine and address the special skills needed for teaching minority males to encourage cultural competency, and endorse and fund the replication of successful models for recruiting, training, and retraining men of color as teachers.
- Nationally evaluate the No Child Left Behind Act to determine its fairness and equity in serving young men of color and promote legislative action or litigation to ensure full funding of activities required under the act.
- Invest more financial resources in college readiness programs to increase the number of young men of color in postsecondary education.
- Implement more community-based models for change that target high-risk youth and reclaim former high school dropouts.

Family Support and Child Welfare

- Strengthen and expand the role of federal leadership and funding to increase the number of stable foster homes and increase the incentives for adoption.
- Connect family service agencies with "grass roots" leaders who can help them build community-based family support networks.
- Address the lack of cultural competency in the foster care system, such as the lack of adequate bilingual services.
- Promote positive social network experiences for boys and young men of color by supporting the creation of in-school and out-of-school engagements with positive peer groups.
- Strengthen the assurance that children in foster care will receive early and periodic assessment of physical, mental, and oral health, diagnosis, care planning, treatment, and visitation to monitor and support health and health care.

- Pursue a model of reform like the John H. Chafee Foster Care Independence Program, which incorporates and expands the former Independent Living Program (ILP) and expands services for aftercare youth ages 18-21 who have exited foster care at age 18 or after, but have not reached age 21.

Workforce and Economic Development

- Increase the minimum wage at the federal level or the state and local level.
- Identify, fund, and promote micro- and macro-economic development opportunities in distressed communities (e.g., to establish viable business initiatives, access to government contracts and technical assistance to potential entrepreneurs).
- Vigorously enforce existing anti-discrimination laws in the area of employment, housing, and credit markets.
- Encourage businesses to pursue models of innovation for workforce development, such as the Hillside Work-Scholarship Connection and California's "Double Bottom Line" initiative.

Juvenile and Criminal Justice

- Provide a continuum of care that begins in detention and continues in the community as part of the transition process; improve alcohol, drug treatment, and ancillary services for inmates and detained youth during incarceration.
- Establish effective re-entry programs for juveniles, reducing recidivism by providing education during detention and a "one-stop service" that provides mental health and social services, drug and family counseling, and employment training and placement for students returning from incarceration; adequately fund local re-entry programs that are performance-based; support additional funding for aftercare services to reduce the high rate of recidivism of youth leaving detention; and strengthen and expand the quality of on-site education and vocational programs and assist inmates in re-entry by effective release planning, including potential employment.

- Mandate better legal counsel for young men of color and strengthen the public defender system.
- Support the call of Justice Kennedy and other prominent justice officials to repeal mandatory minimums, including the mandatory 100-to-1 powder cocaine/crack cocaine ratio and other sentencing requirements that incarcerate nonviolent offenders for long periods; expand youth courts, drug courts, and community-based counseling as alternatives to incarceration for low-risk, nonviolent offenders.
- Employ models of reform and innovation, such as drug policy reforms presented by Roger Goodman, director of the Drug Policy Project at the King County Bar Association; juvenile justice system reforms authored by Mississippi Representative George Flaggs, Jr.; Massachusetts' Youth Advocacy Project, which provides comprehensive legal representation and advocacy for youth charged as delinquent and youthful offenders in Boston's juvenile courts; community courts, such as Brooklyn's Red Hook Community Justice Center, the nation's first multi-jurisdictional community court; and community-based engagement efforts to effectively re-integrate former offenders into society, such as the Family Life Center, based in Providence, Rhode Island.

The Media

- Make state-owned buildings and other facilities available to facilitate engagement—including discussions of news coverage—between media outlets and community groups.
- Media reform activists, foundations, and other nonprofits should organize community-media forums to discuss media practices— including bias and staffing diversity and sourcing—and conduct periodic audits of news coverage.
- The Federal Communications Commission (FCC) should oppose current proposals to further loosen ownership restrictions that would allow media conglomerates to acquire even more broadcasting properties.
- Repeal the 1996 Telecommunications Act and restore the Fairness Doctrine in broadcasting.
- Pass legislation that would provide subsidies to help finance new

minority-owned Internet enterprises and other digital media to promote more diversity in communications and more public service media.

- News organizations should adopt "best practices" proposals, such as those produced by the Columbia University Journalism School, and consult journalism-improvement institutes such as the Poynter Institute and the Maynard Institute and media-community engagement institutes such as the UCLA-based Center for Communications and Community.

- Pursue models of innovation such as the National Credibility Roundtables Project of the Associated Press Managing Editors, which is one of a number of Ford Foundation-sponsored media projects designed to promote ongoing communication between the public and the press and to encourage journalists to use what they learn to improve news practices.

CONCLUSIONS AND RECOMMENDATIONS

The policy recommendations for education, child welfare, economic, justice, and health care systems are directed to policymakers, legislators, public administrators, and key influential leaders within communities. The Joint Center, through its Health Policy Institute, adds its voice to recent efforts by the 21st Century Fund, the National Urban League, the Harvard Civil Rights Project, the Advancement Project, the Children's Defense Fund, and several other organizations in asking our nation to address the barriers faced by African American and other minority youth. This effort focuses on the male population, not to diminish the crisis of women, but to recognize the disproportionate and unfair burden that young men carry and its far-reaching implications for family and community health. This report captures the key points of several detailed background papers that were used by the Commission to understand the issues more fully and inform its deliberations in formulating an ambitious but realistic action plan.

While elected officials at all levels of government can create policies and direct and redirect resources, the impetus, indeed the pressure, for such decisions must come from informed and galvanized constituencies. This work is therefore also directed to a larger audience. The Joint Center Health Policy Institute will form multi-sectoral partnerships (public, labor, education, and private sectors) to rigorously pursue these recommendations. As Chairman

Dellums stated, "Once we have developed the appropriate recommendations, we must come together to lay out tactics and strategies so that at the end of the day, this does not end up being simply another report gathering dust."

It is true that our collective quality of life is intricately connected. As such, life outcomes of young men of color, in many ways, depict the health and capability of our nation. The Commission strongly believes that just as failed policies led us here, a thoughtful policy agenda can light the way forward. Such government innovation is essential, not just because it delivers benefits, but because successful policy changes remind us of our persistent power to create the society that we desire. America must now decide that the society we desire is one in which children of color, no less than others, are expecting life, enjoying liberty, and pursuing the happiness promised to us all. Ultimately, it is in our nation's best interest to intervene on behalf of young men of color and embrace them as true partners for our nation's security and prosperity.

THE DELLUMS COMMISSION

CHAIRMAN
The Honorable Ronald Dellums

HONORARY VICE CHAIR
Alvin Poussaint, MD

COMMISSION MEMBERS

Estela Mara Bensimon
The Honorable Arthur L. Burnett, Sr.
The Honorable George Flaggs
Reverend Dr. James A. Forbes Jr.
Badi Foster, PhD
Frank Fountain
The Honorable Nancy Gist

Roger Goodman
Gloria Grantham, PhD
Norbert Hill
Sherry Hirota
Loretta Jones
The Honorable Arthenia Joyner
The Honorable Bob Knight
The Honorable Alexander Lipsey, Esq.
The Honorable John McCoy
Joseph McDonald, EdD
The Honorable Robert McEwyn
The Honorable Thelma Wyatt Moore
The Honorable Felix w. Ortiz
The Honorable Bernadette M. Sanchez
Ronald Walters, PhD
The Honorable William F. Winter

DELLUMS COMMISSION BACKGROUND PAPERS

The Dellums Commission's final report and background papers listed below are available on the Joint Center's Web site at www.jointcenter.org.

Men and Communities: African American Males and the Well-Being of Children, Families, and Neighborhoods
by James B. Hyman

A New Generation of Native Sons: Men of Color and the Prison-Industrial Complex
by Adolphus G. Belk, Jr.

Public Policies and Practices in Child Welfare Systems that Affect Life Options for Children of Color
by Ernestine F. Jones

***Black Male Students at Public Flagship Universities in the U.S. –
Status, Trends, and Implications for Policy and Practice,***
by Shaun R. Harper

***How the Juvenile Justice System Reduces Life Options of
Minority Youth***
by Edgar S. Cahn

***The Impact of Waivers to Adult Court, Alternative Sentencing,
and Alternatives to Incarceration on Young Men of Color***
by Michael L. Lindsey

Correctional Policy — Re-entry and Recidivism
by Sandra Edmonds Crewe

***Community Health Strategies to Better the Life Options of Boys
and Young Men of Color: Policy Issues and Solutions***
by Kay Randolph-Back

Indigenous Men in Higher Education
by Bryan McKinley Jones Brayboy

***State Public Education Policy and Life Pathways for Boys and
Young Men of Color,***
by Kay Randolph-Back

***Conditions that Affect the Participation and Success of Latino
Males in College,***
by Octavio Villalpando

NOTES

1. Certain subgroups of minority males have lower life expectancies than do white males. Life expectancy at birth is listed by race/ethnicity in descending order: Asian American men in California (80.9), Hispanic or Latino men in California and Puerto Rico (77.7–73), white non-Hispanic men (75.4), African American men (69.2), and American Indian men (67.4). See W. A. Leigh and D. Huff, *Women of Color Health Data Book: Adolescents to Seniors*, 3rd ed. (Bethesda, MD: National Institutes of Health, 2006), 65, Figure 4. However, aggregate life expectancy rates do not tell the whole story. For example, young men of color in particular have greater rates of mortality from two important preventable causes of death: homicide and HIV/AIDS. See National Center for Health Statistics, *Health, United States, 2005 With Chartbook on Trends in the Health of Americans* (Hyattsville, MD: 2005).

2. See recent publications such as P. Edelman, H. Holzer, and P. Offner, *Reconnecting Disadvantaged Young Men* (Washington, D.C.: Urban Institute Press, 2006); R. Mincy, ed., *Black Males Left Behind* (Washington, D.C.: Urban Institute Press, 2006).

3. See Appendix for a summary of the Dellums Commission background papers.

4. The World Health Organization Commission on Social Determinants of Health, http://www.who.int/social_determinants/en.

5. See, e.g., I. K Crombie, L. Irvine, L. Elliott, and H. Wallace, *Closing the Health Inequalities Gap: An International Perspective* (Cophenhagen: World Health Organization, 2005), and generally, the Health Inequality resources Web site of the World Health Organization, http://www.who.int/health-systems-performance/docs/healthinequality_docs.htm.

6. On the decline of good jobs in inner cities, see W. J. Wilson, *When Work Disappears: The World of the New Urban Poor* (New York: Random House, 1997). On segregation, see D. S. Massey and N. A. Denton, *American Apartheid: Segregation and the Making of the Underclass* (Harvard University Press, 1993). For statistics on residential segregation, see the University of Michigan Population Studies Center, http://enceladus.isr.umich.edu/race/races-tart.asp.

7. R. B. Hill, "Social Welfare Policies and African American Families," *Black Families, Third Edition*, ed. H. P. McAdoo (Thousand Oaks: Sage Publications, 1997).

8. C. B. Swanson, *Who Graduates? Who Doesn't? A Statistical Portrait of Public High-School Graduation, Class of 2001* (Washington, D.C.: The Urban Institute, 2004).

9. T. P. Bonczar, *Prevalence of Imprisonment in the U.S. Population, 1974-2001* (Washington, D.C.: U.S. Department of Justice, 2003).

10. National Center for Health Statistics, Health data for all ages warehouse Web site, Data tables: Adults, mortality, http://www.cdc.gov/nchs/health_data_for_all_ages.htm.

11. E. S. Cahn, *How the Juvenile Justice System Reduces Life Options of Minority Youth* (Washington, D.C.: Joint Center for Political and Economic Studies, 2006), 7. Cahn lists these trip wires as "'zero tolerance,' 'the war on drugs,' truancy, mental health problems, lack of parental support, learning disability, and enforced custodial care stemming from abuse and neglect."

12. Cahn, *How the Juvenile Justice System Reduces Life Options of Minority Youth*, 9.

13. A. G. Belk Jr., *A New Generation of Native Sons: Men of Color and the Prison-Industrial Complex* (Washington, D.C.: Joint Center for Political and Economic Studies, 2006), v.

14. Cahn, *How the Juvenile Justice System Reduces Life Options of Minority Youth*, 21. See also U.S. Department of Health and Human Services, *Youth Violence: A Report of the Surgeon General* (Washington, D.C.: GPO, 2001), 117.

15. U.S. Census Bureau, *American Community Survey 2005*, American Factfinder, http:/factfinder.census.gov.

16. R. M. Entman, *Young Men of Color in the Media: Images and Impacts* (Washington, D.C.: Joint Center for Political and Economic Studies, 2006).

[1] *This Essay is excerpted from the Dellums Commission's final report, available on the Joint Center's Web site at www.jointcenter.org.*

REPORT FROM THE NATIONAL URBAN LEAGUE POLICY INSTITUTE

Invisible Men: The Urgent Problems of Low-Income African-American Males

National Urban League Policy Institute
Renee Hanson, Mark McArdle, and Valerie Rawlston Wilson, Ph.D.

T his edition of *The State of Black America*, 2007 has been dedicated to various aspects of the plight of African-American males. While we celebrate the individuality of black boys and black men living in America and the diversity of perspective, talents and experiences that exist among them, we also acknowledge a shared experience that in some cases has resulted in triumph, and in others, tragedy. In many ways, two different worlds exist for African-American males. In one world, the number of black men graduating from college has quadrupled since the passage of the 1964 Civil Rights Act; in the other, more black men are earning high school equivalency diplomas in prison each year than are graduating from college. In one world, black families consisting of a father and a mother have a median family income nearly equal to white families; in the other, more than half of the nation's 5.6 million black boys live in fatherless households, 40 percent of which are impoverished. The existence of these two worlds is both an example of what is possible, and a warning about the consequences of racism, inequality and marginalization.

After decades of neglect, the glaring disparities and injustices faced by black males in America are finally beginning to receive the national attention they deserve. Over the course of the previous year, black males have been the focus of a number of symposia, research and policy initiatives, and news reports. Some of these include the Washington Post series, *Being a Black Man*; the Dellums Commission's, *A Way Out: Creating Partners for Our Nation's Prosperity by Expanding Life Paths of Young Men of Color,* released by the Health Policy Institute of the Joint Center for Political and Economic Studies; and the book, *Black Males Left Behind*, edited by Ronald Mincy and published by the Urban Institute. While many in the civil rights community are pleased that the challenges facing black males are receiving the serious thought and consideration they deserve, it seems to have come at a time when the urgency of these problems can no longer be ignored.

As powerful as the words published in this book and elsewhere are, the old adage, "a picture is worth a thousand words", remains true. The following graphs, prepared by the research staff of the National Urban League Policy Institute, illustrate some of the incredible challenges facing African-American males—particularly in the areas of employment, education and incarceration.

Unemployment

Unemployment is in many ways the canary in coal mine for black men. As demonstrated by Figure 1, although the unemployment rate for all racial and ethnic groups follows the economic cycle (higher during recessions, lower during recoveries), black male unemployment is consistently higher than any other group and usually twice that of whites. Figure 2 shows that if broken down by age group, nearly a third of black teens were unemployed in 2006, compared with only 15% of white teens. Although unemployment declines as men age, black unemployment is still double that of whites for each age group. These high rates of unemployment among black males have been attributed to a lack of skills necessary for participation in today's mainstream labor force, a shortage of relatively well-paying jobs for those with less than a college education, and disproportionately high rates of incarceration, accompanied by discrimination against former prisoners. The graphs in the next two sections detail some of the factors contributing to these disparities.

Education

One explanation for why black men experience higher rates of unemployment is the fact that the average level of educational attainment is lower for this group. In many inner cities, more than half of all black men do not finish high school[1], and in 2004, 72 percent of black male high school dropouts in

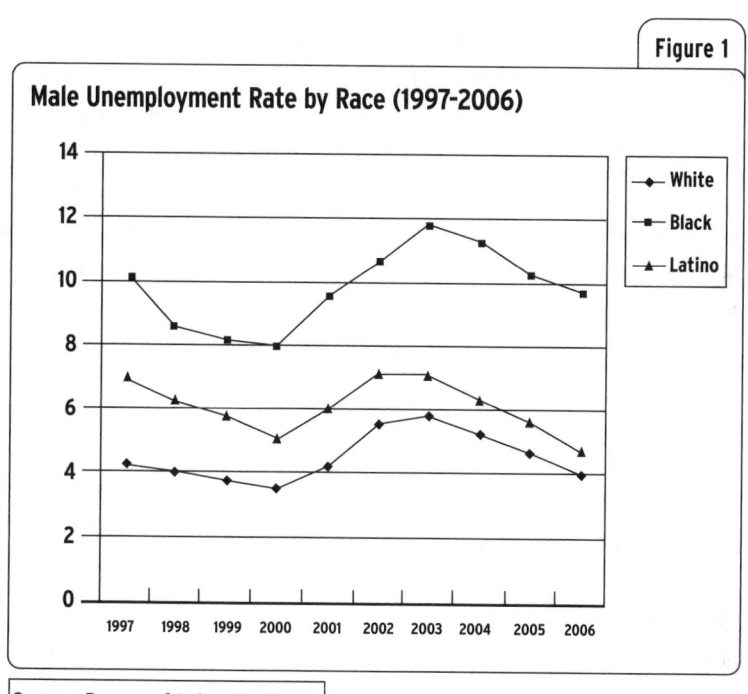

Figure 1

Male Unemployment Rate by Race (1997-2006)

Source: Bureau of Labor Statistics

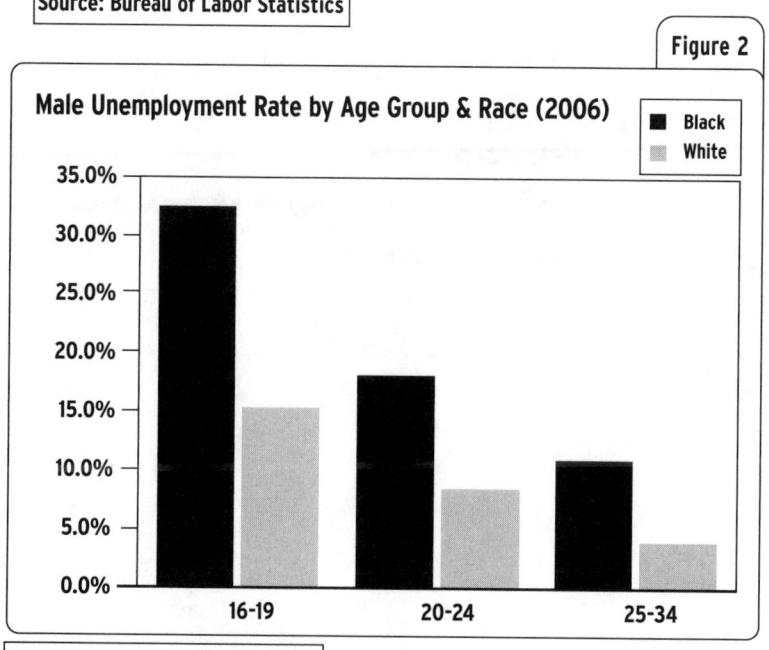

Figure 2

Male Unemployment Rate by Age Group & Race (2006)

Source: Bureau of Labor Statistics

their twenties were jobless.[2] As can be seen in Figure 3, nearly 20 percent of all black men over age 25 have no high school diploma compared with only 10 percent of white men. At the upper end of the educational spectrum, black men are getting master's degrees, PhDs and professional degrees at half the rate of white men. It has been well-documented that education is a major determinant of earning power and employability. Figure 4 shows that in 2005 college graduates earned over twice as much as high school dropouts. It also shows that the unemployment rate of those without a high school diploma was nearly three times the unemployment rate of college graduates.

Figure 3

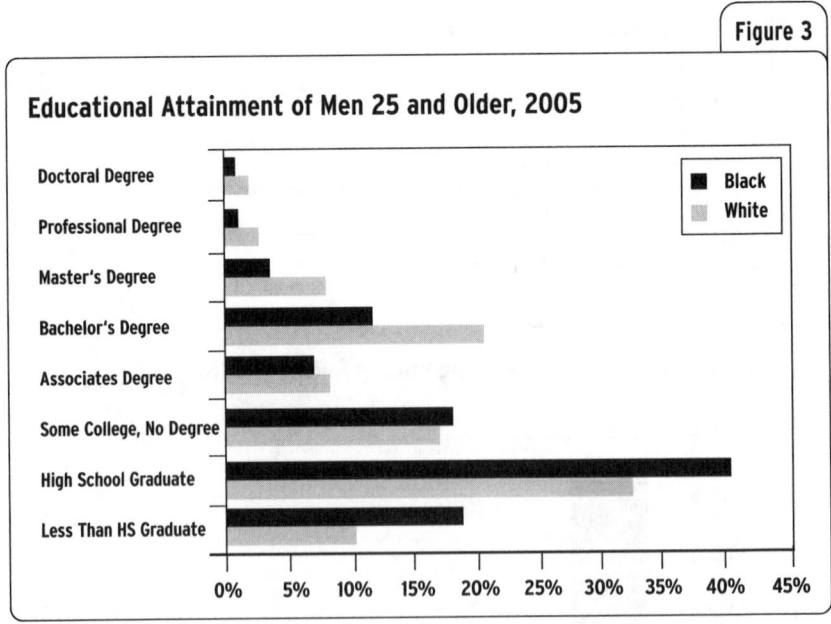

Educational Attainment of Men 25 and Older, 2005

Source: U.S. Census

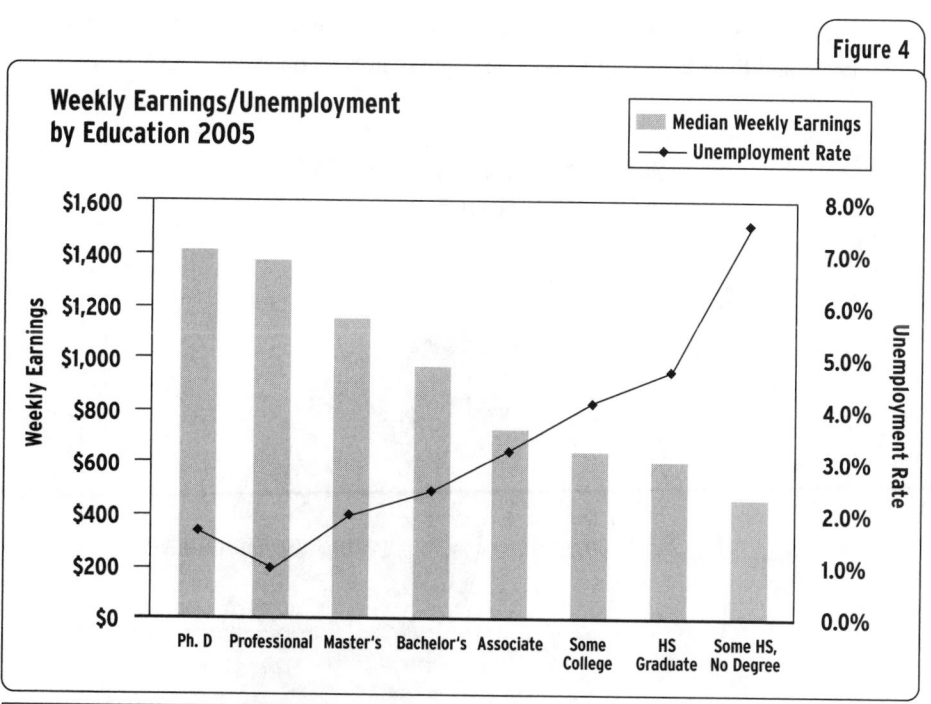

Figure 4

Weekly Earnings/Unemployment by Education 2005

Median Weekly Earnings
Unemployment Rate

Source: Bureau of Labor Statistics

Incarceration

Another contributing factor to higher unemployment for black men is their much higher incarceration rates. Although comprising only 12 percent of the U.S. population, nearly 40 percent of all prison inmates were black in 2005 (see Figure 5), and the black incarceration rate was *over 6 times* the incarceration rate for whites (see Figure 6). The rate of incarceration is highest for men between the ages of 25 and 29, when over 8% of black men are in prison, compared with only 1% of white men (see Figure 7). The rate of incarceration among black males has been increasing since the 1990s due in large part to harsher punishments for repeat offenders (e.g. "three strikes law") and drug laws that impose harsher sentences on those found in pos-

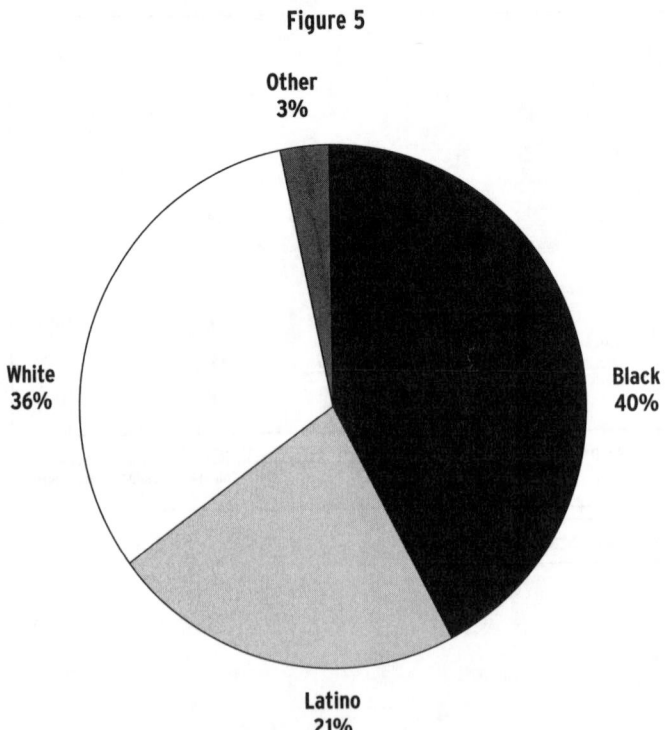

Race/Ethnicity of Prisoners, 2005
Figure 5

Other
3%

White
36%

Black
40%

Latino
21%

Source: Bureau of Justice Statistics

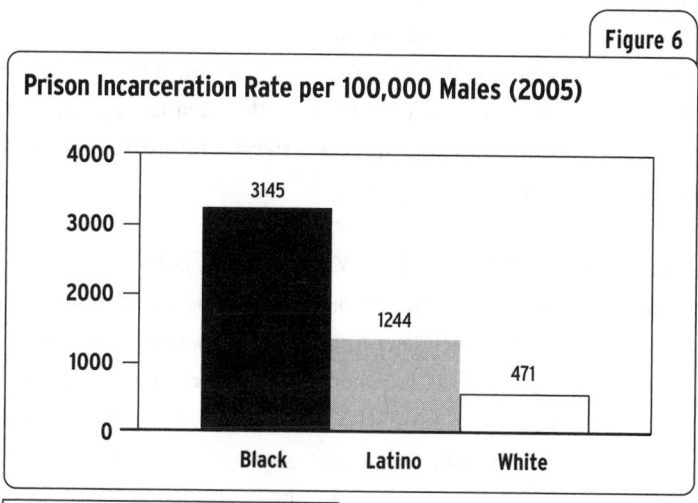

Source: Bureau of Justice Statistics

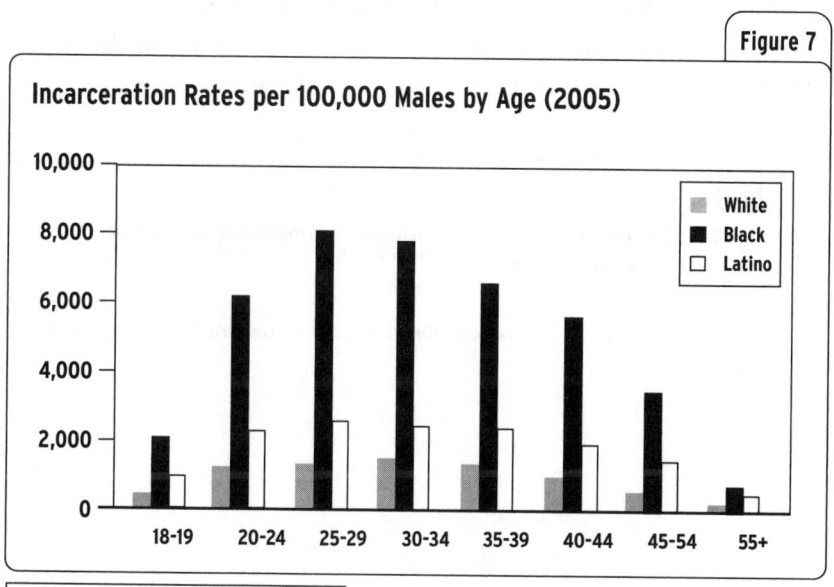

Source: Bureau of Justice Statistics

session of crack cocaine. In 2005, drug offenders comprised 20 percent of state prisoners and almost 55 percent of federal prisoners. The U.S. now has the highest reported incarceration rate in the world, at 737 inmates per 100,000 persons in the population (followed by Russia at 611 per 100,000). A history of incarceration not only interferes with educational attainment, but also becomes a significant employment barrier; therefore, the effect of even a short imprisonment lasts a lifetime.

CONCLUSION AND RECOMMENDATIONS

The graphs presented in this report, along with the findings of other researchers and policymakers demonstrate how joblessness, low educational attainment and high rates of incarceration all work together to create a vicious downward cycle for those who become disconnected from school or work, or become involved in the justice system at any point. Taking all of these factors into consideration, it is absolutely critical that there be a well-defined pipeline that not only seeks to engage young black males early in the educational process, but also provides options for them as they transition into the labor market – be it directly out of high school, college or correctional facilities. Whatever the particular solutions, they must be approached from the standpoint that it is never too early, nor too late, to change a life.

NOTES

[1] Orfield, Gary ed. (2004). *Dropouts in America: Confronting the Graduation Rate Crisis*. Cambridge: Harvard Education Press.

[2] Western, Bruce (2006). *Punishment and Inequality in America*. New York: Russell Sage Foundation.

THE NATIONAL URBAN LEAGUE: EMPOWERING BLACK MALES TO REACH THEIR FULL POTENTIAL

by Aaron Thomas and James Reed

The National Urban League's Black Male Commission, launched in 2004 by President Marc H. Morial, is a national, coordinated effort to address the alarming inequities, disparities and social trends disproportionately affecting black males. Through the advocacy of policies and implementation of programs that support black men through job development, academic achievement, early childhood education and prisoner re-entry strategies, the Commission works to improve the status, life hopes and prospects for Black males at every level of society.

Since its inception, the Black Male Commission has established national strategic partnerships and internal and external taskforces to research and tackle problems that impede the economic and social success of black men and boys in this nation. Bringing together educators, public officials, scholars, policy experts and practitioners and others, the National Urban League is creating realistic solutions to the problems facing black American males.

In coordination with the Black Male Commission, the National Urban League is developing innovative and effective programs to advance job development, provide educational opportunities, and enhance black men's ability to be strong, effective fathers. In addition, the Black Male Commission addresses the critical and significant need for quality and rigorous early childhood education for black boys as a long term strategy against incarceration and low academic achievement. The Black Male Commission's comprehensive prisoner re-entry strategy's holistic and systemic change approach to redirecting and supporting ex-prisoners is designed to reduce recidivism and improve their chances of a successful life.

The National Urban League is partnered with the U.S. Department of Labor on a multi-year effort to break the cycle of unemployment, incarceration and recidivism facing many black families. Focusing on out-of-school

217

and/or adjudicated young adults, ages 18-24, the *Urban Youth Empowerment Program (UYEP)* is making a difference in 27 local Urban League affiliate sites across the country.

The goal of the UYEP is to prepare youth for entry into the world of work through their participation in a comprehensive set of services; including case management, community service with faith-based organizations, educational upgrades including GEDs, mentoring, internships, on-the-job training, occupational stills training, personal development, and unsubsidized employment. More than 4,000 youth (53% male) will participate in this three-year demonstration program. The highly successful program has produced the following results through 2006:

- 83% of at-risk and ex-offender participants stayed with the program's activities;
- 33% of participants earned their GEDs and/or high school diplomas;
- 40% of participants increased their reading and math scores;
- 37% of participants got jobs or other positive outcomes
- Average earnings increased by 12% over the targeted goal of $7.00 per hour;
- Recidivism rate for participants was 50% less than anticipated.

For more information on the Black Male Commission and the Urban Youth Empowerment Program, please visit our website: www.nul.org

Losing Our Children in America's *Cradle to Prison Pipeline*®

by Marian Wright Edelman

G ay cancer"—that's what they called AIDS, the mysterious killer of white homosexual men in the early 1980s before medical researchers isolated the virus that causes the disease. Some religious leaders claimed it was God's punishment for sinful behavior. The administration of President Ronald Reagan failed to adequately fund the research focused on identifying its cause. Some leaders in the black community looked the other way because they thought it was something that only white gay men could catch.

We now know in retrospect that as a result of widespread ignorance and negligence, precious years were lost in discovering effective treatments for AIDS that would have saved so many lives. As the disease spread beyond our means to contain it, millions died needlessly. Those most endangered by the disease are no longer gay white men. Currently, HIV-AIDS infection rates among black females exceed the rates for males of all races and ethnic groups except African Americans, according to Centers for Disease Control and Prevention data. For three-quarters of infected black females, the disease was transmitted through heterosexual contact.

I bring to mind our national experience with AIDS to shed light on another growing epidemic plaguing our communities and nation, about which many are blind or choose to remain conveniently ignorant. I'm referring to America's Cradle to Prison Pipeline crisis that funnels tens of thousands of poor children every year down life paths that lead to arrest, conviction, incarceration and death. Currently, about 100,000 youths languish in detention centers across the country. Millions of children are at risk of entering the prison pipeline from the moment they come into the world as poor, low-birthweight babies born to parents unprepared to care for them and lacking sufficient supports. A large portion of these vulnerable children come under the care of an inadequate child welfare system that is often unable to make their lives better and sometimes makes them worse.

For the past two years, through our new Cradle to Prison Pipeline® Initiative, the Children's Defense Fund (CDF) has been researching the entry and exit points of the prison pipeline. Our study has involved the children and families who live their lives in and out of daily proximity to the prison pipeline as well as educators, health care professionals, judges, law enforcement and juvenile justice officials, and advocates for improved child welfare and early childhood development policies and practices.

The Cradle to Prison Pipeline is made up of a complex combination of social and economic factors and political choices that converge to reduce the odds that poor children, especially poor minority children, will grow up to become productive, responsible, and contributing members of their families, communities and nation. These factors include stressed, poor and often single-parent families; disparities in access to health and mental health care; lack of quality early childhood experiences; underperforming schools with low expectations and zero tolerance discipline policies; broken child welfare and juvenile justice systems; a pervasive popular culture that glorifies violence, conspicuous consumption, promiscuity, narcissism, celebrity and misogyny; and far too few positive role models and alternatives to the streets.

Children who enter the prison pipeline represent all races and ethnic groups, but in a majority of cases, those caught at the intersection of poverty and race are most vulnerable because our society does not offer all children a level playing field on which to develop and grow. Although a black boy born in 2001 has a one-in-three chance of going to prison in his lifetime, girls are the fastest growing group among imprisoned children and teens. What is most alarming is that poor children are arrested, convicted and incarcerated at younger and younger ages.

Regrettably, like the AIDS epidemic in its early stages, many of our political leaders, pastors and heads of community organizations are silent, ignorant or indifferent about the increasing damage the prison pipeline is visiting upon our communities. This is another missed diagnosis that is costing lives and eroding our nation's future. We all must recognize this unfolding tragedy in our rich nation and act now to dismantle the Cradle to Prison Pipeline.

First, we must acknowledge that the prison pipeline exists and understand its dangerous and synergistic architecture. At its base is poverty compounded by decades of racial exclusion that, in combination, have concentrated poor minorities into dense, economically depressed and crime-ridden inner-city neighborhoods, small towns and rural areas.

A child's family environment is critical in determining whether or not he or she enters the Cradle to Prison Pipeline. Most of the young people who end up behind bars started out in poor and unstable families unable to weather the pressures of economic hardship and persistent poverty—physical and spiritual. The 13 million children living in poverty, including the 5.6 million living in extreme poverty, are more involved in serious delinquency than youngsters from families with higher incomes, the "Rochester Youth Development Study" reports.

Too many absent fathers leave too many poor and minority children in families headed by single mothers struggling financially and straining to hold their households together. With frayed or sundered extended family networks, few single working mothers have the time, supports or energy to nurture and guide their children, read to them at night, help with their homework, take them to a health clinic, or advocate for them at their schools. They are too busy merely trying to survive.

Starting Behind—Staying Behind

Another important factor in determining whether a child enters the Cradle to Prison Pipeline is whether she or he gets a healthy start in life. A healthy start for any child begins in the womb even before conception, but many low-income pregnant women do not receive prenatal care or health counseling. A 2004 article in *The Journal of Pediatrics*, titled "The Lingering Academic Deficits of Low Birth Weight Children," says that a low-birthweight child is 50 percent more likely to score below average on measures of both reading and mathematics. Low-birthweight children are more likely when they start school to experience educational disadvantages that can persist into early adulthood.

According to data from Mental Health America, a national organization focused on mental health, about 10 percent of all children and adolescents have a serious mental or emotional disorder such as attention deficit/hyperactivity disorder, depression, post-traumatic stress disorder, dyslexia or mental retardation. These and other unaddressed health problems, including early hearing or vision loss and learning disabilities, can turn into deficits and developmental delays. If caught early, many of these problems can be effectively treated. This is less likely among black children, large numbers of whom do not receive routine health care including the standard battery of vaccinations against diseases like measles, mumps and rubella. Today, more than nine million children in our country lack health insurance—of those, 16 percent or 1.5 million are black. Our nation can guarantee health insurance for *every* child and pregnant woman living at or below 300 percent of the federal poverty level. Advancing this goal is CDF's top priority in 2007.

Throughout the American experience, children born into poverty and depressed conditions have elevated themselves through education. That's difficult to do at a poorly funded, understaffed and low-achieving school. Fourth-graders in U.S. public elementary schools with the highest poverty levels have significantly lower reading scores than students from schools with higher family incomes. Statistics from the U.S. Department of Education's National Assessment of Educational Progress (NAEP) reveal that, of all black fourth-graders, only 13 percent read at or above grade level. The figure is nine percent for math.

Too many poor black children begin school so far behind that they never catch up. Already burdened by health and nutrition deficiencies and little preschool preparation, they often attend schools that are generally ill-equipped to identify or remedy the developmental delays of children who need help. To compound this problem, schools with the highest percentages of minority, limited English proficient and low-income students are more likely to employ beginning teachers, teachers who are less educated, and those who teach subjects in which they are not certified or in which they did not major in college. And black children are unlikely to be taught by teachers who look like them. A 2006 Harvard University Civil Rights Project report, "The Segregation of American Teachers," found that 83 percent of public school teachers were White and just eight percent were African Americans. Low expectations for children from marginalized families are too common among teachers and administrators lacking the cultural competence to understand and respond adequately to their problems.

Less effort is made to work with children whose behavior is perceived as insubordinate, disruptive or unruly. "Zero tolerance" disciplinary standards are too frequently applied. A disturbing outgrowth of the zero tolerance approach is that schools are becoming a major point of entry into the juvenile justice system as children are now regularly arrested on school grounds at younger and younger ages. Their offenses are often subjectively and loosely defined behaviors such as "disorderly conduct" and "malicious mischief." An Advancement Project study, "Derailed: The Schoolhouse to Jailhouse Track," found that student arrests in Miami-Dade County, Florida, have tripled since 1999. One need only recall the case in 2005 of five-year-old Ja'eisha Scott who was handcuffed and arrested by three St. Petersburg, Florida police officers for having a temper tantrum at school.

The growth in school expulsions and suspensions contributes to increasing numbers of children and teens entering the prison pipeline. In 2002, 3.1 million children were suspended from school. Black students were nearly three times more likely to be suspended than white students according to U.S. Department of Education, Office for Civil Rights statistics. Discouraged teens who are suspended or pushed out of school are almost invariably placed at greater risk. Numerous studies demonstrate that students who are suspended or expelled are more likely than their peers to drop out of school altogether. Left at home without adult supervision if their parents work, some students simply hang out on street corners where they socialize with ex-offenders who are neither in school nor employed. The corner is not a place where values like academic achievement or deferred gratification are taught. It is a place that teaches the negative values of not accepting responsibility, rationalizing harm, and blaming others or the system for one's problems.

The Bureau of Justice Statistics report, "Educational and Correctional Populations," reveals that high school dropouts are almost three times as likely to be incarcerated as youths who have graduated from high school. According to the Justice Policy Institute, in 1999, 52 percent of black men who had dropped out of high school had prison records by their early thirties. The fallout from zero tolerance school disciplinary policies leading to increased suspensions and expulsion is making the street corner a gaping entry way into the Cradle to Prison Pipeline.

Many children are locked up not because they commit crimes but because they have a mental or emotional disorder. Parents who don't know how to deal with this behavior are sometimes left with no option other than relinquishing them to the foster care or juvenile justice system hoping that they will get the mental health treatment they need. Thousands of children are sentenced to juvenile detention facilities because they are awaiting treatment that does not exist in their communities. "If your family has money, you get psychiatric intervention...if they don't, you get the prison psychologist," says Dr. Edward J. Latessa, a University of Cincinnati criminologist. Comprehensive health coverage, including mental health coverage, is crucial to stopping these destructive trends.

Crammed Dockets

Poor children and teens sent to juvenile courts often face an overcrowded system where they are unlikely to be treated fairly. The overburdened juvenile justice system handles more than 1.5 million cases a year. Many of these are infractions by children that used to be handled by families, school principals and community organizations. About two-thirds of all children behind bars are locked up for non-violent offenses. Among youths charged with drug offenses, African Americans are 48 times as likely to be incarcerated as White youths.

A poor child charged with an offense may appear before a court with no member of his family or community to stand with him, and he may not understand the legal process or the gravity of his circumstances. His case may be assigned to a public defender whom he meets for the first time on the day of his trial. With crammed dockets, judges pressed to process as many cases as possible often dispense in minutes verdicts that define a lifetime. Juvenile courts have become another major feeder system for the Cradle to Prison Pipeline.

Once they enter the juvenile justice system, the odds that poor and minority children and teens will get a second chance are not good. Too few judges offer poor youthful defendants productive alternatives to incarceration—restitution, community service, drug treatment, or placement in a "staff secure" but not locked community corrections facility. The deeper a poor child gets into the justice system, the harder it is for him to get out. Some never do. In

January 2006, 14-year-old Martin Lee Anderson died of suffocation at a state-run boot camp in Florida after seven guards beat and restrained him. His death occurred the day after he was sent to the camp for violating parole by taking his grandmother's car.

Hardened by long terms of incarceration, criminalized youngsters return to communities that are ill-equipped to positively reintegrate them. Outcast and unemployed, they become the teachers and role models for a new crop of youngsters pushed onto the street corners of America's most depressed neighborhoods. This cycle of re-infection works to perpetuate the prison pipeline and enlarge the tragic scope of its damage to our society.

The Prison Pipeline Must Be Demolished

The Cradle to Prison Pipeline must be demolished along with the structures and policies that feed and support it. This will require an active, vocal and persistent commitment from families, community organizations, faith networks and policy makers from every segment of our society. First, adults must take responsibility for children and provide positive role models and alternatives to the streets. And adults must stand up for children when political leaders slash essential investments in successful programs for children and youth. We must speak out against policies that contribute to criminalizing children at younger and younger ages, and fight for policies that put children on a trajectory to productive adulthood. The costs are too great. In dollars alone, we save more than $1.5 million for each child we divert from the criminal justice system, states the Department of Justice report, "Treatment, Services and Intervention Programs for Child Delinquents."

This year, we should stand together and insist that our Congress and President guarantee health and mental health care in 2007 for *all* children and pregnant women in America. The reauthorization of the State Children's Health Insurance Program (SCHIP) presents an opportunity to finish the job of insuring all of our nation's children. God did not make two classes of children and we should not permit America to. And shame on us if Katrina's children continue to be abandoned by adults in positions of responsibility who are entrusted with their care, protection and education.

We must invest far greater resources in proven early childhood development programs that build healthy bodies and minds including Early Head

Start and Head Start as well as home visiting and other parent supports that prevent children from going into the child welfare system. Zero tolerance school discipline that is escalating suspensions and abusive treatment of young children must be terminated. Education must be better funded and teachers better prepared to support children—including the 80 percent of black children who do not read at grade level in fourth grade.

We can also begin to dismantle the prison pipeline at home. Parents must get the help they need to become the best parents they can and want to be. We must all take personal responsibility to mentor and advocate for children and to be change agents in our communities. Families can set another place at the dinner table once or twice a week for an at-risk child. If you are taking your children to a museum or the zoo, make room in the car for another child. Buy an extra ticket to a ball game or play.

There are a variety of opportunities for communities to make a difference by working to keep schools, churches, mosques and temples open after school hours and during idle summer months as safe havens from the dangerous influences of the streets. Much of the trouble children and teens get into occurs after school and before their parents return home from work, between 3:00 and 6:00 p.m. There are numerous examples of successful partnerships of parents, educators, community organizations, pastors and local governments coming together that need to be replicated on a much greater scale like the Harlem Children's Zone, the Boston Ten Point Coalition and the CDF Freedom Schools[SM] program.

We ignore the human devastation caused by the Cradle to Prison Pipeline at our peril. Our failure to act on the lack of health coverage for the uninsured, shortfalls in fixing underperforming schools, and neglect of broken child welfare and juvenile justice systems and increasing child poverty will perpetuate the cycle of despair and erode the hard won gains of the Civil Rights Movement. We must reclaim our children and our future by reweaving the fabric of family and community. We must emphasize the importance of and support for parenting so our children can grow up to be strong, self-sufficient adults who are good parents and productive citizens. Black America has fought slavery, segregation and apartheid. In each of those struggles, we had valuable allies. Now we must fight for the lives of our children and our nation's soul threatened by the Cradle to Prison Pipeline and the increasing gap between rich and poor. All of the forces of common sense, faith and good will in our society must join this nation-defining struggle. For the sakes of all of our children and ourselves, we must stand up together and act. *For more information on CDF's Healthy Child plan, go to www.ElectSusie.com.*

REFERENCES

Breslau, Naomi, Paneth, Nigel S., and Lucia, Victoria C. 2004. "The Lingering Academic Deficits of Low Birth Weight Children." *Journal of Pediatrics*, 114:4, pp. 1035-1040.

Browne, Judith A. 2003. "Derailed: The Schoolhouse to Jailhouse Track." Washington, DC: Advancement Project.

Burns, Barbara J., Howell, James C., Wiig, Janet K., Augimeri, Leena K., Welsh, Brendan C., Loeber, Rolf and Petechuk, David. 2003. "Treatment, Services and Intervention Programs for Child Delinquents." Washington, DC: U.S. Department of Justice.

Frankenberg, Erica. 2006. "The Segregation of American Teachers." Cambridge, MA: The Civil Rights Project at Harvard University.

Harlow, Caroline Wolf, 2002, "Educational and Correctional Populations." Washington, DC: Bureau of Justice Statistics, Office of Justice Programs. Calculations by the Children's Defense Fund.

Sexual Fault Lines:
Robbing the Love Between Us

by Michael Eric Dyson, Ph.D.

I f the often tense relationship between black men and black women is to improve, we must confront the social and personal difficulties that plague their togetherness. There are many elements that contribute to strained relations between black men and black women, including black female educational achievements and socioeconomic standing, both of which are higher on average than black men's; the substantial mortality gap between men and women; the disproportionate incarceration of black men; the poor labor force participation of black men; black men's lower occupational status; the dramatically decreasing rate of black men seeking higher education; and the increasing rate of interracial marriage among black men.

The incarceration of black men is a huge problem, especially when it is a zero-sum game between supporting black males in school or in prison. According to the Justice Policy Institute report, "Cellblocks or Classrooms? The Funding of Higher Education and Corrections and Its Impact on African American Men," we have chosen to fund correctional facilities over higher education. During the 1980s and 1990s, state spending for corrections grew at six times the rate of state spending on higher education. One of the tragedies of this state of affairs is that it undercuts the advances of black males in higher education over the last two decades. In 1980, there were 143,000 black men in jail or prison and 463,700 matriculating in higher educational institutions. In 2000, there were 791,600 black men in jail or prison, while only 603,032 were enrolled in colleges or universities. That same year, at least thirteen states had more black men in prison than in college, and from 1980 until 2000, thirty-eight states, along with the federal system, increased the prison population more than they swelled the ranks of higher education.

If black men are in prison and not in college, they have two strikes against them in their bid to become viable partners to black women. Black male imprisonment has a double-whammy effect on black women finding mates among their male peers: it separates black men from society, and it severely erodes their prospects for higher education.

Despite the depleted numbers of black men available for black women, there is the perception that smooth relations between black men and black women are hampered by the perception that black females are just too picky. *Ebony* magazine has through the years addressed the issue, in articles such as "How Black Women Can Deal with the Black Male Shortage," "Black Women/ Black Men: Has Something Gone Wrong Between Them?" and "Do Black Women Set Their Standards for Marriage Too High?" The black male shortage article, from the May 1986 issue, cited Census Bureau statistics that there were at the time 6.4 million more females than males in the United States, and that there were 1.4 million more black females than males.

According to the article, Dr. Ann Ashmore Poussaint and other experts suggested that black women stop blaming black men and society for their dilemma. The experts argued that women should take a closer look at themselves, their attitude about men, and their approach to finding a mate. "There are many single women who complain about loneliness, but when they do meet interesting men, they project a negative attitude or seem to always get into debates over feminist issues. Others aren't shy about flaunting their professional and financial successes, giving men the impression that they either don't need or have time for a meaningful relationship."

These sentiments appear to be informed by the reluctance to embrace feminist principles as a viable alternative for black women, or by a presumption that female success is the catalyst for the downfall of black men. But Poussaint also argued that too many black women eliminated suitors for superficial reasons, including profession, skin color, height, weight, income, education, family background, and social graces or contacts. She said that if a woman felt she was lowering her standards by dating or marrying a particular kind of man, she should reconsider her priorities. Poussaint and others were not suggesting that black women lower their standards, the article said, but that they should broaden their outlooks, including, some experts said, dating men outside their culture, although other experts strongly opposed interracial relationships.

In the higher standards article, printed in January 1981, *Ebony* explored the black male complaint that black women are more interested in what black men do than who they are. It also grapples with the black male perception that black women are more concerned with professional stature, high income, college degrees, and good looks. They tested this perception—which was really a hypothesis about black female behavior put forth by black men—by engaging twenty-five young women at Spelman College in a group discussion. To the question, "Is a man's status really important to a Black woman thinking about marriage?" *Ebony* reports there "was a resounding 'Yes' from the group."

Some of the students claimed that they were attending college to better themselves, and thus, they seek mates who match their efforts and achievement. The gap between a black male bus driver and a black female attorney would be hard to surmount. Since the vast majority of black men in 1981 held blue-collar jobs—a statistic that remains unchanged to this day—and because black women's route to professional achievement was not as difficult as that of black men, the magazine contended, the tensions between the genders would only increase. Many of the young Spelman women recognized that they might have difficulty in finding mates with comparable achievements, and hence believed they could afford to wait.

If the issue of black women having higher standards for relationships was a concern twenty years ago, it is even more prevalent now. According to some research, black women have been less willing than white women to marry men with lower status and undesirable traits—those who are younger, previously married, less educated, or unattractive. In short, black women prefer attractive men who are near their age and who have a stable career. For those black women who have never been married, they prefer mates with no previous wives or children. The younger the black woman, the greater her expectation that her man meet the criteria she deemed important. Further, black women who have higher status are more invested in building careers and less urgent about finding a mate. The economic independence of high-achieving black women, and the deteriorating economic conditions of black males, severely depletes the pool of potentially marriageable black men.

In our nation, people tend to marry folk who have similar educational backgrounds. That poses a huge problem for black men and women, since the ratio of highly educated black men to women has been said to be as small as sixty men available for every one hundred women. There are nearly 400,000 more black women than men enrolled in higher education. Black women are now earning more than sixty-three percent of all college degrees awarded to blacks. There are nearly four million black married couples in the United States, and among them, just under ten percent have marriages where both spouses have a college degree. Slightly more than one percent of them are marriages where both spouses had graduate degrees.

Moreover, black women with higher levels of education are disproportionately affected by the shortage of black men with similar levels of education. In the 1930s, only eleven percent of black women were expected not to marry; today, less than forty percent of black women are expected to marry. One might conclude in analyzing these statistics that there is no shortage of black men for black women to marry, but that black women choose to remain single rather than marry partners who do not meet their expectations. Further, educated professional black women seek to marry only those men they find acceptable by high standards; thus, lack of motivation, not availability, is the critical issue.

But that would be extremely shortsighted. While it is true that such numbers might translate to black women being "picky," the reality is that black women seek to meet and marry those men with whom they have the greatest degree of compatibility. Black male resentment of black female achievement, especially among black men who have not enjoyed the opportunity to succeed, may translate to unwarranted hostility toward black women. Many brothers feel that black women are the pawns of a white establishment that seeks to hold them down. As a result, black female movement through educational and professional ranks is to some black men a symptom of black women's complicity with a racist system. Rather than offer an astute analysis of our condition—that in a patriarchal culture, black men do represent a specific threat to white male power that black women don't, and hence, in some instances, white men prefer the presence of black women in professional settings—black men often confuse the consequences of racism with a desire of black females to undercut them.

Further, for a black man to reach beneath his class station to embrace a black woman reinforces the status quo: as breadwinner, he can provide for his family, and thus remain "head of the house." For a black woman to behave similarly upsets the status quo: if she makes more money and is better educated than her partner, the resentment of her man can become burdensome, sometimes abusive. Many black men feel that they could deal with a woman making more money than them, but once the reality of her higher status sets in, it usually takes on social meanings beyond a paycheck. Issues of control inevitably arise, and the question of who is "in charge" follows in its wake. Since black men struggle with a society that sets up expectations for appropriate masculine behavior—take care of one's family, be gainfully employed, be a financial success—and then undermines their attainment, black women are often the psychological scapegoat of our anger. The rise in black male domestic violence is poignant testimony to such tensions in the black home.

Many college-educated black women marry black men with significantly lower levels of education. In marriages where black women have a college degree, only 45.9 percent of their husbands also have a college degree. More than one quarter of black women who have a college degree are married to men who have never gone to college. And four percent of black women with a college degree are married to black men who didn't graduate from high school. By comparison, nearly seventy percent of white women with a college degree married men who also had a college degree, and only twelve percent of white women with a college degree married men who never went to college. While black women may prefer mates who are educationally compatible, they have often chosen mates whose lower achievement makes their marriages vulnerable to divorce and spousal abuse.

Other black men complain bitterly that many black women prefer the hardcore, "thugged-out" brother, the bad boy, the player. A brilliant young Vanderbilt University professor of mathematics, whom this thinking victimized, wrote an essay about his experience for *Essence* magazine. Jonathan Farley is a tall, slim, attractive brown-skinned young man, a summa cum laude graduate of Harvard who took a doctorate in mathematics from Oxford University and is an outspoken advocate for the Black Panthers. In his essay, he recalls a painful episode: a young lady with whom he fell in love only wanted to be his friend. But the worst of it is that she took him to dinner to heal his wounds by telling him why he struck out. "She outlined the difference between men like me and the men Black women preferred, between mere African Americans and `niggaz': African-Americans are safe, respectable, upwardly mobile and professional Black men. Niggaz are strong, streetwise, hard Black men."

Jonathan pointed out that his erstwhile love had a question posed to her by a friend: if she was walking down a dark street at night, who would she want by her side, an African-American or a 'nigga'? She told Jonathan that black women sought a strong protector. Jonathan writes that he "tried to explain that physical strength had ceased to be a survival trait back in the Stone Age:" Further, he warned her that women who prefer 'niggaz' to African-Americans were making a costly mistake since African-Americans, by virtue of their "higher social and economic status"-and wasn't this what black women wanted?—could better protect them and give them the security they desired. Since many young black women grow up without fathers in the home, even college-educated black women often settled for dropouts and drug dealers.

Because of his experience, Jonathan found himself "resisting my own impulses to open a door, start a conversation or even say hello to many young black women I meet, for fear of appearing too gentlemanly and hence unworthy of their attention." Jonathan argued that even black men who were "raised in the suburbs don the attire and attitude of street thugs so that they, too, will be chosen." He concluded his essay by admonishing sisters to "leave the players in the playground," and that "Knights in shining armor don't have to have gold teeth."

Many black women have admitted that this is far too frequent a flaw among their sisters. Many sisters claim to have outgrown such an inclination, chalking it up to their youth and their failure to know what kind of man would really be a good partner. Once they mature, many black women are attracted to brothers whose stability and substance are prized above the flashy danger of destructive black men.

As big a barrier to the flow of love between black men and women as the issues I've discussed are, perhaps none is more controversial, or as hurtful, as the rejection many black women experience when black men date and marry white women. As I lecture and preach across the country, black women of every station corner me, or ask me before an auditorium of hundreds, sometimes thousands, a version of the question: "Why do so many brothers despise us and chase white women?"

Of course, I am always reluctant to speak for all black men, especially when it comes to something as personal and subjective—though obviously not without serious social overtones—as who one likes or loves. And many of my heroes—Quincy Jones and Sidney Poitier among them—married white women at a time when doing so bravely challenged the nation's apartheid. In the sixties and seventies, interracial marriage, whether intended or not, represented a rejection of white supremacist values and indicated that love was a matter between individuals, not races. Few could miss the heroic gesture of loving across racial lines. Those who did often risked their reputations and social status while enduring cultural stigma. In short, it was apparent that interracial romance was unavoidably interpreted in political terms.

But if we are honest, interracial love has rarely, if ever, been simply about love. It has always borne political implications. From the very beginning of the black presence on American soil, stereotypes have distorted relations between the races, including those involving sex. Black males were brought to this nation in chains to be studs. Their virility was placed in the service of slavery. Black females were raped at will; their wombs became the largely unprotected domain of white male desire. Their sexuality was harnessed to perpetuate slavery through procreation. Later, of course, many more stereotypes of black men and women flourished, from the docile Uncle Tom, the fiery "field nigger," the compliant "house nigger," and the uppity buck, to the nurturing Mammy, the sarcastic sapphire, the promiscuous Jezebel, and now, in our day, the sex-crazed lothario, the unrepentant rapist, the welfare queen and the hoochie mama. These stereotypes often expressed the stunted social perceptions of black identity put forth by a white culture that refused to own up to its heavy hand in their creation.

Moreover, white society was ambivalent about black sexual identity—they wanted their blacks highly sexed to support slavery and white male pleasure. Otherwise, they wanted blacks to be constrained, even sexless if possible. Black men were feared and envied for their mythically large sexual organs. White male sexual desire was linked to strengthening patriarchal culture. As a result, white men sought to exploit black female eroticism, and to minimize sexual competition by outlawing black male sexual interactions with white women. The rise of lynching and castration are tied to the white male attempt to control the exaggerated threat of black male sexual desire. Long after the demise of such vicious social acts, the strong taboo on interracial sex prevails.

Anti-miscegenation laws prohibiting interracial marriage between whites and people of color existed in forty states until 1967, when the U.S. Supreme Court struck down these laws as unconstitutional in the landmark, and aptly named, *Loving v. Virginia*. Moreover, after emancipation, vicious sexual stereotypes served in part as a smoke screen to divert attention from how white men sought to prevent black men from enjoying the privileges of economic stability, middle-class status and the freedom to raise their families. Still, the white woman defined the norm of beauty for the culture. She remained the prized erotic possession to be fought over by black and white men. Black women were largely excluded from this economy of desire, except in the crudest fashion.

This history must be kept in mind as we ponder the sexual fault lines in black America, and the tensions between black men and women around the perception that black men are aggressively marrying white women. Interracial marriage among black men and white women has risen dramatically in the last few years. Nearly eight percent of all black men between the ages of twenty-five and thirty-four who were married in 1990 married nonblack women, compared to just four percent for white men in the same age cohort who married outside their race. Region, occupation, and education play a huge role in determining the interracial marriages of black men. In the Pacific Northwest, thirty-two percent of black men marry white women; in California, it's twenty percent; in the Rocky Mountain states, its thirty percent; and in the New England states, nineteen percent of black men marry white women. Military service hikes the numbers for black men marrying women outside their race, as fourteen percent of black males in the military are married to nonblacks.

By contrast, only seven percent of black men who didn't serve in the military married nonblacks. More than ten percent of black men who complete college marry outside of their race, compared to only six percent for black men who didn't complete high school. And for black men who have attended graduate school, the number jumps to thirteen percent who marry nonblack women. In fact, black men with graduate school experience are thirty percent more likely to marry outside their race than even black men with a college

degree. Overall, more than 200,000 black men are married outside their ra
mostly to white women.

On the surface, despite the soaring rates of intermarriage for black men, that number might not seem particularly disturbing, but from the perspective of educated black women, it represents a significant draining of the pool of available black men from which to choose a potential mate. As more black men go to prison, die early from crime or from AIDS, are severely unemployed or underemployed, or choose an alternative sexual lifestyle, the numbers of compatible black men begin to significantly diminish for educated black women. And given the hostility that black men without higher education often harbor toward educated black women, the numbers of black men available for black women dwindle even more.

Each of the situations I have just outlined has in its own right negatively affected the relationships between black men and black women. In the quest for an ideal mate, black women not only fight against trends in the economy, employment and education, but they fight a far more elusive opponent: the mythological eroticization of a standard of beauty that by definition excludes them from competition. Furthermore, black women are subject to stereotypes among black men about their being "difficult," "demanding," "bossy," "full of attitude," "aggressive" and the like, ruling them out of play as possible mates, often by the relatively small pool of highly educated, or highly achieving, black men.

The factors that rob black men and women of more love between us— imprisonment, early death, educational disparities and self-destructive habits such as snobbishness, skin-color bias, the preference for bad boys, and worship of white standards of beauty—can only be combated through conscientious response to our plight.

Breaking the "Hip Hop" Hold: Looking Beyond the Media Hype

by Mark A. Boles

"How much y'all make?"

This was the predominant question from a group of young black men during a recent career day panel with other marketing professionals at a predominantly black school in the South End of Boston.

What they really wanted to know was *"How can I make as much as you make - NOW?"*

It is not surprising that many of our young black men are so intent on achieving instant gratification, getting paid and pursuing the "bling." Millions of African-American men take care of their business every day. They build strong families, pay their taxes, and give back to their communities. But too many of our young black men do not see these role models portrayed in the media, but are instead bombarded with images that reinforce and promulgate stereotypes and negatively impact the development and expectations of young African-American males. This media distortion provokes two distinct outcomes, resulting in further exacerbation of existent social and cultural inequities:

• an insatiable desire for immediate financial gratification
• the overshadowing and devaluation of attainable, positive role models

It's not hard to understand how this happens. Among other factors, African Americans consume far more media than the national average. According to the 2005 PCAG Multicultural Kids Study, Cable TV plays a greater role in the lives of African-American kids. Significantly more black kids have cable TV in their bedrooms then do kids in other ethnic segments.

And the messages they receive do little to instill the values needed to close the glaring equality gaps that plague black Americans in general and black men in particular.

In his book *Is Bill Cosby Right?* Michael Eric Dyson contends that "status is internal to black culture . . . Rarely has a secular black culture as proudly and defiantly, embraced the extravagant excess and exaggerated of poor black identity as they do hip hop."

The media has done much to perpetuate the impact of hip hop, incorporating it into efforts to draw the attention and influence the buying habits of young African Americans, especially males. For example, a recent beer commercial, titled "Jet Bet," opens with rapper Lil Jon lounging on a private plane with an attractive female companion. The plane lands and taxis to an empty tarmac where Jermaine Dupri waits near a chauffeur-driven luxury vehicle. Lil Jon hands Dupri a 12-pack of the sponsor's beer - a wager being paid off.

This display of over-the-top extravagance is barely attainable for even the uber-wealthy, much less the average American. Yet it is typical of what many of our young black men see in the media on a daily basis.

These images go beyond merely reinforcing unattainable goals and misplaced values. The ubiquitous "get rich or die tryin'" messages are outright irresponsible and possibly dangerous. For example, recently, DefJam and Electronic Arts released a street fighting video game called ICON, a gang street-fighting game.

"With the hottest music seamlessly infused into the world around you, the game's environments pulsate, crumble, and explode to life with every bone-jarring beat," the bestselling game's description blares. "Time your attacks to the driving bass and use falling debris and exposed environmental hazards to pound your rivals. Featuring an all-new single-player story, the game takes you deep into the life of a high-rolling hip hop mogul to build a record label, discover new superstars, and become a hip hop ICON."

The disproportionate media coverage and glorification of black entertainers and sports figures (especially those engaging in bad behavior) plays a large role in the immediate desire for riches. However, there is a considerable difference between being rich and being wealthy. Most would agree that most of the hip hop artists and professional athletes held up to acclaim are "rich" but not "wealthy." In fact, when their fame ends, many have already outspent their riches. Nevertheless, with rare exceptions, the popular media focuses our children's attention on the acquisition of quick money, not lasting wealth.

Given black children's increased exposure to the media, the promulgation of negative images of their older selves is likely to have an even more detrimental impact on their perspectives and their futures. As author Todd Boyd wrote "[I]n the same way that MLK demanded that people be judged not by the 'color of their skin, but by the content of their character' hip hop prefers to be 'judged by twelve' instead of being 'carried by six'. The reality of this perceived short life span has ushered in a force unrivaled before in American popular culture and a force that has surpassed previous political exploits."

Moreover, this holds even greater power given how much trends are adopted by other ethnic segments from baggy jeans and flat brimmed hats adorned by action sports athletes to Daddy Yankee being a top-10 video on MTVs *Direct Effect*. In addition to the fact that from the PCAG Multicultural Kids Study, most among kids age 6-14, whites, Asian and Hispanics all feel overwhelmingly that African Americans have the greatest knowledge of "sports and sports teams, coolest fashions and latest music." Inevitably, young black males may feel the pressure to live up to expectations determined by popular culture.

Clearly, we're not going to be able to scream louder than the collective voice of the media, but if we can redirect our children's focus from the largely unattainable glory of hip hop and sports fame and promote "everyday role models" whose accomplishments are more attainable and sustaining, we must do it — and do it before it's too late. We must turn our children's question away from, "How much do y'all make?" to "What can I make of myself?"

Universal Fatherhood: Black Men Sharing the Load

by Steven Ivory

Three black men sit at a table in a Los Angeles restaurant one Saturday afternoon, engaged in animated conversation.

One, in a green Ralph Lauren Polo shirt and khakis, looks to be about 50. The other two, citizens of the Hip Hop nation in dutifully sagging jeans and cocked baseball caps, might be thirty, tops.

Ignoring High Definition sports blaring out of a flatscreen television above the bar, the three are preoccupied with the digital images each have pulled up on their cell phones, which they enthusiastically pass around to one another.

Naked women? Video games? Strategic eavesdropping reveals the images on the cell screens to be those of children - specifically, their sons and daughters. On a lazy Saturday afternoon usually reserved for decidedly more exciting fare, these men pridefully share their stories of the challenge, universal mystery and the unrelenting joy of fatherhood.

They swig imported brew and exchange opinions regarding private school and college tuition, the conundrum of teenage clothing trends (Humph—the brothers in the sagging designer denim should talk) and the expense of feeding youngsters with furnaces for digestive systems.

They grasp for the secret to braiding the perfect little girl's pigtail, and joke about the proverbial shotgun that will subtly greet the mannish boys who come calling on said little girl. They speak over one another, often boisterously, about the miscellaneous woe and probity of nurturing "little people" who ultimately morph into adults with independent ideas and concepts, and perhaps one day, children of their own.

Fatherhood is arguably the closest mortal man comes to Godliness.

After all, according to the Good Book, God created man in His own image. Man, with profound assistance from a woman, more or less does the same thing when his seed creates a child.

It is the miracle of miracles, man's capacity to physically engineer another human being who innately purses their lips in like fashion as he; whose nose and fingernail bed uncannily resemble his own.

However, biology is usually where the comparisons to God end. For fatherhood is also where mortal man's love, pride and ego can intersect to create a shameless, impassioned mélange of self-importance, starkly manifested in the bouncing baby boy dubbed "Junior." Or the little girl who becomes "Daddy's girl" with a moniker to match, as in Michael becoming Michaela or Frank becoming Frankie.

While the three celebrants of fatherhood in the restaurant may or may not have considered the divinity of it all, honorable black fathers, despite what the world has been told, are not an anomaly. The truth is that the institution of American black fatherhood has suffered largely from a monumental case of bad public relations.

The smear campaign dates back to slavery, when the slave master, curious, bewildered and scared to death of the African he dragged to these shores to dominate, sell and trade like farm equipment, systematically extricated the black man from his family unit - effectively diminishing the father's role as leader and chief influence in the lives of his loved ones.

It was by sheer, sinister design that a female slave was often the sole parent charged with looking after her children; the little ones, after all, were the slave master's fledgling stock. The father, separated from his own family, was emotionally castrated. Thus, a culturally debilitating dysfunction was born.

Nevertheless, the lousy black dad does exist, and he is not entirely the fault of the white man, not by a long shot. Black men, like all emotionally sound men, make their own choices.

Black men fail as fathers for many of the same reasons fathers of any hue and background fail. Quite often, they themselves lack strong, sound examples of fatherhood. Indeed, the shadowy, baleful urban gang is nothing more than a collective of lovelorn boys and men (and women) in search of Daddy, seeking to fill the hole in their hearts with the camaraderie of other fearful, fatherless souls.

And what, beyond the absence of a fatherly example, could be reason a man needs to be hauled into court to do right fiscally by the children of his own creation? Look up "trifling" in the dictionary and there an image of this man (I use the word loosely) will be.

But more than anyone else, when a black person is in hot water, their paternal heritage is likely to come under scrutiny.

Timothy McVeigh's merciless 1995 bombing of the Alfred P. Murrah Building in Oklahoma City reflected something seriously wrong in the man's life. Still, I don't recall a federal case being made as to the whereabouts of his father or what dark kernel in their relationship led McVeigh to fill a rented Ryder truck with homemade explosives and slaughter men, women and children.

Unlike the nagging perpetuation of a lack of principled black parenting in the Community, great black fatherhood doesn't usually make headlines. That is, unless you are Wesley Autrey, the 50 year-old construction worker who, as his frightened four- and five-year old daughters looked on, began 2007 by jumping onto the tracks of a Manhattan subway one morning to save Cameron Hollopeter, a first year film student whose sudden epileptic seizure caused him to fall into the path of the subway. As the train roared just inches above their bodies, Autrey lay atop Hollopeter between the tracks inside the trough, keeping him still, and thus, alive.

After the media hoopla subsided, Autrey went back to what he was doing before he saved a man's life - fathering his two little girls. No reality show contract, no clothing line, just day-to-day dignity.

I don't know if McVeigh had children, but Autrey's girls aren't likely to one day end up some playa's bitch or ho; thanks to Daddy's stunning illustration of heroism and selfless, dynamic compassion, a seed has been planted in their young psyche as to what a real man is.

That, however, is what black fathers do everyday, anonymously and without fanfare: they instill in their progeny, by deed and example, wholesale self-esteem and worth. They nurture, provide, and guide.

Fathers communicate, through the setting and loving enforcement of boundaries and unspoken family by-laws, the importance of walking the walk and talking the talk. They demonstrate what it is to be a man by being one in a society where, despite the Oprahs, Tigers and Obamas, he still can on any given day be referred to as boy.

These things don't deter a real man from being a father. How he deals with what the world hands him becomes yet another parable from which his young ones will glean something valuable toward the shaping of their spirits. When we encounter this father's children, whether adolescents or adults, we encounter him.

Granted, it is difficult to witness the often garish sights, sounds and general incivility of popular culture and not conclude that black youth is headed to hell in a pimped-out SUV. But be assured that in park sandboxes, on college campuses, behind the cash registers of fast food establishments—everywhere—there are plenty of kids who know better. They are proud to do the right thing, even when no one is watching. They learned to be this way under the mindful tutelage of a conscientious dad.

The earnest father comes in many configurations. The clichéd image of Cosby's Heathcliff Huxtable TV character is overtaken by the reality that a father's sustaining love and guidance emanates just as sincerely from a stepfather or the dad divorced from the mother of his children or the man who never wed his child's mom.

And then there is the man to whom I shall refer as the universal father. He is without offspring, and at any time may be without an intimate connection to anyone with a son or daughter.

But having had one, he knows the value of a proud, loving father. He has also witnessed the sad consequence of men and women who limp through life without such a father. And he believes that all men can find a certain responsibility in the fatherhood concept.

The universal father embraces the notion that we are all connected, and that the emotional, spiritual and academic success of anyone's child is an investment in his own future. This is a man who understands that in an age where profit can cast a softer light on even the most unseemly act, the way in which he merely walks down the street - how he conducts his life in the presence of a youngster—can serve as a subtle, yet powerful act of mentoring.

Though its inhabitants are now linked by technology, he knows it still takes a village to raise a child.

The universal dad is comfortable in his skin in the village—okay with being asked how'd THAT happen, him not having had kids and all—even if the kids themselves can get a little rambunctious in the village. Especially on the weekends.

I know all about the universal dad. I happen to be one.

As my three friends in the restaurant contemplate the rite of fatherhood, one of them utters the mantra of parents everywhere: Having a child changes your life forever. My life has not been altered in the way they describe. However, as a card-carrying villager, I've been told that I have changed a life or two, and knowing this is my joy.

Whether or not we are biological or step or universal dads, all men shoulder some responsibility in how children turn out. It's simply a matter of stepping up and taking our share of the load. Period.

The National Urban League's Prescriptions For Change

To help empower African Americans, especially young black males, to reach their full potential, the National Urban League recommends the following Prescriptions for Change:

Universal Early Childhood Education

All children in this nation have a right to comprehensive early childhood education. Early childhood programs such as Head Start have proven effective in narrowing the gap between low-income children and their more affluent peers. The National Urban League proposes that early childhood education be provided to all children to prepare them for a lifetime of learning.

Greater Experimentation with All-Male Schools, Longer School Days and Mentoring

All-male schools, combined with mentoring and longer school days, help keep young boys focused on education and away from the distractions that could lead them down the wrong paths. The National Urban League proposes the establishment of more all-male schools, longer school days and active, engaged mentoring to guide and foster black male students' educational and social growth.

More Second Chance Programs for High School Drop-Outs, Ex-Offenders

Second-Chance programs help to steer more Americans, especially those at-risk, back on track by providing assistance in getting GEDs, skills training and new jobs. The National Urban League proposes the establishment and full funding of more Second-Chance programs to bring ex-offenders and disadvantaged individuals who are out of school and out of work back into the mainstream.

Restore The Federal Summer Jobs Program to Its Previous State

At the end of the 21st Century, federal lawmakers agreed to "reinvent" the federal Summer Jobs Program that had been in place for decades by changing its status from a stand alone mandatory program to one of 10 optional youth services programs. Under this reform, cities and municipalities had the option of offering the program or not; the result was a major scale back of this successful federal program. The National Urban League proposes reimplementation of the Summer Jobs Program in its previous form.

Drive Home the Message That Education Pays Dividends in the Long Run

Parents need to instill in their children the value of education in achieving their dreams and improving their financial security. The National Urban League encourages parents to engage in an on-going conversation with their children on the benefits of graduating from high school and college. Parents must help their children understand that their opportunities for professional and economic advancement are much greater with a college degree or higher than without.

APPENDIX I

In Memoriam

Ed Bradley

Ed Bradley is one of the premier journalists in media history. He spent most of his 39-year journalistic career with CBS News. He began on CBS Evening News and on CBS News documentaries, but he was best known for his work on *60 Minutes*, where he showed his journalistic talents in both interviewing and investigative work.

Born Edward Rudolph Bradley on June 22, 1941 in Philadelphia, he earned a teaching degree from Cheyney State College in 1964 and taught sixth grade for three years in Philadelphia. While moonlighting at WDAS radio doing odd jobs, like spinning records, reading the news, and covering sporting events, Bradley discovered his love of journalism. In the late 1960s, he offered to cover the Philadelphia riots for the radio station. He never looked back.

He soon got a job at WCBS radio in New York, and then in 1972 was offered a job at CBS News to cover the Vietnam War. This made him one of the first African-American journalists to make a name for himself on national television. Bradley was injured during war coverage in Cambodia, and was briefly assigned to the Washington Bureau to cover Capitol Hill. But this was too boring for Bradley. He volunteered to cover the fall of Vietnam and Cambodia and was one of the last reporters to leave both war zones when they fell to the Communists in 1975.

Though the winner of countless journalism awards, 20 Emmys, and much critical success, Bradley never forgot his roots. He spent much of his free time talking to young minority journalists and provided money to establish an annual monetary award given each year in his name to a promising minority journalist.

Mr. Bradley was a reporter's reporter and has left a high mark to which future journalists can aspire. He died from complications of leukemia on November 9, 2006. He was 65.

James Brown

Known as the "Godfather of Soul," "Mr. Dynamite," and "Soul Brother Number One," James Brown was a singer, songwriter, and performer who, without question, greatly influenced 20th Century musical genres. Some rock critics have referred to him as *the* most important Black musician of the rock era.

Brown was born on May 3, 1933, in Barnwell, South Carolina. After his parents separated when he was four, he moved to Augusta, Georgia where he was taken in by his aunt. Growing up, he earned money picking cotton, shining shoes, and buck-dancing for soldiers. In the late 1940s, he was imprisoned for armed robbery. While in prison, he met his life-long friend Bobby Byrd.

Byrd invited Brown to join a gospel singing group; they eventually called themselves the Flames, and eventually changed their focus to R&B. They were signed to King Records and immediately had a hit with "Please Please Please" in 1956. By this time, the group had become known as James Brown & the Famous Flames. Brown's powerful voice, boundless energy, and athletic dancing had pushed him to the forefront.

Brown was among the first African-American entertainers to take complete control of his own career, propelling himself to critical and commercial success. He won Grammy Awards for "Papa's Got a Brand New Bag" (1965) and "Living in America" (1987). In 1986, he was an inaugural inductee to the Rock and Roll Hall of Fame and in 2003, he received a Kennedy Center Honor. Over his career, Brown had a total of 114 entries on Billboard's R&B charts; 17 of those went to number one.

He was "the hardest working man in show business." James Brown is an icon whose musical legacy is astounding. His talent has been and will be an inspiration to many generations of musicians. He died from congestive heart failure on December 25, 2006. He was 73.

Bebe Moore Campbell

Bebe Moore Campbell was one of the best-selling African-American novelists of our time. She was among the first-wave of black novelists to write about successful black lives for popular fiction. Her books notably explored black and white race relations, and she used her writings to debunk the stereotypes of the social and economic lives of African Americans.

Campbell was born Elizabeth Bebe Moore in Philadelphia on February 19, 1950. She earned a bachelor's degree in elementary education from the University of Pittsburgh in 1971 and taught in Atlanta for several years before becoming a freelance journalist. Her first book, published in 1986, was a work of nonfiction called "Successful Women, Angry Men: Backlash in the Two-Career Marriage.".

But it was her first novel, *Your Blues Ain't Like Mine*, that got everyone's attention. Published in 1992, the story is based on the 1955 real-life murder of young Emmett Till. Her next three novels were *New York Times* best-sellers. They include *Brothers and Sisters* (1994), *Singing in the Comeback Choir* (1998), and *What You Owe Me* (2001). Her interest in mental health issues inspired her to write her first children's book, *Sometimes My Mommy Gets Angry* (2003). She continued this theme and became a visible advocate on mental-health issues with her first play, "Even with the Madness" (2003) in her most recent novel *72 Hour Hold* (2005).

As a journalist, Campbell has written for the *New York Times Magazine*, the *Washington Post*, and *Ebony* among others. She was a regular commentator for National Public Radio's *Morning Edition* and a contributing editor to *Essence*.

Bebe Moore Campbell was a social commentator as well as a writer whose books will be remembered for their intelligence and passion. She died due to complications related to brain cancer on November 27, 2006 at her home in Los Angeles. She was 56.

Katherine Dunham

Katherine Dunham was a dancer, choreographer, activist, anthropologist, writer, and teacher. She combined her study of anthropology with her love of dance to revolutionize American modern dance by uniting it with Caribbean and African movements and rhythms.

Katherine Mary Dunham was born on June 22, 1909 in Chicago to an African-American father and a French-Canadian and Native American mother. Dunham began her formal dance training in her late teens. While studying anthropology at the University of Chicago, she was inspired to consider dance from an academic standpoint as a function of culture. She continued to dance, forming the first African-American ballet company in 1931(which would ultimately become the Katherine Dunham Dance Company); but she also continued her studies, earning her degree in 1936 in social anthropology.

She opened her first dance school in 1933. After receiving a grant from the Rosenwald Fund, she traveled to the West Indies to conduct field research in dance and anthropology 1935-36. This trip was the basis of her master's thesis and established her unique dance vocabulary. In high demand, she and her company performed in theaters across America. Dunham refused to perform in any venue that was segregated. She filed lawsuits and made public condemnations against hotels, restaurants and theaters that were segregated. Her dance company traveled the world, going to 57 countries on 6 continents throughout the 40's and early 60's.

Throughout her career, she wrote several books, articles, and short stories and lectured around the world. She danced and choreographed for Broadway (*Cabin in the Sky*) and Hollywood (*Carnival of Rhythm* and *Stormy Weather*). In 1963, she became the first African American to choreograph for the Metropolitan Opera in New York.

The recipient of numerous honors, awards, and honorary doctorates, Dunham will be remembered as a humanitarian as well as a scholar and artist. She died on May 21, 2006. She was 96.

Mike Evans

Mike Evans was best known for his role as "Lionel Jefferson" on two classic sitcoms, *All in the Family* and *The Jeffersons*.

Michael Jonas Evans was born on November 3, 1949 in Salisbury, North Carolina. His family moved to Los Angeles when he was a child. In 1971, while studying acting at Los Angeles City College, he landed the role of Lionel, the next door neighbor to the Bunkers, on *All in the Family*. Evans continued to play the character when spin-off *The Jeffersons* was created in 1975.

The next year, Evans left to concentrate on the *Good Times*, the series he helped co-create with his college friend Eric Monte. *Good Times* ran from 1974-79. After it ended, Evans returned to the role of Lionel and *The Jeffersons* for two years. The show ended its run in 1986.

Evans also appeared in *Love American Style, The Streets of San Francisco*, and the miniseries *Rich Man, Poor Man*. His last acting role was in 2000 on the show *Walker, Texas Ranger*. Aside from acting, Evans was a real estate investor and owned properties in California's Inland Empire.

Mike Evans succumbed to throat cancer on December 14, 2006. He was 57.

Coretta Scott King

Coretta Scott King partnered with her husband, civil rights leader Dr. Martin Luther King, Jr., to bring about social change. After his death, she continued the efforts they had begun, speaking out about justice, racial peace, and human rights throughout the world.

Coretta Scott was born in Marion, Alabama on April 27, 1927. She graduated as valedictorian of her high school class and received a scholarship to attend Anitoch College in Yellow Springs, Ohio. She earned a bachelor's degree in music and education and received a scholarship to study concert singing at the New England Conservatory of Music in Boston, Massachusetts. There she earned a degree in voice and violin.

While at the conservatory, she met Dr. King, at the time, a theology student pursuing a doctorate at Boston University. They married on June 18, 1953 in her hometown of Marion and subsequently moved to Montgomery, AL where Dr. King was to be pastor of the Dexter Avenue Baptist Church.

The mother of four, Mrs. King worked tirelessly for the civil rights movement. She organized marches and sit-ins, gave speeches, and organized and performed in the Freedom Concerts, a series of fundraisers for the Southern Christian Leadership Conference. In 1962, she attended the Disarmament Conference in Geneva, Switzerland as a delegate.

After Dr. King's death, she continued her husband's civil rights work, by building and developing The Martin Luther King, Jr. Center for Non-Violent Social Change in Atlanta, GA and working to establish Dr. King's birthday as a national holiday.

A woman of grace, she was an inspiration to the world. Coretta Scott King died on January 31, 2006. She was 78 years old.

Gerald Levert

Known for his powerful and smooth baritone voice, Gerald Levert was also an accomplished songwriter, arranger and producer. He consistently topped the charts during his two-decade career as a member of two different groups and as a solo artist.

Levert was born on July 13, 1966 in Canton, Ohio. He is the son of R&B legend Eddie Levert, Sr. of the group The O'Jays. Exposed to music and the music industry early on, Gerald formed the group Levert, along with his brother Sean and friend Marc Gordon, in the mid-80s. Eventually signing with Atlantic Records, the group had five number one singles, seven top ten singles, and 4 top twenty singles on Billboard's R&B charts. Their hits include "Pop Pop Pop Pop (Goes My Mind) (1986) and "Cassanova" (1987).

In the late 80s, Gerald Levert and Marc Gordon formed their own production company, Trevel Productions. They worked with Anita Baker, Men at Large, the O'Jays, and Miki Howard, among others. Now a genuine hitmaker for others as well as his own group, Gerald Levert was ready for more.

In 1991, Levert went solo and released his debut album; this and the subsequent string of albums marked him as a successful solo artist. But Levert was not finished collaborating. In 1997, he joined with singers Johnny Gill and Keith Sweat to form the group LSG. The group's self-titled album sold more than two million copies.

Known to his fans as "the Teddy Bear," Gerald Levert was a gifted artist. He died from a fatal combination of medication on November 10, 2006. He was 40 years old.

Gordon Parks

Gordon Parks was a highly esteemed photographer, filmmaker, writer, and composer who used his artistic talents to chronicle African-American life. Largely self-taught, he was the first African American photographer for magazines *Life* and *Vogue*, and he was also the first Black artist to produce, direct, and score a major Hollywood film, *The Learning Tree*.

Parks was born Gordon Roger Alexander Buchanan Parks on November 30, 1912 in Fort Scott, Kansas, the youngest of 15 children. His mother died when he was a teenager, and he was sent to live with his sister in St. Paul, MN. Eventually, Parks departed, leaving school, to work in a variety of jobs before obtaining a position as a waiter with the railroad. In the late 1930s, after looking through a magazine left by a passenger that contained documentary photos of migrant workers, Parks determined to become a professional photographer to articulate his point of view.

He bought his first camera in 1938, and before long was working as a portrait and fashion photographer. Later, he went to work in the photography section of the Farm Security Administration, which was created to produce a historical record of social and cultural conditions in the US. In 1944, he went to work for *Vogue,* and in 1948, for *Life,* where he worked for almost 25 years documenting everyday life as well as extraordinary events.

The first film Parks wrote and directed was a documentary; his second film was *The Learning Tree* (1963), which was based on his 1962 autobiography. Parks directed Shaft (1971) and Leadbelly (1976) among other films. In 1970, he helped to found *Essence* magazine.

His oeuvre includes his memoirs, novels, books of poetry, as well as his films, musical compositions, and photographs. His art was a challenge and a gift to our humanity. Gordon Parks died March 7, 2006. He was 93 years old.

June Pointer

Best known as a vocalist with the group The Pointer Sisters, award-winning recording artist June Pointer had a voice that has been described as soulful and pure. For over 30 years she toured the world with her sisters and as a solo performer.

June Antoinette Pointer was born on November 30, 1953 in Oakland, CA. She was the youngest of six children. June and her sister Bonnie began singing as a duo. With the 1969 addition of their sister Anita, they became The Pointer Sisters. Their sister Ruth would join the group in 1973. Dressed in 1940's era clothing, they sang a mixture of jazz, gospel, and soul. They released their self-titled debut in 1973 to critical and commercial success. Their next album earned them a country cross-over hit single and a Grammy. In 1974, The Pointer Sisters were the first African-American women to play in Nashville's Grand Ole Opry.

The Pointer Sisters had such hits singles as "He's So Shy" (1980), "Slow Hand" (1981), and "I'm So Excited" (1982). Their 1983 album, "Break Out" gave them three top five singles, including "Automatic," "Jump (For My

Love)," and "The Neutron Dance." June would also release two solo albums; 1983's "Baby Sister," and 1989's "June Pointer," which included the hit "Tight on Time (I'll Fit U In).

The winner of many awards and honors, June Pointer's music was an inspiration. She died of cancer on April 11, 2006. She was 53 years old.

Lou Rawls

Lou Rawls was the ultimate soul singer known for his strong baritone stylings. With a five decade-career, he became just as well known for his charitable efforts as for his music.

Louis Allen Rawls was born on December 1, 1933 in Chicago, Illinois. He was raised on the South Side of Chicago by his grandmother. Inspired by the music he heard as a teenager attending shows at the Regal Theatre, Rawls began singing in a group with schoolmate Sam Cooke, singing gospel. They sang with a couple of different groups until 1956, when Rawls quit to join the Army. After his discharge in 1958, he returned to join Cooke's group on tour. They were in a fatal car accident that left one person dead. Cooke escaped with minor injuries, but Rawls was pronounced dead on the way to the hospital. He was revived, but slipped into a coma for 5 days, suffered memory loss, and took a full year to recover. Once he did, he came back with a vengeance.

With direction and purpose, Rawls hit the club circuit, now as a solo act and singing secular music. He was signed to Capitol Records, and released his 1962 solo debut, *"I'd Rather Drink Muddy Water."* Rawls would eventually release over seventy-five albums (one platinum and five gold). He also would earn three Grammy Awards. Some of his hits were "Natural Man" (1971), "You'll Never Find Another Love Like Mine" (1976), and "Lady Love" (1978).

In 1980, Rawls established The Annual Lou Rawls Parade of Stars telethon to benefit the United Negro College Fund. Because of his devoted efforts, the telethon has raised over $200 million.

Singing in a variety of genres, Low Rawls epitomized cool and class. He died of cancer on January 6, 2006. He was 72 years old.

Urban League Member

Helen E. Harden

Helen Harden was born on March 22, 1903. A New York native, Ms. Harden attended public schools and graduated with honors from Jamaica High School. She earned both her B.S. and M.A. degrees in education and counseling from the City College of New York, and enjoyed a long career as a teacher and guidance counselor in the New York City Public Schools.

Ms. Harden joined the Urban League sixty years ago. She began her service in the Urban League Movement as a volunteer with the Queens Branch of the New York Urban League. In 1942, she became a founding member of the National Urban League Guild, a volunteer auxiliary designed to help raise funds for the National Urban League. In addition to her work with the Guild, she served on the Advisory Council of the Salvation Army's Services for Children and the League of Women Voters Criminal Justice Committee. She was also a dedicated member of the St. James Presbyterian Church for over fifty years.

Ms. Harden received a number of awards over the years. In 2001, the National Urban League Guild hosted a luncheon in her honor for her excellent service as a dedicated volunteer to the National Urban League and the Guild Movement.

Ms. Harden died November 1, 2006. She was 103.

APPENDIX II

About the Authors

Barbara R. Arnwine, J.D.

Barbara R. Arnwine is the Executive Director of the Lawyers Committee for Civil Rights Under Law, whose principal mission is to secure equal justice under the law.

William C. Bell

William C. Bell is President and Chief Executive Officer of Casey Family Programs, the nation's largest operating foundation with a mission focused solely on foster care.

Mark A. Boles

Mark A. Boles is Founder and President of Juice Market Research, an urban account planning and strategy firm. He is a member of the National Urban League Board of Trustees.

Mercedes R. Carnethon, Ph.D.

Dr. Mercedes Carnethon is an Assistant Professor of Preventive Medicine in the Feinberg School of Medicine at Northwestern University. Her research focuses on risk factors for cardiovascular disease and diabetes in the population.

Michael Eric Dyson, Ph.D.

Dr. Michael Eric Dyson is the Avalon Foundation Professor in the Humanities at the University of Pennsylvania. He is the author of several books; his most recent book is *Debating Race*.

Marian Wright Edelman

Marian Wright Edelman is the Founder and President of the Children's Defense Fund, a non-profit whose Leave No Child Behind® mission is to ensure every child a passage to adulthood with the help of caring families and communities.

Renee Hanson

Renee Hanson is the Hewlett Emerging Scholar at the National Urban League Policy Institute. Her areas of specialization are sociology and poverty.

Harry J. Holzer, Ph.D.

Dr. Harry J. Holzer is a Professor of Public Policy at Georgetown University and a Visiting Fellow at the Urban Institute in Washington, DC. His research focuses on the labor market problems of low-wage workers and other disadvantaged groups.

Steven Ivory

Steven Ivory is a Los Angeles-based music and culture journalist. He is the author of several books, including *Fool in Love*.

David J. Johns

David J. Johns is an educator and consultant who has researched and written extensively on black male issues. He currently serves as a Congressional Black Caucus Fellow.

Christopher B. Knaus, Ph.D

Dr. Christopher B. Knaus is a Lecturer in African American Studies at Berkeley University. His research focuses on critical cultural expression and the role of education in promoting social identity formation.

Silas Lee, Ph.D

Dr. Silas Lee is a pollster and research and strategic analyst. He is President of Dr. Silas Lee & Associates, a public opinion research and communications strategy firm.

Mark McArdle

Mark McArdle is a Research Analyst at the National Urban League Policy Institute.

Barack Obama

Barack Obama is the junior U.S. Senator from Illinois. He is the author of two books, *Dreams From My Father: A Story of Race and Inheritance* and *The Audacity of Hope: Thoughts on Reclaiming the American Dream.*

James Reed

James Reed is the Vice President for Workforce Development at the National Urban League. He serves as Director of the National Urban League's Urban Youth Empowerment Program.

William M. Rodgers III, Ph.D.

Dr. William M. Rodgers III is a professor at the Edward J. Bloustein School of Planning and Public Policy and Chief Economist for the John J. Heldrich Center for Workforce Development at Rutgers, The State University of New Jersey. Professor Rodgers' research examines issues in labor economics and the economics of social problems.

Theodore M. Shaw, J.D.

Theodore M. Shaw is the President and Director-Counsel of the NAACP Legal Defense and Educational Fund, Inc.

Aaron Thomas

Aaron Thomas is Senior Director, Education and Youth at the National Urban League. He serves as the Co-Chair of the National Urban League's Black Male Commission.

Valerie R. Wilson, Ph.D.

Dr. Valerie Rawlston Wilson is Senior Resident Scholar at the National Urban League Policy Institute where she is responsible for directing the Policy Institute's research agenda. Her research focuses on labor economics, economics of higher education, poverty and discrimination.

APPENDIX III

Index of Authors and Articles 1987–2007

In 1987, the National Urban League began publishing *The State of Black America* in a smaller, typeset format. By so doing, it became easier to catalog and archive the various essays by author and article name.

The 2007 edition of *The State of Black America* is the thirteenth to contain an index of the authors and articles that have appeared since 1987. The articles have been divided by topic and are listed in the alphabetical order of their authors' names.

Reprints of the articles catalogued herein are available through the National Urban League, 120 Wall Street, New York, New York 10005; 212/558-5316.

Affirmative Action

Arnwine, Barbara R., "The Battle Over Affirmative Action: Legal Challenges and Outlook," **2007**, pp. 159-172.

Special Section. "Affirmative Action/National Urban League Columns and Amici Brief on the Michigan Case," **2003**, pp. 225–268.

Afterword

Daniels, Lee A., "Praising the Mutilated World," **2002**, pp. 181–188

AIDS

Rockeymoore, Maya, "AIDS in Black America and the World," **2002**, pp. 123–146

An Appreciation

National Urban League, "Ossie Davis: Still Caught in the Dream," **2005**, pp. 137-138.

Jones, Stephanie J., "Rosa Parks: An Ordinary Woman, An Extraordinary Life," **2006**, pp. 245-246.

Black Males

Bell, William C., "How are the Children? Foster Care and African-American Boys," **2007,** pp. 151-157.

Carnethon, Mercedes R., "Black Male Life Expectancy in the United States: A Multi-level Exploration of Causes," **2007**, pp. 137-150.

Dyson, Eric Michael, "Sexual Fault Lines: Robbing the Love Between Us," **2007**, pp. 229-237.

Hanson, Renee, Mark McArdle, and Valerie Rawlston Wilson, "Invisible Men: The Urgent Problems of Low-Income African-American Males," **2007**, pp. 209-216.

Holzer, Harry J., "Reconnecting Young Black Men: What Policies Would Help," **2007**, pp. 75-87.

Johns, David J., "Re-imagining Black Masculine Identity: An Investigation of the 'Problem' Surrounding the Construction of Black Masculinity in America," **2007**, pp. 59-73.

Lanier, James R., "The Empowerment Movement and the Black Male," **2004**, pp. 143–148.

Lanier, James R., "The National Urban League's Commission on the Black Male: Renewal, Revival and Resurrection Feasibility and Strategic Planning Study," **2005**, pp. 107–109.

Morial, Marc H., "Empowering Black Males to Reach Their Full Potential," **2007**, pp. 13-15.

Reed, James, and Aaron Thomas, The National Urban League: The National Urban League: Empowering Black Males to Reach Their Full Potential, **2007**, pp. 217-218.

Rodgers III, William, M., "Why Should African Americans Care About Macroeconomic Policy," **2007**, pp. 89-103.

Wilson, Valerie Rawlston, "On Equal Ground: Causes and Solutions for Lower College Completion Rates Among Black Males," **2007**, pp. 123-135.

Business

Emerson, Melinda F., "Five Things You Must Have to Run a Successful Business," **2004**, pp. 153–156.

Glasgow, Douglas G., "The Black Underclass in Perspective," **1987**, pp. 129–144.

Henderson, Lenneal J., "Empowerment through Enterprise: African-American Business Development," **1993**, pp. 91–108.

Price, Hugh B., "Beacons in a New Millennium: Reflections on 21st-Century Leaders and Leadership," **2000**, pp. 13–39.

Tidwell, Billy J., "Black Wealth: Facts and Fiction," **1988**, pp. 193–210.

Turner, Mark D., "Escaping the 'Ghetto' of Subcontracting," **2006**, pp. 117–131.

Walker, Juliet E.K., "The Future of Black Business in America: Can It Get Out of the Box?," **2000**, pp. 199–226.

Children and Youth

Bell, William C., "How are the Children? Foster Care and African American Boys," **2007,** pp. 151-157.

Comer, James P., "Leave No Child Behind: Preparing Today's Youth for Tomorrow's World," **2005**, pp.75–84.

Cox, Kenya L. Covington, "The Childcare Imbalance: Impact on Working Opportunities for Poor Mothers," **2003**, pp.197–224d.

Edelman, Marian Wright, "The State of Our Children," **2006**, pp. 133–141.

Edelman, Marian Wright, "Losing Our Children in America's *Cradle to Prison Pipeline*," **2007**, pp. 219-227.

Fulbright-Anderson, Karen, "Developing Our Youth: What Works," **1996**, pp. 127–143.

Hare, Bruce R., "Black Youth at Risk," **1988**, pp. 81–93.

Howard, Jeff P., "The Third Movement: Developing Black Children for the 21st Century," **1993**, pp. 11–34.

Knaus, Christopher B., "Still Segregated, Still Unequal: Analyzing the Impact of No Child Left Behind on African-American Students," **2007**, pp. 105-121.

McMurray, Georgia L. "Those of Broader Vision: An African-American Perspective on Teenage Pregnancy and Parenting," **1990,** pp. 195–211.

Moore, Evelyn K., "The Call: Universal Child Care," **1996**, pp. 219–244.

Scott, Kimberly A., "A Case Study: African-American Girls and Their Families," **2003**, pp. 181–195.

Williams, Terry M., and William Kornblum, "A Portrait of Youth: Coming of Age in Harlem Public Housing," **1991**, pp. 187–207.

Civil Rights

Archer, Dennis W., "Security Must Never Trump Liberty," **2004**, pp. 139–142.

Burnham, David, "The Fog of War," **2005**, pp. 123-127.

Jones, Nathaniel R., "The State of Civil Rights," **2006**, pp. 165–170.

Ogletree, Jr., Charles J., "Brown at 50: Considering the Continuing Legal Struggle for Racial Justice," **2004**, pp. 81–96.

Shaw, Theodore M., "The State of Civil Rights," **2007,** pp. 173-183.

Criminal Justice

Curry, George E., "Racial Disparities Drive Prison Boom," **2006**, pp. 171–187.

Drucker, Ernest M., "The Impact of Mass Incarceration on Public Health in Black Communities," **2003**, pp. 151–168.

Edelman, Marian Wright, "Losing Our Children in America's *Cradle to Prison Pipeline*," **2007**, pp. 219-227.

Lanier, James R., "The Harmful Impact of the Criminal Justice System and War on Drugs on the African-American Family," **2003**, pp. 169–179.

Diversity

Bell, Derrick, "The Elusive Quest for Racial Justice: The Chronicle of the Constitutional Contradiction," **1991**, pp. 9–23.

Cobbs, Price M., "Critical Perspectives on the Psychology of Race," **1988**, pp. 61–70.

Cobbs, Price M., "Valuing Diversity: The Myth and the Challenge," **1989**, pp. 151–159.

Darity, William Jr., "History, Discrimination and Racial Inequality," **1999**, pp. 153–166.

Jones, Stephanie J., "Sunday Morning Apartheid: A Diversity Study of the Sunday Morning Talk Shows," **2006**, pp. 189-228.

Watson, Bernard C., "The Demographic Revolution: Diversity in 21st-Century America," **1992**, pp. 31–59.

Wiley, Maya, "Hurricane Katrina Exposed the Face of Diversity," **2006**, pp. 143–153.

Drug Trade

Lanier, James R., "The Harmful Impact of the Criminal Justice System and War on Drugs on the African-American Family," **2003**, pp. 169–179.

Economics

Alexis, Marcus and Geraldine R. Henderson, "The Economic Base of African-American Communities: A Study of Consumption Patterns," **1994**, pp. 51–82.

Bradford, William, "Black Family Wealth in the United States," **2000**, pp. 103-145.

———, "Money Matters: Lending Discrimination in African-American Communities," **1993**, pp. 109–134.

Burbridge, Lynn C., "Toward Economic Self-Sufficiency: Independence Without Poverty," **1993**, pp. 71–90.

Edwards, Harry, "Playoffs and Payoffs: The African-American Athlete as an Institutional Resource," **1994**, pp. 85–111.

Hamilton, Darrick, "The Racial Composition of American Jobs," **2006**, pp. 77-115.

Henderson, Lenneal J., "Blacks, Budgets, and Taxes: Assessing the Impact of Budget Deficit Reduction and Tax Reform on Blacks," **1987**, pp. 75–95.

———, "Budget and Tax Strategy: Implications for Blacks," **1990**, pp. 53–71.

———, "Public Investment for Public Good: Needs, Benefits, and Financing Options," **1992**, pp. 213–229.

Holzer, Harry J., "Reconnecting Young Black Men: What Policies Would Help," **2007**, pp. 75-87.

Jeffries, John M., and Richard L. Schaffer, "Changes in the Labor Economy and Labor Market State of Black Americans," **1996**, pp. 12-77.

Malveaux, Julianne M., "The Parity Imperative: Civil Rights, Economic Justice, and the New American Dilemma," **1992**, pp. 281–303.

Morial, Marc H. and Marvin Owens, "The National Urban League Economic Empowerment Initiative," **2005**, pp. 111-113.

Myers, Jr., Samuel L., "African-American Economic Well-Being During the Boom and Bust," **2004**, pp. 53–80.

National Urban League Research Staff, "African Americans in Profile: Selected Demographic, Social and Economic Data," **1992**, pp. 309–325.

———, "The Economic Status of African Americans During the Reagan-Bush Era: Withered Opportunities, Limited Outcomes, and Uncertain Outlook," **1993**, pp. 135–200.

———, "The Economic Status of African Americans: Limited Ownership and Persistent Inequality," **1992**, pp. 61–117.

———, "The Economic Status of African Americans: 'Permanent' Poverty and Inequality," **1991**, pp. 25–75.

———, "Economic Status of Black Americans During the 1980s: A Decade of Limited Progress," **1990**, pp. 25–52.

———, "Economic Status of Black Americans," **1989**, pp. 9–39.

———, "Economic Status of Black 1987," **1988**, pp. 129–152.

———, "Economic Status of Blacks 1986," **1987**, pp. 49–73.

Rodgers III, William, M., "Why Should African Americans Care About Macroeconomic Policy," **2007**, pp. 89–103.

Shapiro, Thomas M., "The Racial Wealth Gap," **2005**, pp. 41–48.

Taylor, Robert D., "Wealth Creation: The Next Leadership Challenge," **2005**, pp. 119–122.

Tidwell, Billy J., "Economic Costs of American Racism," **1991**, pp. 219–232.

Turner, Mark D., "Escaping the 'Ghetto' of Subcontracting," **2006**, pp. 117-131.

Watkins, Celeste, "The Socio-Economic Divide Among Black Americans Under 35," **2001**, pp. 67-85.

Webb, Michael B., "Programs for Progress and Empowerment: The Urban League's National Education Initiative," **1993**, pp. 203-216.

Education

Allen, Walter R., "The Struggle Continues: Race, Equity and Affirmative Action in U.S. Higher Education," **2001**, pp. 87-100.

Bailey, Deirdre, "School Choice: The Option of Success," **2001**, pp. 101-114.

Bradford, William D., "Dollars for Deeds: Prospects and Prescriptions for African-American Financial Institutions," **1994**, pp. 31–50.

Comer, James P., Norris Haynes, and Muriel Hamilton-Leel, "School Power: A Model for Improving Black Student Achievement," **1990**, pp. 225–238.

Comer, James P., "Leave No child Behind: Preparing Today's Youth for Tomorrow's World," **2005**, pp.75–84.

Dilworth, Mary E. "Historically Black Colleges and Universities: Taking Care of Home," **1994**, pp. 127–151.

Edelman, Marian Wright, "Black Children In America," **1989,** pp. 63–76.

Freeman, Dr. Kimberly Edelin, "African-American Men and Women in Higher Education: 'Filling the Glass' in the New Millennium," **2000**, pp. 61–90.

Gordon, Edmund W., "The State of Education in Black America," **2004**, pp. 97–113.

Guinier, Prof. Lani, "Confirmative Action in a Multiracial Democracy," **2000**, pp. 333–364.

Journal of Blacks in Higher Education (reprint), "The 'Acting White' Myth," **2005**, pp.115–117.

Knaus, Christopher B., "Still Segregated, Still Unequal: Analyzing the Impact of No Child Left Behind on African American Students," **2007**, pp. 105-121.

McBay, Shirley M. "The Condition of African American Education: Changes and Challenges," **1992**, pp. 141–156.

McKenzie, Floretta Dukes with Patricia Evans, "Education Strategies for the 90s," **1991**, pp. 95–109.

Robinson, Sharon P., "Taking Charge: An Approach to Making the Educational Problems of Blacks Comprehensible and Manageable," **1987**, pp. 31–47.

Rose, Dr. Stephanie Bell, "African-American High Achievers: Developing Talented Leaders," **2000**, pp. 41–60.

Ross, Ronald O., "Gaps, Traps and Lies: African-American Students and Test Scores," **2004**, pp. 157–161.

Sudarkasa, Niara, "Black Enrollment in Higher Education: The Unfulfilled Promise of Equality," **1988**, pp. 7–22.

Watson, Bernard C., with Fasaha M. Traylor, "Tomorrow's Teachers: Who Will They Be, What Will They Know?" **1988**, pp. 23–37.

Willie, Charles V., "The Future of School Desegregation," **1987,** pp. 37–47.

Wilson, Reginald, "Black Higher Education: Crisis and Promise," **1989**, pp. 121–135.

Wilson, Valerie Rawlston, "On Equal Ground: Causes and Solutions for Lower College Completion Rates Among Black Males," **2007**, pp. 123-135.

Wirschem, David, "Community Mobilization for Education in Rochester, New York: A Case Study," **1991**, pp. 243-248.

Emerging Ideas

Huggins, Sheryl, "The Rules of the Game," **2001**, pp. 65-66.

Employment

Anderson, Bernard E., "African Americans in the Labor Force,: **2002**, pp. 51-67

Darity, William M., Jr., and Samuel L.Myers, Jr., "Racial Earnings Inequality into the 21st Century," **1992**, pp. 119–139.

Hamilton, Darrick, "The Racial Composition of American Jobs," **2006**, pp. 77–115.

Hammond, Theresa A., "African Americans in White-Collar Professions," **2002**, pp. 109–121

Thomas, R. Roosevelt, Jr., "Managing Employee Diversity: An Assessment," **1991**, pp. 145–154.

Tidwell, Billy, J., "Parity Progress and Prospects: Racial Inequalities in Economic Well-being," **2000**, pp. 287–316.

Tidwell, Billy J., "African Americans and the 21st- Century Labor Market: Improving the Fit," **1993**, pp. 35–57.

———, "The Unemployment Experience of African Americans: Some Important Correlates and Consequences," **1990**, pp. 213–223.

———, "A Profile of the Black Unemployed," **1987**, pp. 223–237.

Equality

Raines, Franklin D., "What Equality Would Look Like: Reflections on the Past, Present and Future, **2002**, pp. 13-27.

Equality Index

Global Insight, Inc., The National Urban League Equality Index, **2004**, pp. 15-34.

Global Insight, Inc., The National Urban League Equality Index, **2005**, pp. 15-40.

Thompson, Rondel and Sophia Parker of Global Insight, Inc.,The National Urban League Equality Index, **2006**, pp. 13-60.

Thompson, Rondel and Sophia Parker of Global Insight, Inc., The National Urban League Equality Index, **2007** pp. 17-58.

Families

Battle, Juan, Cathy J. Cohen, Angelique Harris, and Beth E. Richie, "We Are Family: Embracing Our Lesbian, Gay, Bisexual, and Transgender (LGBT) Family Members," **2003**, pp. 93-106.

Billingsley, Andrew, "Black Families in a Changing Society," **1987**, pp. 97–111.

———, "Understanding African-American Family Diversity," **1990**, pp. 85–108.

Cox, Kenya L. Covington, "The Childcare Imbalance: Impact on Working Opportunities for Poor Mothers," **2003**, pp. 197-224d.

Drucker, Ernest M., "The Impact of Mass Incarceration on Public Health in Black Communities," **2003**, pp. 151-168.

Dyson, Eric Michael, "Sexual Fault Lines: Robbing the Love Between Us," **2007**, pp. 229-237.

Hill, Robert B., "Critical Issues for Black Families by the Year 2000," **1989**, pp. 41–61.

Hill, Robert B., "The Strengths of Black Families' Revisited," **2003**, pp. 107-149.

Ivory, Steven, "Universal Fatherhood: Black Men Sharing the Load," **2007**, pp. 243-247.

Rawlston, Valerie A., "The Impact of Social Security on Child Poverty," **2000**, pp. 317–331.

Scott, Kimberly A., "A Case Study: African-American Girls and Their Families," **2003**, pp. 181-195.

Shapiro, Thomas M., "The Racial Wealth Gap," **2005**, pp. 41-48

Stafford, Walter, Angela Dews, Melissa Mendez, and Diana Salas, "Race, Gender and Welfare Reform: The Need for Targeted Support," **2003**, pp. 41-92.

Stockard (Jr.), Russell L. and M. Belinda Tucker, "Young African-American Men and Women: Separate Paths?," **2001**, pp. 143-159.

Teele, James E., "E. Franklin Frazier: The Man and His Intellectual Legacy," **2003**, pp. 29-40

Thompson, Dr. Linda S. and Georgene Butler, "The Role of the Black Family in Promoting Healthy Child Development," **2000**, pp. 227–241.

West, Carolyn M., "Feminism is a Black Thing"?: Feminist Contribution to Black Family Life, **2003**, pp. 13-27.

Willie, Charles V. "The Black Family: Striving Toward Freedom," **1988**, pp. 71–80.

Foreword

Obama, Barack, Foreword, **2007**, pp. 9-12.

From the President's Desk

Morial, Marc H., "The State of Black America: The Complexity of Black Progress," **2004**, pp. 11-14.

Morial, Marc H., "The State of Black America: Prescriptions for Change," **2005**, pp. 11–14

Morial, Marc H., "The National Urban League Opportunity Compact," **2006**, pp. 9–1..

Morial, Marc H., "Empowering Black Males to Reach Their Full Potential," **2007**, pp. 13-15.

Health

Carnethon, Mercedes R., "Black Male Life Expectancy in the United States: A Multi-level Exploration of Causes," **2007**, pp. 137-150.

Christmas, June Jackson, "The Health of African Americans: Progress Toward Healthy People 2000," **1996**, pp. 95–126.

Leffall, LaSalle D., Jr., "Health Status of Black Americans," **1990**, pp. 121–142.

McAlpine, Robert, "Toward Development of a National Drug Control Strategy," **1991**, pp. 233–241.

Nobles, Wade W., and Lawford L. Goddard, "Drugs in the African-American Community: A Clear and Present Danger," and **1989**, pp. 161–181.

Primm, Annelle and Marisela B. Gomez, "The Impact of Mental Health on Chronic Disease," **2005**, pp. 63–73.

Primm, Beny J., "AIDS: A Special Report," **1987**, pp. 159–166.

———, "Drug Use: Special Implications for Black America," **1987**, pp. 145–158.

Smedley, Brian D., "Race, Poverty, and Healthcare Disparities," **2006**, pp. 155–164.

Williams, David R., "Health and the Quality of Life Among African Americans," **2004**, pp. 115-138.

Housing

Calmore, John O., "To Make Wrong Right: The Necessary and Proper Aspirations of Fair Housing," **1989**, pp. 77–109.

Clay, Phillip, "Housing Opportunity: A Dream Deferred," **1990**, pp. 73–84.

Freeman, Lance, "Black Homeownership: A Dream No Longer Deferred?," **2006**, pp. 63–75.

James, Angela , "Black Homeownership: Housing and Black Americans Under 35," **2001**, pp. 115-129.

Leigh, Wilhelmina A., "U.S. Housing Policy in 1996: The Outlook for Black Americans," **1996**, pp. 188–218.

In Memoriam

National Urban League, "William A. Bootle, Ray Charles, Margo T. Clarke, Ossie Davis, Herman C. Ewing, James Forman, Joanne Grant, Ann Kheel, Memphis Norman, Max Schmeling," **2005**, pp. 139–152.

National Urban League, "Renaldo Benson, Shirley Chisholm, Johnnie Cochran, Jr., Shirley Horn, John H. Johnson, Vivian Malone Jones, Brock Peters, Richard Pryor, Bobby Short, C. Delores Tucker, August Wilson, Luther Vandross, and NUL members Clarence Lyle Barney, Jr., Manuel Augustus Romero;" **2006**, pp. 279–287.

National Urban League, "Ossie Davis: Still Caught in the Dream," **2005**, pp. 137–138.

National Urban League, "Ed Bradley, James Brown, Bebe Moore Campbell, Katherine Dunham, Mike Evans, Coretta Scott King, Gerald Levert, Gordon Parks, June Pointer, Lou Rawls, and Helen E. Harden," **2007,** pp. 249-257.

Jones, Stephanie J., "Rosa Parks: An Ordinary Woman, An Extraordinary Life," **2006**, pp. 245–246.

Military Affairs

Butler, John Sibley, "African Americans and the American Military," **2002**, pp. 93-107

Music

Boles, Mark A., "Breaking the 'Hip Hop' Hold: Looking Beyond the Media Hype," **2007**, pp. 239-241.

Brown, David W., "Their Characteristic Music: Thoughts on Rap Music and Hip-Hop Culture," **2001**, pp. 189–201

Bynoe, Yvonne, "The Roots of Rap Music and Hip-Hop Culture: One Perspective," **2001**, pp. 175–187.

Op-Ed

Archer, Dennis W., "Security Must Never Trump Liberty," **2004**, pp. 139–142.

Boles, Mark A., "Breaking the 'Hip Hop' Hold: Looking Beyond the Media Hype," **2007**, pp. 239-241.

Burnham, David, "The Fog of War," **2005**, pp. 123–127.

Covington, Kenya L., "The Transformation of the Welfare Caseload," **2004**, pp. 149–152.

Dyson, Eric Michael, "Sexual Fault Lines: Robbing the Love Between Us," **2007**, pp. 229-237.

Edelman, Marian Wright, "Losing Our Children in America's *Cradle to Prison Pipeline*," **2007**, pp. 219-227.

Emerson, Melinda F., "Five Things You Must Have to Run a Successful Business," **2004**, pp. 153–156.

Ivory, Steven, "Universal Fatherhood: Black Men Sharing the Load," **2007**, pp. 243-247.

Journal of Blacks in Higher Education (reprint), "The 'Acting White' Myth," **2005**, pp. 115–117.

Lanier, James R., "The Empowerment Movement and the Black Male," **2004**, pp. 143–148.

Ross, Ronald O., "Gaps, Traps and Lies: African-American Students and Test Scores," **2004**, pp. 157–161.

Taylor, Robert D., "Wealth Creation: The Next Leadership Challenge," **2005**, pp. 119–122.

West, Cornel, "Democracy Matters," **2005**, pp. 129–132.

Overview

Morial, Marc H., "Black America's Family Matters," **2003**, pp.9-12.

Price, Hugh B., "Still Worth Fighting For: America After 9/11," **2002**, pp. 9-11

Politics

Coleman, Henry A., "Interagency and Intergovernmental Coordination: New Demands for Domestic Policy Initiatives," **1992**, pp. 249–263.

Hamilton, Charles V., "On Parity and Political Empowerment," **1989**, pp. 111–120.

———, "Promoting Priorities: African-American Political Influence in the 1990s," **1993**, pp. 59–69.

Henderson, Lenneal J., "Budgets, Taxes, and Politics: Options for the African-American Community," **1991**, pp. 77–93.

Holden, Matthew, Jr., "The Rewards of Daring and the Ambiguity of Power: Perspectives on the Wilder Election of 1989," **1990**, pp. 109–120.

Kilson, Martin L., "African Americans and American Politics 2002: The Maturation Phase," **2002**, pp. 147–180

———, "Thinking About the Black Elite's Role: Yesterday and Today," **2005**, pp. 85-106.

Lee, Silas, "Who's Going to Take the Weight? African Americans and Civic Engagement in the 21st Century," **2007,** pp. 185-192.

McHenry, Donald F., "A Changing World Order: Implications for Black America," **1991,** pp. 155–163.

Persons, Georgia A., "Blacks in State and Local Government: Progress and Constraints," **1987**, pp. 167–192.

Pinderhughes, Dianne M., "Power and Progress: African-American Politics in the New Era of Diversity," **1992**, pp. 265–280.

Pinderhughes, Dianne, "The Renewal of the Voting Rights Act," **2005**, pp. 49–61.

———, "Civil Rights and the Future of the American Presidency," **1988**, pp. 39–60.

Price, Hugh B., "Black America's Challenge: The Re-construction of Black Civil Society," **2001**, pp. 13-18.

Tidwell, Billy J., "Serving the National Interest: A Marshall Plan for America," **1992**, pp. 11–30.

West, Cornel, "Democracy Matters," **2005**, pp. 129–132.

Williams, Eddie N., "The Evolution of Black Political Power", **2000**, pp. 91–102.

Poverty

Edelman, Marian Wright, "The State of Our Children," **2006**, pp. 133–141.

Prescriptions for Change

National Urban League, "Prescriptions for Change," **2005**, pp. 133-135.

Religion

Lincoln, C. Eric, "Knowing the Black Church: What It Is and Why," **1989**, pp. 137–149.

Richardson, W. Franklyn, "Mission to Mandate: Self-Development through the Black Church," **1994**, pp. 113–126.

Smith, Dr. Drew, "The Evolving Political Priorities of African-American Churches: An Empirical View," **2000**, pp. 171–197.

Taylor, Mark V.C., "Young Adults and Religion," **2001**, pp. 161–174.

Reports from the National Urban League

Hanson, Renee, Mark McArdle, and Valerie Rawlston Wilson, "Invisible Men: The Urgent Problems of Low-Income African-American Males," **2007**, pp. 209-216.

Lanier, James, "The National Urban League's Commission on the Black Male: Renewal, Revival and Resurrection Feasibility and Strategic Planning Study," **2005**, pp. 107–109.

Jones, Stephanie J., "Sunday Morning Apartheid: A Diversity Study of the Sunday Morning Talk Shows" **2006**, pp. 189–228.

Reports

Joint Center for Political and Economic Studies, A Way Out: Creating Partners for Our Nation's Prosperity by Expanding Life Paths for Young Men of Color - *Final Report of the Dellums Commission*, **2007**, pp. 193-207.

Reed, James and Aaron Thomas, The National Urban League: Empowering Black Males to Meet Their Full Potential, **2007**, pp. 217-218.

Sexual Identity

Battle, Juan, Cathy J. Cohen, Angelique Harris, and Beth E. Richie, "We Are Family: Embracing Our Lesbian, Gay, Bisexual, and Transgender (LGBT) Family Members," **2003**, pp. 93-106.

Sociology

Teele, James E., "E. Franklin Frazier: The Man and His Intellectual Legacy," **2003**, pp. 29-40.

Special Section: Katrina and Beyond

Brazile, Donna L., "New Orleans: Next Steps on the Road to Recovery," **2006**, pp. 233–237.

Morial, Marc H., "New Orleans Revisited," **2006**, pp. 229–232.

National Urban League, "The National Urban League Katrina Bill of Rights," **2006**, pp. 239–243.

Surveys

The National Urban League Survey, **2004**, pp. 35-51.

Stafford, Walter S., "The National Urban League Survey: Black America's Under-35 Generation," **2001**, pp. 19-63.

Stafford, Walter S., "The New York Urban League Survey: Black New York—On Edge, But Optimistic," **2001**, pp. 203-219.

Technology

Dreyfuss, Joel, "Black Americans and the Internet: The Technological Imperative," **2001**, pp. 131-141.

Wilson Ernest J., III, "Technological Convergence, Media Ownership and Content Diversity," **2000**, pp. 147–170.

Urban Affairs

Allen, Antonine, and Leland Ware, "The Socio-Economic Divide: Hypersegregation, Fragmentation and Disparities Within the African-American Community," **2002**, pp. 69–92

Bates, Timothy, "The Paradox of Urban Poverty," **1996**, pp. 144–163.

Bell, Carl C., with Esther J. Jenkins,"Preventing Black Homicide," **1990**,pp. 143–155.

Bryant Solomon, Barbara, "Social Welfare Reform," **1987**, pp. 113–127.

Brown, Lee P., "Crime in the Black Community," **1988**, pp. 95–113.

Bullard, Robert D. "Urban Infrastructure: Social, Environmental, and Health Risks to African Americans," **1992**, pp.183–196.

Chambers, Julius L., "The Law and Black Americans: Retreat from Civil Rights," **1987**, pp. 15–30.

———, "Black Americans and the Courts: Has the Clock Been Turned Back Permanently?" **1990**, pp. 9–24.

Edelin, Ramona H., "Toward an African-American Agenda: An Inward Look," **1990**, pp. 173–183.

Fair, T. Willard, "Coordinated Community Empowerment: Experiences of the Urban League of Greater Miami," **1993**, pp. 217–233.

Gray, Sandra T., "Public-Private Partnerships: Prospects for America...Promise for African Americans," **1992**, pp. 231–247.

Harris, David, " 'Driving While Black' and Other African-American Crimes: The Continuing Relevance of Race to American Criminal Justice," **2000**, pp. 259–285.

Henderson, Lenneal J., "African Americans in the Urban Milieu: Conditions, Trends, and Development Needs," **1994**, pp. 11–29.

Hill, Robert B., "Urban Redevelopment: Developing Effective Targeting Strategies," **1992**, pp. 197–211.

Jones, Dionne J., with Greg Harrison of the National Urban League Research Department, "Fast Facts: Comparative Views of African-American Status and Progress," **1994**, pp. 213–236.

Jones, Shirley J., "Silent Suffering: The Plight of Rural Black America," **1994**, pp.171–188.

Massey, Walter E. "Science, Technology, and Human Resources: Preparing for the 21st Century," **1992**, pp. 157–169.

Mendez, Jr. Garry A., "Crime Is Not a Part of Our Black Heritage: A Theoretical Essay," **1988**, pp. 211–216.

Miller, Warren F., Jr., "Developing Untapped Talent: A National Call for African-American Technologists," **1991**, pp. 111–127.

Murray, Sylvester, "Clear and Present Danger: The Decay of America's Physical Infrastructure," **1992**, pp. 171–182.

Pemberton, Gayle, "It's the Thing That Counts, Or Reflections on the Legacy of W.E.B. Du Bois," **1991**, pp. 129–143.

Pinderhughes, Dianne M., "The Case of African-Americans in the Persian Gulf: The Intersection of American Foreign and Military Policy with Domestic Employment Policy in the United States," **1991**, pp. 165–186.

Robinson, Gene S. "Television Advertising and Its Impact on Black America," **1990**, pp. 157–171.

Sawyers, Dr. Andrew and Dr. Lenneal Henderson, "Race, Space and Justice: Cities and Growth in the 21st Century," **2000**, pp. 243–258.

Schneider, Alvin J., "Blacks in the Military: The Victory and the Challenge," **1988**, pp. 115–128.

Smedley, Brian, "Race, Poverty, and Healthcare Disparities," **2006**, pp. 155–164.

Stafford, Walter, Angela Dews, Melissa Mendez, and Diana Salas, "Race, Gender and Welfare Reform: The Need for Targeted Support," **2003**, pp. 41–92.

Stewart, James B., "Developing Black and Latino Survival Strategies: The Future of Urban Areas," **1996**, pp. 164–187.

Stone, Christopher E., "Crime and Justice in Black America," **1996**, pp. 78–94.

Tidwell, Billy J., with Monica B. Kuumba, Dionne J. Jones, and Betty C. Watson, "Fast Facts: African Americans in the 1990s," **1993**, pp. 243–265.

Wallace-Benjamin, Joan, "Organizing African-American Self-Development: The Role of Community-Based Organizations," **1994**, pp. 189–205.

Walters, Ronald, "Serving the People: African-American Leadership and the Challenge of Empowerment," **1994**, pp. 153–170.

Ware, Leland, and Antoine Allen, "The Socio-Economic Divide: Hypersegregation, Fragmentation and Disparities Within the African-American Community," **2002**, pp. 69–92

Wiley, Maya, "Hurricane Katrina Exposed the Face of Poverty," **2006**, pp. 143–153.

Welfare

Bergeron, Suzanne, and William E. Spriggs, "Welfare Reform and Black America," **2002**, pp. 29–50.

Covington, Kenya L., "The Transformation of the Welfare Caseload," **2004**, pp. 149–152.

Spriggs, William E., and Suzanne Bergeron, "Welfare Reform and Black America," **2002**, pp. 29–50.

Stafford, Walter, Angela Dews, Melissa Mendez, and Diana Salas, "Race, Gender and Welfare Reform: The Need for Targeted Support," **2003**, pp. 41-92.

Women's Issues

Stafford, Walter, Angela Dews, Melissa Mendez, and Diana Salas, "Race, Gender and Welfare Reform: The Need for Targeted Support," **2003**, pp. 41–92.

West, Carolyn M., "Feminism is a Black Thing"?: Feminist Contribution to Black Family Life, **2003**, pp. 13–27.

History of the National Urban League

T he National Urban League grew out of that spontaneous grass-roots movement for freedom and opportunity that came to be called the Black Migrations. When the U.S. Supreme Court declared its approval of segregation in the 1896 *Plessy v. Ferguson* decision, the brutal system of economic, social and political oppression the White South quickly adopted rapidly transformed what had been a trickle of African Americans northward into a flood.

Those newcomers to the North soon discovered that while they had escaped the South, they had by no means escaped racial discrimination. Excluded from all but menial jobs in the larger society, victimized by poor housing and education, and inexperienced in the ways of urban living, many lived in terrible social and economic conditions.

Still, in the North and West blacks could vote; and in that and other differences between living in the South and not living in the South lay opportunity—and that African Americans clearly understood.

But to capitalize on that opportunity, to successfully adapt to urban life and to reduce the pervasive discrimination they faced, they would need help. That was the reason the Committee on Urban Conditions Among Negroes was established on September 29, 1910 in New York City. Central to the organization's founding were two extraordinary people: Mrs. Ruth Standish Baldwin and Dr. George Edmund Haynes, who would become the Committee's first executive secretary. Mrs. Baldwin, the widow of a railroad magnate and a member of one of America's oldest families, had a remarkable social conscience and was a stalwart champion of the poor and disadvantaged. Dr. Haynes, a graduate of Fisk University, Yale University, and Columbia University (he was the first African American to receive a doctorate from the latter), felt a compelling need to use his training as a social worker to serve his people.

A year later, the Committee merged with the Committee for the Improvement of Industrial Conditions Among Negroes in New York (founded in 1906), and the National League for the Protection of Colored Women (founded in 1905) to form the National League on Urban Conditions Among Negroes. In 1920, the name was later shortened to the National Urban League.

The interracial character of the League's board was set from its first days. Professor Edwin R. A. Seligman of Columbia University, one of the leaders in progressive social service activities in New York City, served as chairman from 1911 to 1913. Mrs. Baldwin took the post until 1915.

The fledgling organization counseled black migrants from the South, helped train black social workers, and worked in various other ways to bring educational and employment opportunities to blacks. Its research into the problems blacks faced in employment opportunities, recreation, housing, health and sanitation, and education spurred the League's quick growth. By the end of World War I the organization had 81 staff members working in 30 cities.

In 1918, Dr. Haynes was succeeded by Eugene Kinckle Jones who would direct the agency until his retirement in 1941. Under his direction, the League significantly expanded its multifaceted campaign to crack the barriers to black employment, spurred first by the boom years of the 1920s, and then, by the desperate years of the Great Depression. Efforts at reasoned persuasion were buttressed by boycotts against firms that refused to employ blacks, pressures on schools to expand vocational opportunities for young people, constant prodding of Washington officials to include blacks in New Deal recovery programs and a drive to get blacks into previously segregated labor unions.

As World War II loomed, Lester Granger, a seasoned League veteran and crusading newspaper columnist, was appointed Jones' successor.

Outspoken in his commitment to advancing opportunity for African Americans, Granger pushed tirelessly to integrate recalcitrant trade unions, and led the League's effort to support A. Philip Randolph's March on Washington Movement to fight discrimination in defense work and in the armed services. Under Granger, the League, through its own Industrial Relations Laboratory, had notable success in cracking the color bar in numerous defense plants. The nation's demand for civilian labor during the war also helped the organization press with greater urgency its programs to train black youths for meaningful blue-collar employment. After the war those efforts expanded to persuading Fortune 500 companies to hold career conferences on the campuses of Negro Colleges and place blacks in upper-echelon jobs.

Of equal importance to the League's own future sources of support, Granger avidly supported the organization of its volunteer auxiliary, the National Urban League Guild, which, under the leadership of Mollie Moon, became an important national force in its own right.

The explosion of the civil rights movement provoked a change for the League, one personified by its new leader, Whitney M. Young, Jr., who became executive director in 1961. A social worker like his predecessors, he substantially expanded the League's fundraising ability—and, most critically, made the League a full partner in the civil rights movement. Indeed, although the League's tax-exempt status barred it from protest activities, it hosted at its New York headquarters the planning meetings of A. Philip Randolph, Martin Luther King, Jr., and other civil rights and labor leaders for the 1963 March on Washington. Young was also a forceful advocate for greater government and private-sector involvement in efforts to eradicate poverty. His call for a domestic Marshall Plan, a ten-point program designed to close the huge social and economic gap between black and white Americans, significantly influenced the discussion of the Johnson Administration's War on Poverty legislation.

Young's tragic death in 1971 in a drowning incident off the coast of Lagos, Nigeria brought another change in leadership. Vernon E. Jordan, Jr., formerly Executive Director of the United Negro College Fund, took over as the League's fifth Executive Director in 1972 (the title of the office was changed to President in 1977).

For the next decade, until his resignation in December 1981, Jordan skillfully guided the League to new heights of achievement. He oversaw a major expansion of its social-service efforts, as the League became a significant conduit for the federal government to establish programs and deliver services to aid urban communities, and brokered fresh initiatives in such League programs as housing, health, education and minority business development.

Jordan also instituted a citizenship education program that helped increase the black vote and brought new programs to such areas as energy, the environment, and non-traditional jobs for women of color—and he developed *The State of Black America* report.

In 1982, John E. Jacob, a former chief executive officer of the Washington, D.C. and San Diego affiliates who had served as Executive Vice President under Jordan, took the reins of leadership, solidifying the League's internal structure and expanding its outreach even further.

Jacob established the Permanent Development Fund in order to increase the organization's financial stamina. In honor of Whitney Young, he established several programs to aid the development of those who work for and with the League: The Whitney M. Young, Jr. Training Center, to provide training and leadership development opportunities for both staff and volunteers; the Whitney M. Young, Jr. Race Relations Program, which recognizes affiliates doing exemplary work in race relations; and the Whitney M. Young, Jr. Commemoration Ceremony, which honors and pays tribute to long-term staff and volunteers who have made extraordinary contributions to the Urban League Movement. Jacob established the League's NULITES youth-development program and spurred the League to put new emphasis on programs to reduce teenage pregnancy, help single female heads of households, combat crime in black communities, and increase voter registration.

Hugh B. Price, appointed to the League's top office in July 1994, took its reins at a critical moment for the League, for Black America, and for the nation as a whole. The fierce market-driven dynamic known as "globalization," swept the world, fundamentally altering economic relations among and within countries, including the United States. Price, a lawyer by training, with extensive experience in community development and other public policy issues, intensified the organization's work in three broad areas: in education and youth development, in individual and community-wide economic empowerment, and in the forceful advocacy of affirmative action and the promotion of inclusion as a critical foundation for securing America's future as a multi-ethnic democracy.

In the spring of 2003, Price stepped down after a productive nine-year tenure, and Marc H. Morial, the former two-term Mayor of New Orleans, Louisiana, was appointed president and chief executive officer. Since taking the helm, Morial has helped thrust the League into the forefront of major public policy issues, research and effective community-based solutions.

From Hurricane Katrina and the extension of the Voting Rights Act to creating jobs and housing through effective economic strategies, he is considered one of the nation's foremost experts on a wide range of issues related to cities and their residents. He has also been recognized by the *Non-Profit Times* as one of America's top 50 non-profit executives and has been named by *Ebony Magazine* as one of the 100 "Most Influential Blacks in America."

Upon his appointment to the League, Morial established an ambitious five-point empowerment agenda encompassing Education & Youth, Economic Empowerment, Health & Quality of Life, Civic Engagement and Civil Rights & Racial Justice that informs the League's programs, research and advocacy efforts. He created the new quantitative "Equality Index" to effectively measure the disparities in urban communities across these five areas. The Index is now a permanent part of the League's annual and much-heralded *The State of Black America* report.

In 2004, Mr. Morial launched the League's first Annual Legislative Policy Conference (LPC) in Washington, D.C. Armed with a common agenda of jobs, education and civil rights, the Urban League leadership (staff, board and volunteers) from across the country served as frontline advocates in discussions with congressional lawmakers.

A Black Male Commission was formed to explore and formulate concrete recommendations, solutions and programs to address the alarming inequities, disparities and social trends disproportionately affecting black males. Morial also established the Urban Entrepreneur Partnership (UEP), combining public and private sector resources to support business development growth among minority entrepreneurs.

Under Morial's economic agenda, five economic empowerment centers have been established; and $127.5 million has been secured in new market tax credits for business financing.

**National
Urban League**

CHAIRMAN
Michael J. Critelli

CHAIRMAN-ELECT
John Hofmeister

PRESIDENT AND CHIEF EXECUTIVE OFFICER
Marc H. Morial

**SENIOR VICE PRESIDENT
DEVELOPMENT**
Chandra Y. Anderson

**SENIOR VICE PRESIDENT
PROGRAMS**
Donald E. Bowen

**SENIOR VICE PRESIDENT
AFFILIATE SERVICE**
Annelle Lewis

**SENIOR VICE PRESIDENT
MARKETING AND COMMUNICATIONS**
Michele M. Moore

**SENIOR VICE PRESIDENT
FINANCE AND OPERATIONS**
Paul Wycisk

NATIONAL URBAN LEAGUE POLICY INSTITUTE

EXECUTIVE DIRECTOR
Stephanie J. Jones

VICE PRESIDENT & CHIEF OF STAFF
Lisa Bland Malone

SENIOR RESIDENT SCHOLAR
Valerie Rawlston Wilson

SENIOR LEGISLATIVE DIRECTOR
Suzanne M. Bergeron

RESIDENT SCHOLAR
Renee R. Hanson

RESEARCH ANALYST
Mark McArdle

PUBLICATIONS MANAGER
Rose Jefferson-Frazier

OFFICE MANAGER
Thea J. Sanders

ASSISTANT
Clarissa McKithen

RECEPTIONIST
Richard E. Lawrence

Roster of National Urban League Affiliates

AKRON, OHIO
Akron Community Service Center
And Urban League

ALEXANDRIA, VIRGINIA
Northern Virginia Urban League

ANCHORAGE, ALASKA
Urban League of Anchorage-Alaska

ALTON, ILLINOIS
Madison County Urban League

ANDERSON, INDIANA
Urban League of Madison County, Inc.

ATLANTA, GEORGIA
Atlanta Urban League

AURORA, ILLINOIS
Quad County Urban League

AUSTIN, TEXAS
Austin Area Urban League

BALTIMORE, MARYLAND
Greater Baltimore Urban League

BATTLE CREEK, MICHIGAN
Southwestern Michigan Urban League

BINGHAMTON, NEW YORK
Broome County Urban League

BIRMINGHAM, ALABAMA
Birmingham Urban League

BOSTON, MASSACHUSETTS
Urban League of Eastern Massachusetts

BUFFALO, NEW YORK
Buffalo Urban League

CANTON, OHIO
Greater Stark County Urban League, Inc.

CHAMPAIGN, ILLINOIS
Urban League of Champaign County

CHARLESTON, SOUTH CAROLINA
Trident Urban League

CHARLOTTE, NORTH CAROLINA
Urban League of Central Carolinas, Inc.

CHATTANOOGA, TENNESSEE
Urban League Greater Chattanooga, Inc.

CHICAGO, ILLINOIS
Chicago Urban League

CINCINNATI, OHIO
Urban League of Greater Cincinnati

CLEVELAND, OHIO
Urban League of Greater Cleveland

COLORADO SPRINGS, COLORADO
Urban League of Pikes Peak Region

COLUMBIA, SOUTH CAROLINA
Columbia Urban League

COLUMBUS, GEORGIA
Urban League of Greater Columbus, Inc.

COLUMBUS, OHIO
Columbus Urban League

DALLAS, TEXAS
Urban League of Greater Dallas and

DAYTON, OHIO
Dayton Urban League

DENVER, COLORADO
Urban League of Metropolitan Denver

DETROIT, MICHIGAN
Detroit Urban League

ELIZABETH, NEW JERSEY
Urban League of Union County

ELYRIA, OHIO
Lorain County Urban League

ENGLEWOOD, NEW JERSEY
Urban League for Bergen County

FARRELL, PENNSYLVANIA
Urban League of Shenango Valley

FLINT, MICHIGAN
Urban League of Flint

FORT LAUDERDALE, FLORIDA
Urban League of Broward County

FORT WAYNE, INDIANA
Fort Wayne Urban League

GARY, INDIANA
Urban League of Northwest Indiana, Inc.

GRAND RAPIDS, MICHIGAN
Grand Rapids Urban League

GREENVILLE, SOUTH CAROLINA
The Urban League of the Upstate

HARTFORD, CONNECTICUT
Urban League of Greater Hartford

HOUSTON, TEXAS
Houston Area Urban League

INDIANAPOLIS, INDIANA
Indianapolis Urban League

JACKSON, MISSISSIPPI
Urban League of Greater Jackson

JACKSONVILLE, FLORIDA
Jacksonville Urban League

JERSEY CITY, NEW JERSEY
Urban League of Hudson County

KANSAS CITY, MISSOURI
Urban League of Kansas City

KNOXVILLE, TENNESSEE
Knoxville Area Urban League

LANCASTER, PENNSYLVANIA
Urban League of Lancaster County

LAS VEGAS, NEVADA
Las Vegas- Clark County Urban League

LEXINGTON, KENTUCKY
Urban League of Lexington-Fayette
County

LONG ISLAND, NEW YORK
Urban League of Long Island

LOS ANGELES, CALIFORNIA
Los Angeles Urban League

LOUISVILLE, KENTUCKY
Louisville Urban League

MADISON, WISCONSIN
Urban League of Greater Madison

MEMPHIS, TENNESSEE
Memphis Urban League

MIAMI, FLORIDA
Urban League of Greater Miami

MILWAUKEE, WISCONSIN
Milwaukee Urban League

MINNEAPOLIS, MINNESOTA
Minneapolis Urban League

MORRISTOWN, NEW JERSEY
Morris County Urban League

MUSKEGON, MICHIGAN
Urban League of Greater Muskegon

NASHVILLE, TENNESSEE
Urban League of Middle Tennessee

NEW ORLEANS, LOUISIANA
Urban League of Greater New Orleans

NEW YORK, NEW YORK
New York Urban League

NEWARK, NEW JERSEY
Urban League of Essex County

NORFOLK, VIRGINIA
Urban League of Hampton Roads

OKLAHOMA CITY, OKLAHOMA
Urban League of Oklahoma City

OMAHA, NEBRASKA
Urban League of Nebraska

ORLANDO, FLORIDA
Metropolitan Orlando Urban League

PEORIA, ILLINOIS
Tri-County Urban League

PHILADELPHIA, PENNSYLVANIA
Urban League of Philadelphia

PHOENIX, ARIZONA
Phoenix Urban League

PITTSBURGH, PENNSYLVANIA
Urban League of Pittsburgh

PORTLAND, OREGON
Urban League of Portland

PROVIDENCE, RHODE ISLAND
Urban League of Rhode Island

RACINE, WISCONSIN
Urban League of Racine & Kenosha,Inc.

RALEIGH, NORTH CAROLINA
Triangle Urban League

RICHMOND, VIRGINIA
Urban League of Greater Richmond, Inc.

ROCHESTER, NEW YORK
Urban League of Rochester

SACRAMENTO, CALIFORNIA
Sacramento Urban League

SAINT LOUIS, MISSOURI
Urban League Metropolitan St. Louis

SAINT PAUL, MINNESOTA
St. Paul Urban League

SAINT PETERSBURG, FLORIDA
Pinellas County Urban League

SAN DIEGO, CALIFORNIA
Urban League of San Diego County

SEATTLE, WASHINGTON
Urban League of Metropolitan Seattle

SOUTH BEND, INDIANA
Urban League of South Bend
and St. Joseph County

SPRINGFIELD, ILLINOIS
Springfield Urban League, Inc.

SPRINGFIELD, MASSACHUSETTS
Urban League of Springfield

STAMFORD, CONNECTICUT
Urban League of Greater Fairfield County
Connecticut, Inc.

TACOMA, WASHINGTON
Tacoma Urban League

TALLAHASSEE, FLORDIA
Tallahassee Urban League

TAMPA, FLORIDA
Tampa/Hillsborough Urban League, Inc.

TOLEDO, OHIO
Greater Toledo Urban League

TUCSON, ARIZONA
Tucson Urban League

TULSA, OKLAHOMA
Metropolitan Tulsa Urban League

WARREN, OHIO
Greater Warren-Youngstown Urban
League

WASHINGTON, D.C.
Greater Washington Urban League

WEST PALM BEACH, FLORIDA
Urban League of Palm Beach County, Inc.

WHITE PLAINS, NEW YORK
Urban League of Westchester County

WICHITA, KANSAS
Urban League of Kansas, Inc.

WILMINGTON, DELAWARE
Metropolitan Wilmington Urban League

WINSTON-SALEM, NORTH CAROLINA
Winston-Salem Urban League

Acknowledgments

The editors acknowledge with sincere appreciation the invaluable assistance of the staff and trustees of the National Urban League in the publication of *The State of Black America* 2007 report.

Notes

Notes

Notes

Notes